The Demise of Religion

Also Available from Bloomsbury

Reframing the Masters of Suspicion, Andrew Dole
Spirituality, Corporate Culture, and American Business, James Dennis LoRusso
UFOs, Conspiracy Theories and the New Age, David G. Robertson

The Demise of Religion

How Religions End, Die, or Dissipate

Edited by Michael Stausberg,
Stuart A. Wright, and Carole M. Cusack

BLOOMSBURY ACADEMIC
LONDON • NEW YORK • OXFORD • NEW DELHI • SYDNEY

BLOOMSBURY ACADEMIC
Bloomsbury Publishing Plc
50 Bedford Square, London, WC1B 3DP, UK
1385 Broadway, New York, NY 10018, USA
29 Earlsfort Terrace, Dublin 2, Ireland

BLOOMSBURY, BLOOMSBURY ACADEMIC and the Diana logo are
trademarks of Bloomsbury Publishing Plc

First published in Great Britain 2020
This paperback edition published in 2022

Copyright © Michael Stausberg, Stuart A. Wright, Carole M. Cusack, and contributors, 2020

Michael Stausberg, Stuart A. Wright, and Carole M. Cusack have asserted their right under
the Copyright, Designs and Patents Act, 1988, to be identified as Editors of this work.

For legal purposes the Acknowledgments on p. ix constitute
an extension of this copyright page.

Cover design: Tjaša Krivec
Cover image © hansslegers/Getty Images

This work is published open access subject to a Creative Commons Attribution-NonCommercial-NoDerivatives 3.0 licence (CC BY-NC-ND 3.0, https://creativecommons.org/licenses/by-nc-nd/3.0/). You may re-use, distribute, and reproduce this work in any medium for non-commercial purposes, provided you give attribution to the copyright holder and the publisher and provide a link to the Creative Commons licence.

Bloomsbury Publishing Plc does not have any control over, or responsibility for, any third-party websites referred to or in this book. All internet addresses given in this book were correct at the time of going to press. The author and publisher regret any inconvenience caused if addresses have changed or sites have ceased to exist, but can accept no responsibility for any such changes.

A catalogue record for this book is available from the British Library.

Library of Congress Control Number: 2020945435.

ISBN:	HB:	978-1-3501-6291-4
	PB:	978-1-3501-9530-1
	ePDF:	978-1-3501-6292-1
	eBook:	978-1-3501-6293-8

Typeset by Integra Software Solution Pvt. Ltd.

To find out more about our authors and books visit www.bloomsbury.com
and sign up for our newsletters

Contents

Contributor Biographies ... vii
Preface and Acknowledgments ... ix

Introduction: The Demise of Religions: Or Do Religions End?
Michael Stausberg ... 1

1 How Religions End: Terms and Types
   Stuart A. Wright, Michael Stausberg, and Carole M. Cusack ... 13
2 When Does a Sacrifice Become "Just Meat"? A Sketch for a
   Theory of How Religions Stop Working *Joel Robbins* ... 31
3 Did Aum Shinrikyō Really End? *Erica Baffelli* ... 49
4 The Dissolution of a Religious Community: The Case of Knutby
   Filadelfia in Sweden *Liselotte Frisk* ... 67
5 Demise and Persistence: Religion after the Loss of "Direct Divine
   Control" in the Panacea Society *Alastair Lockhart* ... 83
6 Denominationalization or Death? Comparing Processes of
   Change within the Jesus Fellowship Church and the Children
   of God aka The Family International *Eileen Barker* ... 99
7 The Fall of Mars Hill Church in Seattle: How Online
   Counter-Narratives Catalyzed Change *Jessica Johnson* ... 119
8 Playing the Religion Card: The Creation and Dissolution
   of Rajneeshism *Michael Stausberg* ... 135
9 State Actions in Western Democracies Leading to the
   Dissolution of Religious Communities *Stuart A. Wright* ... 155
10 Mass Suicides and Mass Homicides: Collective Violence
   and the Demise of New Religious Movements
   Carole M. Cusack and James R. Lewis ... 175

Index ... 191

Contributor Biographies

Carole M. Cusack is Professor of Religious Studies in the Department of Studies in Religion at the University of Sydney, Australia. Her latest book publication is *The Sacred in Fantastic Fandom: Essays on the Intersection of Religion and Pop Culture* (co-edited with John W. Morehead and Venetia Laura Delano Robertson, 2019).

Erica Baffelli is Senior Lecturer in Japanese Studies at the University of Manchester (UK). Her latest book publication is *Dynamism and the Ageing of a Japanese "New" Religion: Transformations and the Founder* (with Ian Reader, 2018).

Eileen Barker, FAcSS, FBA, OBE is Professor Emeritus of the Sociology of Religion at the London School of Economics and the founder of INFORM (www.Inform.ac), an educational charity providing information that is as reliable, contextualized, and up-to-date as possible about minority religions.

Liselotte Frisk is Professor of Religious Studies at Dalarna University, Sweden. Her latest book publication is *Children in Minority Religions: Growing Up in Controversial Religious Groups* (with Sanja Nilsson and Peter Åkerbäck, 2018).

Jessica Johnson is a Visiting Assistant Professor of Religious Studies at the College of William & Mary in Williamsburg, Virginia. Her latest book publication is *Biblical Porn: Affect, Labor, and Pastor Mark Driscoll's Evangelical Empire* (2018).

James R. Lewis is Professor of Philosophy in the School of Philosophy at Wuhan University, China. His most recent monograph is *Falun Gong: Spiritual Warfare and Martyrdom* (2018).

Alastair Lockhart is an Affiliated Lecturer in the Faculty of Divinity at the University of Cambridge, and Academic Co-Director at the Centre for the Critical Study of Apocalyptic and Millenarian Movements. His latest book publication is *Personal Religion and Spiritual Healing: The Panacea Society in the Twentieth Century* (2019).

Joel Robbins is Professor of Social Anthropology at the University of Cambridge. His latest book publication is *Theology and the Anthropology of Christian Life* (2020).

Michael Stausberg is Professor of the Study of Religions, University of Bergen, Norway. His latest book publication in English is *The Oxford Handbook of the Study of Religion* (co-edited with Steven Engler, 2016).

Stuart A. Wright is Professor of Sociology and Chair of the Department of Sociology, Social Work and Criminal Justice at Lamar University in Beaumont, Texas. His latest book publication is *Storming Zion: Governments Raids on Religious Communities* (with Susan J. Palmer, 2016).

Preface and Acknowledgments

Much has been written about secularization. As far as we know, this is the first edited volume in English on the demise of religions. The contributors selected for this volume represent scholars with years of research invested in the religious communities they write about. We believe we have made compelling arguments for each chapter and for our collaborative work. Others may disagree or challenge our arguments. Indeed, we welcome such scholarly debate and hope that our efforts are the beginning of a more in-depth discussion of religious demise going forward. As a relatively neglected field of study, there is certainly much more to be studied and explored.

This volume has grown out of the research group "The Demise of Religions" directed by Michael Stausberg and James Lewis at the Centre for Advanced Study (CAS) at the Norwegian Academy of Science and Letters in Oslo. The project ran in the academic year 2018–2019. We wish to thank CAS for providing an extremely collegial and stimulating research environment. We also thank CAS for a grant covering the costs for Open Access publication.

The research group comprised the following colleagues, whose contributions can be sensed in this book (names with asterisk have chapters in the present volume): Janne Arp-Neumann, Erica Baffelli*, Jan Bremmer, Carole Cusack*, Laura Feldt, Albert de Jong, James Lewis*, Richard Lim, Joel Robbins*, Jörg Rüpke, Michael Stausberg*, Olof Sundqvist, and Stuart Wright*. Liselotte Frisk* joined the team as a visiting guest. We are also grateful to Venetia Robertson who compiled the index.

The editors, May 2020

Introduction: The Demise of Religions: Or Do Religions End?

Michael Stausberg

The religious field is in flux and religions change. There are innovation and solidification, but also torpor and attrition in the sphere of religions. Usually, it is heightened religious change that draws public and academic attention, for example, the creation of movements of reform or the emergence of new groups, especially those surrounded by tension or conflict with their environments. Much less attention tends to be paid to later stages of these movements or groups, once they no longer are considered a challenge or have disappeared from the news.[1] While these groups become older—perhaps more mature or maybe more fragile—other developments divert attention from them. The beginnings of religions are often well documented by enthusiastic insiders and interested outsiders, but little is known about how and why religions end.[2]

Religion Death and Language Death

That lack of attention toward ends distinguishes religions from languages. Apart from artificial or constructed languages like Esperanto or revived languages like Modern Hebrew, which both have main individual founding figures, the beginnings of natural languages are more obscure and opaque than the beginnings of religions. Yet, the disappearance of languages—language death or language extinction—is widely documented and studied (see, e.g., Crystal 2014). The passing away of the "last (fluent/native) speaker" of some language even makes it into the news, where headlines follow a stereotypical pattern. For example, in 2010 the *BBC* reported: "Last speaker of ancient language of Bo dies in India"³ (Aka-Bo was spoken on the west central coast of North Andaman and on North Reef Island of the Andaman Islands in the Bay of Bengal). In 2012 a *CNN* headline declared: "Last native speaker of Scots dialect dies" (referring to the Cromarty dialect of North Northern Scots in Scotland).⁴ In 2013 *The Times* reported that "the last ever speaker of Livonian passed away at age 103"⁵ (Livonian was a Finno-Ugric language closely related to Estonian), and in 2016 *Fox News* announced that "Edwin Benson, last-known fluent speaker of Mandan, passes away at 85"⁶ (Mandan was a Siouan language spoken in North Dakota). Sometimes, the reports come out before death has incurred. In 2017, *The New York Times* profiled the last-known living speaker of Taushiro, a nearly extinct language formerly spoken in the Peruvian Amazon region.⁷ Contrary to the other dialects/language mentioned above that belong to so-called language families, Taushiro is a language isolate, that is, a language with no demonstrable genealogical ties to other languages.

In the domain of religions, the write-up on the looming extinction of Taushiro resembles reports on the Shakers. In 2017, several newspapers including *The Guardian* and *The Economist* reported on the death of one of the three remaining members of the last active Shaker community in Sabbathday Lake Shaker village in Maine, USA.⁸ As a living entity, the Shakers appear to be doomed to disappear, even though some of their villages and crafts will be preserved as cultural heritage and museums and their history can be traced in archives. Contrary to many other tiny religious groups or communities the Shakers have attracted outside attention (including tourists) for a long time, given their peculiar lifestyle, including celibacy and prohibition of procreation, which greatly contributed to their demographic limitations and eventual disappearance. Other small groups are widely unknown. Consider the Muggletonians, a small English nonconformist group founded in 1652 that was already in the late nineteenth century erroneously written off as extinct; after the death of the last known member in 1979, the records of the group that he had kept were transferred to the British library. That was the start of renewed public and academic interest in the group that first became more widely known through published scholarly work (Lamont 2006) and an exceptional case of a group whose demise did not occur in silence. Ironically, it was their death that gained them attention and their relative longevity over the centuries could even be regarded as a success, the eventual eclipse of the group notwithstanding.

Similar to the news about the Shakers, *The New York Times* reported on the fate of Mepkin Abbey, a Trappist monastery in South Carolina with an aging and declining population.[9] Mepkin would not be the first monastery to be closed down in the United States or other countries for that matter. In Germany, for example, the closures of landmark abbeys like the former Trappist Abbey of Mariawald, the former Cistercian Abbey of Himmerod, or the former Benedictine Michaelsberg Abbey (Siegburg) have been reported on more widely (even internationally) in the media, while the fate of many other Christian monasteries, congregations, innumerable parish churches, and a host of other religious institutions such as chapels, shrines, or educational facilities run by religious congregations, is the subject of local news only.

The large-scale and widespread closure of religious facilities and institutions and the decreasing membership in mainline churches are an evident index of the process of the erosion of mainstream Christendom, but nobody would go so far as to jump from this observation to predicting the imminent extinction of Christianity (even though some would hope for this to happen). These developments are not limited to Europe or North America. In Japan, for example, mainstream Buddhist factions like the Nichiren or the Sōtō Zen schools have experienced a drastic decline in numbers of temples, resident priests, and death-related ritual services; people possess fewer devotional items and use them less often and less devotedly; there is a decline in common practices like pilgrimages and visits to religious sites, acquisition of talismans and amulets, prayers for health and good luck (Reader 2012). Yet few scholars, as far as I can see, would share Ian Reader's prediction that "in two decades we are … likely to be saying 'Religion R.I.P.'" in Japan (Reader 2012: 34). It seems premature to say that Buddhism faces imminent death.

Claims for timelessness, eternity, and primordial origins are figures of speech in discourses that we tend to classify as religious. In other words, religions can seem like extraordinarily robust entities. Features connected to religions like myths and rituals grounded in commitments to asserted transcendent agents, and realities could potentially increase the robustness and longevity of groups or institutions (Sosis and Bressler 2003). Yet, from a critical academic perspective that regards religions as human creations—as historical, cultural, and social creations—the disappearance of religious phenomena is not unlike developments in other domains: forms of sports and specimen of arts are forgotten, games and dances are no longer practiced, and languages keep on disappearing on a massive scale in front of our eyes. According to one authoritative source, the *Catalogue of Endangered Languages*, around 46 percent of the languages currently spoken are in acute danger of extinction. As mentioned above, there is evidence that similar processes are underway in the domain of religion, but we fail to perceive this because we think of religions in terms of larger units than scholars of language do for languages; we would not account for the disappearance of single groups, institutions, ideas, or practices as amounting to the demise of an entire religion. Consider once again the case of the Muggletonians. If we would introduce a classification similar to that adopted by scholars of language, we could refer to them as a dialect of a language we might wish to call English dissenters (or dissenterism, to coin a new word). Several other dissenting groups (dialects of dissenterism) originating in early modern England have since disappeared; for example, there were the Fifth Monarchists, the Grindletonians, the Levellers, the Philadelphians, the Ranters, the Seekers, and the Socinians, to mention only some. Few others like the Puritans and the Quakers have survived, albeit in transformed versions. In religious studies, we would not account for the disappearance or extinction of the above-mentioned groups as examples of religion death or religion extinction, because Christianity is still alive, to bring home the comparison with language scholarship: when we think of the end of religions, we tend to think of the end of a larger taxonomic unity like a family of religions, similar to what scholars of language call a language family. Dialects and languages that are part of language families share genetic or genealogical relationships in terms of common descent. That is similar to religions; for example, all the religion dialects mentioned above refer to the Bible or Jesus Christ and to earlier interpretations of these genealogical points of reference. In sum, if we were to change our taxonomies and shift our attention from families of religion to minor units, we would perceive plenty of cases of religion extinction and disappearances would not be considered exceptional cases but part of ordinary religious history.

Instead, to once again engage with the analogy from the study of language, when searching for cases of religious demise, we tend to look for cases of religion isolates; as mentioned above, language isolates are languages that have no demonstrable genealogical relationship with other languages or, to put it differently, they are cases where a language is the only known member of a language family. Religion isolates would be religions that have not descended from other religions or that do not share significant traits (vocabulary, symbols, practices, etc.) with other religions that could be considered their relatives. While the number of language isolates has been estimated to be 136 in the world (Campbell 2016), it is doubtful that anything like a religion isolate exists. All known religions derive some of their repertoire from preceding religions or adjust their features to extant models to ease their recognition as religions. For example, in the years after its founding the Church of Scientology copied features from Protestant religion into its layout, and ties to the Buddha and other recognized instances of religion were created for establishing the religious credentials of the founder (Urban 2011). New religious formations can also derive features from different extant religions in combination. This genealogical link is prominent among the most successful new religions such as the Latter-day Saints (Mormons), the Bahais, and Soka Gakkai. Something that does not inherit features from known religion could in theory be classified an isolate, but would probably neither be recognized as a religion nor seek recognition as a religion (for in order to succeed it would need to demonstrate its similarity to extant religions). The branch of religious studies that has paid most attention to matters of religious demise is the study of new religious movements (NRMs). In light of the above observations, this is probably so because there is a prevailing conception that NRMs can count as religious isolates; the fact that these groups entertain genealogical ties to other religions is often overshadowed by their apparent novelty, their recruitment outside church milieus, and not the least the rejection and resistance they have encountered among prevailing religions and society at large.

Extinction and Destruction

In sum, the demise of religions, or religious forms of expression, is a dimension of ongoing religious change and transformation. As such it should not be dismissed as a "failure" but as an ingredient in historical developments. Yet, it must be emphasized that religions—or aspects of religion—not only fall into disuse; there are cases of active abrogation of earlier religious practices and even attempts at religiocide (i.e., the active and organized attempt at annihilation or extermination of religions, for example, by conversion, destruction of religious objects or sacred sites, dispossession of religious places, persecution, outlawing of religions, prohibition of religious practices, and forced religious education). In the contemporary period, the killing, enslavement, rape, and forced conversion of Yezidis by ISIS is the most iconic example. It is attempts to erect not only theocracies that may seek to annihilate religions, but also secular or even anti-religious governments (like the Soviet Union and the People's Republic of China in some periods of their respective histories). The Holocaust was targeted against a people, not a religion *per se*—but the annihilation of Judaism was a desired side effect of the planned extermination of the Jews. Also in the present era governments in various countries—including democracies like the United States, France, and Germany—have conducted raids against small religious groups perceived or misrepresented as threatening, thereby driving them underground or out of business (Wright and Palmer 2018). During the past centuries, indigenous cultures have been targets of colonial, imperialist, modernist, and nationalist ideologies and policies; their religious cultures have regularly been either denied, demonized, or repressed, often by missionaries who have operated in synergy with economical forces and discourses of modernization. A variety of factors—demographic, ecological, economic, medical, political, social, technological—have pulled and pushed many indigenous people to adopting forms of Christianity, often as a consequence of or resulting in intensive indoctrination and conformist pressure. Typically, however, unless entire populations were eradicated, elements of pre-missionary religions were maintained and they resurfaced at later stages, either to be targets for further attempts at eradication or as triggers for revitalizations of indigenous religions (e.g., Paldam 2017). It should, however, be added that far from all Christian missionaries used force and violence to eradicate indigenous religions, and that their weakening or disappearance was not always the result of violent repression. There are examples of erosion of earlier religions, or even of unforced and voluntary decisions by the people to abandon and unwind their traditional religions.

The Chapters

In the first chapter of this volume, Stuart A. Wright, Michael Stausberg, and Carole M. Cusack propose a vocabulary to address the processes alluded to in this introduction. The chapter presents definitions of the following terms around the axes of decline (taking the forms of disengagement, disaffiliation, and decrease) and demise (taking the forms of extinction, endangerment, disaggregation, disintegration, fragmentation, mutation, disappearance, dissolution, abolishment, replacement, effacement, and annihilation); both axes describe processes of transformation. Moreover, the chapter outlines nine (non-mutually exclusive) trajectories of demise around the following factors and themes: leadership; economy and resources; intergenerational transmission; violent self-annihilation; cognitive disconfirmation; transmutation and replacement; split and splinter; organized opposition and mobilization; and religiocide and religious cleansing. The latter two can be called exogeneous trajectories.

The persistence or reappearance of elements of a religion that has been replaced by a secondary one—like Christianity, Islam, or Buddhism—could be adduced as evidence for the lingering vitality of that former religion. In the second chapter, Joel Robbins addresses the question of what it means to say that a religion works or no longer works. In the early 1990s Robbins conducted fieldwork among a small language group in a remote part of Papua New Guinea that had some fifteen years prior redefined itself as "Christian" and left "the ways of our ancestors" behind. Revisiting some instances during his fieldwork where practices from the earlier religion seemed to re-emerge, Robbins finds these practices had changed their signification: the signs did not indicate the ontological transition into indexing something else; for instance, the meat of a pig killed according to the procedures of the "ways of the ancestors" was "just meat," nothing more. Robbins re-describes this as a change in the "constitutive rules" of social life: killing no longer counted as sacrifice, the wearing of large wigs no longer counted as initiation, and neither ceremonies were operative in producing the effects they would have had previously—the sacrifices no longer speak to the spirits and the initiations no longer turn young adults into men.

In Chapter 3, Erica Baffelli takes us to Japan, one of the most fertile grounds of religious creativity and experimentation in the modern era, albeit not without tensions. Baffelli mentions several cases of religions that have ceased to exist as a result of media campaigns and state actions. Her chapter discusses the case of Aum Shinrikyō, which was abolished after the murderous gas attacks committed by some members. That was a traumatic event not only for Japanese society but also for committed members who had been caught unaware of this dimension of Aum's activities. Aum collapsed in 1995 as its material infrastructure was erased, economical activities were discontinued, and religious practices came to an end, including communication with their leader. Yet, two new groups continued Aum's legacies. Baffelli asks a question similar to Robbins: what does it mean for a religion to end? But she asks this question from the perspective of ex-members who were confronted with the ending of their religion. For them, even though they have questioned their beliefs and sought to distance themselves from their former religion, this is an experience of loss and they entertain memories of special moments in their lives. Bringing their experience to a closure—ending their emotional attachment to this ex-religion—was made difficult by the virtual impossibility of openly talking about their positive memories to outsiders for whom even speaking about Aum amounts to a taboo.

Chapter 4 presents a case from Sweden. Liselotte Frisk offers a careful account of the developments and interplaying factors that led to the recent end of the controversial Pentecostal community of Knutby Filadelfia. This community suffered but survived a first blow when the wife of a leader was killed and the pastor and one of his mistresses were convicted—a court case that led to a media siege of the community. Some twelve years later the community faced another crisis that led to widespread defection and the official closure of the community. In Frisk's reading, this ultimate dissolution resulted from the way different problems were intertwined: disillusionment with the leaders, the isolation of the leader from the community, failed prophecy, strain and exhaustion among the members, and—at the end—the intervention of outside therapists tied to anti-cult networks.

While the Aum Shinrikyō and Knutby Filadelfia cases discussed by Baffelli and Frisk respectively were triggered by criminal offenses and delusions, Chapter 5 takes us to England and to a breakaway, esotericist Anglican group— the Panacea Society—that has slowly faded out of existence in a process lasting for some seventy years after the death of the second leader until the death of the last formal member. (Here we may think of the cases of language death and the Shakers, above.) While the death of the founding (charismatic) leader and her/his imminent successor did not lead to the imminent demise of a religion, in the long run this loss of gravity was not compensated and membership kept on aging without recruiting younger members and passing the religion on to the next generation. Even though this could seem like an inevitable steady decline resulting in eventual demise, Alastair Lockhart shows that the demise and practices of a religion can survive its institutional core. Moreover, as the eventual demise did not come as a surprise, management of funds was adjusted and the trust survives even though no member of the religion serves on its board. This is an example of extinct religions that have planned for their legacy.

In Chapter 6, Eileen Barker compares the recent fate of two controversial Christian groups (churches or sects) with an emphasis on communal living and a strong sense of mission that originated in the 1960s—one in England (the Jesus Fellowship Church or JFC) and one in California (known sequentially as the Children of God [CoG], The Family of Love, The Family, and The Family International [TFI]). Both have recently been facing imminent demise, even though their futures seemed secure just a decade ago or so. Both had survived earlier moments of crises successfully, but later the number of members started to dwindle. In both cases the closure remains incomplete: the English church saw the revocation of JFC's constitution, but it still has to fulfill legal obligations, while the American organization broke up its communal structures and went online. Both groups were facing accusations involving several issues, among them child abuse (with different trajectories in both cases) and the costs and challenging of sustaining an aging membership (again with very different trajectories and economic resources). Their futures seemed bleak because they both were unable to retain their children in the communities, even though they were fertile and produced many children.

Chapter 7 directs our attention to the demise of an American megachurch (Mars Hill Church) as the result of administrative and financial scandals and severe accusations (but no legal actions) against the co-founder and main pastor of the church. As a result, the controversial pastor resigned and the church collapsed. In this chapter, Jessica Johnson focuses not so much on the scandal and the chain of events but on the tactics used by critics and opponents—former insiders and collaborators as well as outsiders—to bring the celebrity pastor down through social media. His authority was ridiculed, and by constructing and spreading a counter-narrative the pastor lost mastery over the narrative surrounding the church. Johnson flags the successful use of irony, parody, and ridicule. The use of social media with online public testimonies and online archives created a counter-history and encouraged others to become aware of the harm they had been experiencing, in particular women who complained about the abusiveness of the pastor's teaching on sex.

Chapter 8 addresses an eccentric case of religious demise that took place in a commune in rural Oregon (USA). Bhagwan, the main character in the religion, was a guru who in a paradoxical move denied being a religious leader, yet at the same time claimed to be one and acted as one. He publicly declared: "For the first time in the whole history of mankind, a religion has died." The proclamation of the death of this religion was a performative act serving to put the leader back into control in a situation of crisis suffered by the famed and notorious commune as a result of the departure and defection of its main managers. The public statement was also an ironical performative publicity stunt as part of an ongoing campaign against institutional or traditional religion in the name of "real" religion or religiosity. The dissolution of this religion was staged as a liberation from the imposture imposed on the innocent commune and its deceived leader by the managers who had defected. Incidentally, the chief secretary of the guru had also posed as the high priestess of the religion, the creation of which had strong elements of a parody of traditional religions; in the formal founding and acting out of this religion elements of play and seriousness were entangled. Compared to other cases dealt with in this volume, Chapter 8 (by the present author) moves on a meta-level as it employs the category of religion in a reflexive manner, as a strategic maneuver and a deliberate construction and de-construction.

The commune in Oregon (USA) was facing a series of legal challenges, including zoning or land use and immigration laws issues. Together with labour and employment practices, medical issues, and sexual abuse, these are part of a repertoire of accusations that states can use to destabilize religious groups.

In Chapter 9, Stuart A. Wright presents seven cases where prototypical Western-style democracies—the United States and France—that are officially and legally committed to ideals of religious freedom have in recent decades perpetrated actions, most prominently raids, against small religious groups. As a result of the state actions, these religious groups have been effectively extinguished, largely dissolved, and debilitated or put out of business. In some cases, leaders saw no other option but to terminate their activities or to go underground. Groups that wish to defend themselves against legal accusations have to incur expenses that in many cases go beyond their means. Wright reminds us that states play an active role in determining the relative success or failure of religions.

In Chapter 10, by contrast, Carole M. Cusack and James R. Lewis review four cases where religious groups (NRMs) have terminated their existence by committing collective suicide, mass murder, or a combination of both. For only one of the cases, however, there is overwhelming evidence that the act of self-annihilation was performed voluntarily and by consensus. In the other cases, the voluntary character of the violent acts can be disputed; moreover, in these three cases, the male leader of the group had passed the peak of his abilities and was suffering from serious health problems. In all four cases, their violent self-effacement was probably understood by themselves as ultimate tactics of eschatological empowerment.

Notes

1   Frisk (2007) is an exceptional study of later stages of development of formerly controversial religions.
2   Theoretical contributions: Colpe (1986); Robbins (2014); de Jong (2016).
3   http://news.bbc.co.uk/2/hi/south_asia/8498534.stm
4   https://edition.cnn.com/2012/10/05/world/europe/scotland-dead-dialect/index.html
5   https://www.thetimes.co.uk/article/death-of-a-language-last-ever-speaker-of-livonian-passes-away-aged-103-8k0rlplv8xj
6   https://www.kfyrtv.com/content/news/Edwin-Benson-last-known-fluent-speaker-of-Mandan-passes-away-at-85-405723515.html
7   https://www.nytimes.com/2017/12/26/world/americas/peru-amazon-the-end.html
8   https://www.theguardian.com/us-news/2017/jan/03/shakers-maine-sabbathday-lake-frances-carr-death; https://www.economist.com/united-states/2017/01/12/the-dying-out-of-the-sects-last-members-may-not-mean-the-end-for-the-shakers
9   https://www.nytimes.com/2018/03/17/us/trappist-monks-mepkin-abbey.html

References

Campbell, L. (2016), "Language Isolates and Their History, or, What's Weird, Anyway?" in N. Rolle, J. Steffman, and J. Sylak-Glassman (eds.), *Proceedings of the 36th Annual Meeting of the Berkeley Linguistics Society, February 6–7, 2010*, 16–31. Berkeley, CA: University of California: Department of Linguistics.

Colpe, C. (1986), "Was bedeutet «Untergang einer Religion»?" in H. Zinser (eds.), *Der Untergang von Religionen*, 9–33. Berlin: Reimer.

Crystal, D. (2014), *Language Death*. Cambridge: Cambridge University Press.

De Jong, A. (2016), "The Disintegration and Death of Religions," in M. Stausberg and S. Engler (eds.), *Oxford Handbooks Online*, 646–64. London: Oxford University Press.

Frisk, L. (2007), *De nya religiösa rörelserna—vart tog de vägen?* Nora: Nya Doxa.

Lamont, W. M. (2006), *Last Witnesses: The Muggletonian History, 1652-1979*. Aldershot: Ashgate.

Paldam, E. (2017), "Chumash Conversions: The Historical Dynamics of Religious Change in Native California," *Numen*, 64 (5–6): 596.

Reader, I. (2012), "Secularisation, R.I.P.? Nonsense! The 'Rush Hour Away from the Gods' and the Decline of Religion in Contemporary Japan," *Journal of Religion in Japan*, 1: 7–36.

Robbins, J. (2014), "How Do Religions End? Theorizing Religious Traditions from the Point of View of How They Disappear," *Cambridge Anthropology*, 32 (2): 2–15.

Sosis, R. and E. R. Bressler (2003), "Cooperation and Commune Longevity: A Test of the Costly Signaling Theory of Religion," *Cross-Cultural Research*, 37 (2): 211–39.

Urban, H. B. (2011), *The Church of Scientology: A History of a New Religion*. Princeton, NJ: Princeton University Press.

Wright, S. A. and S. J. Palmer (2018), "Countermovement Mobilization and State Raids on Minority Religious Communities," *Journal for the Scientific Study of Religion*, 57 (3): 616–33.

1

How Religions End: Terms and Types

Stuart A. Wright, Michael Stausberg, and Carole M. Cusack

There is a paucity of studies on how religions disband, dissolve, or die. Most of the research appears to be directed toward religious sustainability, growth, or cultural continuity (Robbins 2014; Stark 2012; Stark and Bainbridge 1985), or in the case of secularization theory, how *religion in general* has had a declining influence on institutions of power and authority in modern societies (Berger et al. 2008; Bruce 2011; Chaves 1994; Wilson 1987). Regarding the latter, how a particular religion declines or dissolves is analytically independent of secularization or modernization; one doesn't necessitate the other.

Terms

We will begin by suggesting some distinctions and definitions. To begin with, we need to distinguish between decline and demise, even though they partially overlap. Both terms can be used by outside and inside observers and analysts, even though they may assign a different meaning to this process. Speaking of decline can be a matter of nostalgia, or a rhetorical lament meant to rejuvenate commitment. *Decline* in a religion is here defined as an attenuation or decrease in activities, attitudes, beliefs, and commitments related to this religion (*disengagement*) and a reduction in the number of adherents, members, supporters, and sympathizers (*disaffiliation* or *decrease*). Decline refers to a process, which can gradually spread over several generations, can intensify in certain moments, or can be more sudden (e.g., as a result of a crisis). This process is not inevitable but can also be intercepted and inverted, for example, by revivals. Moreover, decline can be an issue of measurement: what some would define as decline, others would interpret as change or transformation; for example, the decrease in overt religious practice can be interpreted as increasing spiritualization or a notable decline in the number of adherents can be explained as strategic downsizing or evidence for the approaching of the end of times. Decline can lead to demise, but not necessarily so, and demise can set in without extended preceding processes of decline. By *demise* we mean a process that results in the end or *extinction* of a religion (as observers know it). A group that exhibits demographic decline, be it the result of disaffiliation, a discontinuation of inter-generational retention of commitment ("investment," see below), or a continuous demographic decline in population as the result of a negative reproduction rate (*decrease*), can be called *endangered*; this can be used as an alarmist trope or as an analytical category (similar to endangered languages). Demise is not a natural process, nor one that can be diagnosed unequivocally; sometimes the end is expected, but clear-cut and unambiguous finality is the exception rather than the rule. It is a matter of perspective whether the continued use of a word, name, or symbol in other contexts would count for the continued existence of a religion, even in fragmented form; some may interpret the process as *disaggregation*, *disintegration*, or *fragmentation*; others would speak of the end of a religion. The demise of a religion does not exclude its reappearance, reconstruction, or restoration in posterity; this is then a designed and invented tradition, an appropriation, or a rebranding. Rebranding may also signal the end of a religion once it decides to label itself predominantly in non-religious terms. We can call this a *mutation*. A more prosaic and common process of demise is *disappearance*; in many cases there are simply no more traces or sources available, so that there is the theoretical possibility that a religion continues to exist unobserved. A related phenomenon is groups that deliberately have gone into hiding or conceal their religious identity. Rare cases of demise are public acts of *dissolution* or *abolishment*. Such a religion is then declared *defunct*. The opposite phenomenon involves cases of deliberate *replacement*, (attempted) *effacement*, or (achieved) *annihilation* of religions, either because that religion is considered useless, dangerous, and/or inferior or because religion itself is considered a threat or inept.

An analytical framework for examining religious demise must consider the various ways in which this process may take place. In this chapter, we propose nine trajectories of religious demise. The proposed categories relate to both how and why religions end.

Most of the cases discussed in this volume belong to the field of new religious movements (NRMs). A relative latecomer to the field of Religious Studies, it began in the 1930s when scholars from a liberal Protestant background began to study the "anomalous religions at the time, like Christian Science, Spiritualism, Seventh-day Adventism, the Jehovah's Witnesses and Theosophy" (Ashcraft 2018: 9). The study of NRMs as a subfield gained ground in the 1960s and 1970s, and has in the twenty-first century become a major part of the academic study of religion, albeit as an area that presents challenges to traditional definitions of "religion" and which frequently focuses on unorthodox, transgressive, and fringe phenomena. Within the study of NRMs the question of the death (or "failure") of religions, though never so popular as that of the birth of religions (Stark 1985), has received some scant attention (Wilson 1987). Clearly, some groups are able to survive challenges where most others falter or fail. This fact is sometimes acknowledged, for example, for the United States: "Of the plethora of new religions that emerged in the United States after 1965, many are defunct or essentially defunct; some survive but in heavily modified form; and a few survive without massive changes" (Miller 2010: 14). Similarly, for Japan it has been observed that in the study of the great number of Japanese new religions—and their number has vastly increased in the postwar period—research has focused mainly on the rapid growth and expansion of some groups, while the fate of the "losers" has been ignored in scholarship, unless their demise has caught media attention because of criminal charges or because of the involvement of celebrities (Baffelli, Chapter 3, this volume). In the following, we are seeking to put some signposts on an unchartered territory.

Trajectories

We propose that there are at least nine possible categories in which religious demise or dissolution can occur. However, when speaking of categories we refer to constellations of main reasons resulting in demise. It is tempting to place these categories on an axis that distinguishes exogenous (external) from endogenous (internal) forces that impact on the process leading to demise (see also Wilson [1987] and Miller [2010] with different interpretations). The distinction serves to highlight the location of the main disruptive force: are they within the sphere of action of the respective religion or beyond? In actual fact, however, exogeneous and endogenous forces may operate in conjunction: exogeneous factors can accelerate and thrive on endogenous problems, and endogenous forces can make exogeneous forces more challenging than they would have been without any preceding endogenous troubles. For example, internal problems that leak out to the media can be thrown back at a movement as external pressure. A main potential endogenous factor for demise of a religion is if it fails to match up to its promises or fails to meet the expectations of its "investors" (i.e., people who have invested commitment, energy and time in it as adherents, consumers, members, sympathizers, etc.) without providing rationalization for this disappointment, thereby transforming commitment into ongoing "investments." The broader cultural context is difficult to position on the endogenous/exogenous axis, as both insiders and outsiders have to relate it.

Endogenous Forces of Demise

1. Leadership

Some religions face internal crises which may prove to be too great to survive. It is inferred here that the demise of the group is largely the result of factors that are more or less under the control of the religious group and its leaders. For example, leaders may lack the skills, insights, or judgments to ameliorate a crisis. Members may lose faith or confidence in leadership regarding decisions made, or they may be in conflict with leadership over the direction of the group. Of course, there are a number of possible outcomes in this regard. Members may leave over conflicts, and leavers may or may not form new factions. Minor incidences of defection are not likely to impact the sustainability of a religion. On the other hand, the departure of a large faction may break apart the religious community as it is unable to endure deep and intractable divisions. The sexually experimental intentional community Kerista, for example, peacefully disbanded in 1991, after its founder John Peltz Presmont (1923–2009), known as "Brother Jud," was forced to leave due to internal pressure from a majority of members (Cusack 2019a).

The leader's actions may be seen as a betrayal of the group's mission (Frisk and Palmer 2015). In some cases, the leader may even be charged with a crime, arrested and incarcerated, imperiling the viability of the group (e.g., Aumism, Neo-Phare, Nuwaubian Nation/Ansaaru Allah Community, Knutby Filadelfia [see Chapter 4, this volume], and Aum Shinrikyo [see Chapter 3, this volume]). Such a grave crisis in leadership can lead to dissolution, abeyance, splintering, or schism. Yet a simple and inevitable event such as the death of a leader can also precipitate the demise of a new religion. J. Gordon Melton gives examples of groups that ended with their founders or relatively shortly after: for example, Frank B. Robinson (1856–1948) founded Psychiana in 1929, and its demise was 1952, despite the efforts of Robinson's son to keep it going; and the Spirit Fruit Society, incorporated by its founder Jacob Beilhart (1867–1908) in Lisbon, Ohio in 1901, ended in 1930 (Melton 1991: 9).

2. Economy and Resources

Economic problems may beset the group in ways they are unable to overcome. In the case of the Love Israel Family, a communal religious group founded in 1968 in Seattle, economic changes involving commercial ventures, borrowing funds, and acquiring mortgage properties resulted in deep divisions and conflicts with regard to the original goals of the group (LeWarne 2009). Debts accrued, socioeconomic divisions appeared, and the communal character of the group was altered in ways that displeased many members. Also, the growing number of children put a strain on economic resources and "parents felt they were not receiving essential needs in daily life and schooling" (LeWarne 2009: 134).

Another, very different, example of demise due to economic problems is the Synanon therapeutic community, founded by Charles E. "Chuck" Dederich Sr. (1913–97) in 1958 as a drug rehabilitation program in Santa Monica, California (Ofshe 1980). In the 1970s Synanon transformed into a religion, the Church of Synanon, gaining tax-free status as a result. Synanon was involved in a range of dubious activities which attracted the attention of law enforcement agencies, and the Internal Revenue Service revoked its tax-exempt status in 1982, ordering the repayment of almost 20 million dollars in taxes. This legal judgment resulted in bankruptcy, and Synanon was formally dissolved in 1991 (Janzen 2001).

3. Intergenerational Transmission

Intergenerational transmission and retention is a precondition for a religion to flourish. This may pose challenges even for mainstream religions such as Catholicism (Bullivant 2019). For new religions challenges often arise when children are born and the group must make adjustments to family roles, parenting, childhood education, training, and discipline (Palmer and Hardman 1999). First-generation religions can focus on evangelizing, recruitment, fundraising, disseminating religious literature, and other activities that are outwardly directed. But with the advent of the second generation, the focus becomes more inward. This may lead to conflicts with leaders, conflicts among members, and even conflicts within families. Research suggests that these problems are mirrored in processes of religious defection—how and why people leave new religious movements or NRMs (Wright 1983, 1984, 1987, 1988, 2014; Wright and Ebaugh 1993). Religious defection can signal demise or decline.

4. Violent Self-Annihilation

Collective suicide/homicide may result in the demise of the group. Peoples Temple, Heaven's Gate, Order of the Solar Temple, and the Movement for the Restoration of the Ten Commandments of God are examples in recent decades (see Chapter 10, this volume). There is evidence to suggest that in some instances of collective violence, it was a response, at least in part, to the threat of defection or perceived loss of key members which might lead to mass defection and/or disintegration of the group (e.g., Peoples Temple, Movement for the Restoration of the Ten Commandments of God). Thus, it might be instructive to review studies of religious defection to assess how religious demise and defection are intertwined.

The strict analytical distinction between endogenous and exogenous forces may obscure the fact that in some cases, the factors or correlates linked to religious demise may involve the *interaction* of the two. For example, evidence suggests that in the two collective suicide/homicide cases of Peoples Temple and Movement for the Restoration of the Ten Commandments, external pressures from state officials were perceived as threatening the respective missions of the groups. According to John Hall, Jim Jones reacted to the pressure by organized opponents (Concerned Relatives) who had successfully persuaded California Congressman Leo Ryan to visit the Guyana property to investigate claims of abuse. When some of the members in Guyana approached Ryan and asked to leave with him, Jones perceived this as a destructive force threatening to undermine his life's work. He was already prepared for a response in the form of the ritual of "revolutionary suicide" (Hall 1989, 1995; Hall, Schuyler, and Trinh 2000; see also Chidester 1988; Wessinger 2000). In the case of the Movement for the Restoration of the Ten Commandments, our knowledge is hazier because the incident took place in a remote part of Uganda and the forensic evidence and resources were substandard. But Atuhaire (2003) suggests that the leaders of the movement—Credonia Mwerinde, Joseph Kibweteere, and Dominic Kataribabo—were on the verge of being exposed as charlatans and orchestrated the mass deaths. There is also evidence that some of the collective violence were clearly homicides rather than suicides. Following a failed apocalyptic prophecy on January 1, 2000, the Movement began to unravel. Payments to the Church decreased dramatically. Ugandan police believe that some members, who were required to sell their possessions and turn over the money to the Movement, demanded the return of their money. Officials believe that events that followed were engineered by leaders in response to the crisis in the ranks.

Historically, one can think of examples of religious suicide such as the Russian Old Believers (Robbins 1986) or the Jewish zealots at Masada (Ben-Yehuda 2014; Yadin 1966). The Russian Old Believers went underground and developed an apocalyptic mindset after repressive legislation was passed against them in 1684. From approximately 1690 to 1860 tens of thousands of Old Believers actively committed suicide or devised situations in which attackers massacred them (Robbins 2014; [1986]: 35–6). Yet, the movement was sufficiently large that the suicides did not bring about its end; over time, moderation and abandonment of suicide as a religious practice won out.

5. Cognitive Disconfirmation (Failed Prophecy)

The failure of religions not to deliver on its promises causes an inherent frailty, but the promises can be ambiguous, vague, and empirically non-testable, and the assessment of the situation is subject to interpretation and rationalization.

Some promises, however, appear to be more prone to falsification, for instance healing and prophecy, in particular if this takes the form of a precise prediction of events in the near future (see the case of Movement for the Restoration of the Ten Commandments in the previous section). Failed prophecy may lead to religious demise as Wright and Greil (2011) have shown in the case of Chen Tao, a Taiwanese UFO group. In the summer of 1997, approximately 140 emigrant members of a little-known group appeared in Garland, Texas and declared the site a holy place where God would descend from heaven. The group's founder and prophet, Hon-Ming Chen, announced that God would appear on TV Channel 18 on March 25, 1998, six days before the revelatory date (March 31) to warn the population of the coming tribulation. The news made national headlines since the date was only a year removed from the mass suicides of another UFO group, Heaven's Gate, in Rancho Santa Fe, California in which thirty-nine members died. When the prophecy failed to materialize, Master Chen called a press conference and sought to minimize the disconfirmation, announcing that God had pushed the apocalyptic date back to 1999. The group abruptly departed in May and a remnant of thirty-five members relocated to Lockport, New York. Group members who were interviewed by Wright and Greil (2011) dismissed the importance of the previous failed prophecy and remained confident that the new prophecy would be fulfilled. However, the second prophecy also failed to materialize in 1999 and shortly afterwards financial trouble forced members to find outside employment to support the mission. Within a short time Chen Tao disintegrated, and members returned home to Taiwan. In a test of the Festinger et al. (2009 [1956]) thesis that groups typically survive prophetic failure through a readjustment process to cognitive dissonance, this case study found that the group only partly survived the first failed prophecy—only thirty-five members out of 140 remained—and then completely dissolved soon after the second failed prophecy. However, Wright and Greil (2011: 169) acknowledge that there were other social and economic factors likely contributing to the group's failure and which likely weakened the charismatic relationship between Master Chen and his devotees.

Palmer and Finn (1992) studied two Canadian religious groups that experienced failed prophecy—one survived and one did not. In the surviving group, the Institute of Applied Physics (IAM), they found that the leader effectively improvised a reinterpretation of the prophecy by claiming its spiritual fulfillment and by initiating "rituals of apocalypse" that helped to cultivate an emotional catharsis and strong social support. In the failed group, La Mission de l'Esprit Saint, the leader responded by exposing his own doubts and by converting to another apocalyptic religious group (Jehovah's Witnesses) four months after the disconfirmation, convincing many of the members to follow him.

According to Lorne Dawson (2011) who examined fifty studies of prophetic failure involving twenty-eight different religious groups, he found only two entirely unambiguous cases of groups disintegrating after a failed prophecy. Approximately 69 percent survived prophetic failure "quite well with varying degrees of success." However, the fate of 26 percent was more ambiguous: they "border(ed) on being failures because they experienced significant disruptions and losses of membership from which they did not fully recover" (Dawson 2011). In the final analysis, the exact disposition of these groups, he states, "is open to debate." What constitutes survival, he notes, is difficult because we often lack reliable evidence about the exact number of members before and after the prophetic failures. Moreover, the time span covered in these studies is usually too limited. Dawson's study illustrates vividly the definitional dilemmas and conceptual complexities of our project.

6. Transmutation and Replacement

Transmutation refers to the processes of religious change that involve the dissolution of older traditions when they are replaced by newer ones. Ancient Egyptian religion, whose temples were abandoned or ruined, has recently been read as producing a "conglomerate" of old and new (Frankfurter 2018: 2), so that transmutation and replacement are two sides of the same coin. Instances of transmutations can also be found, for example, in the case of the transition from what is called Old Norse pagan religion to medieval Christianity: sacred sites are being continued, iconographic repertoire is adapted, and pagan mythologies are preserved by putting them into a new garb. The entire religious landscape from Europe through the Middle East and South Asia as much as that of the Americas is one of religious replacements and transmutations.

Robbins (2014) discusses the recent "disappearance" of the Urapmin religion in New Guinea through a "passive accommodation" to Christian missionaries. The Urapmin began sending their young people out to study with the missionaries during the early 1960s, resulting in the conversion of these students. The students returned to convert their siblings and parents. A Christian revival swept through the community in 1977, sealing the conversion of the Urapmin and the end of their ancestral religion. Social anthropologist Donald Tuzin (1997) found in a return trip to continue his research on the secret male Tambaran cult among the Ilahita Arapesh in New Guinea that the men had destroyed the sacred paraphernalia and revealed all the secrets to women, thus signaling an end to the cult evidently engineered by the male leaders themselves.

Raymond Firth (2011), who conducted three separate fieldwork expeditions to Tikopia, a Polynesian island, describes in his last visit how the two remaining pagan *ariki* (highest ranking chiefs), along with a hand full of faithful followers, celebrated the *kava* of the departing gods in the final stages of tribal conversion to Christianity. Firth provides a sorrowful account of visiting the old sacrificial site and seeing the sacra in decay.

For NRMs, Carole M. Cusack (2019b) has also examined "demise by transformation" by focusing on two groups, The Process Church of the Final Judgment and the Holy Order of MANS. The Process Church was founded by Mary Ann MacLean and Robert de Grimston in 1966. De Grimston later had an affair with another member and was expelled from the group in 1974. The Process Church remnant under MacLean changed names multiple times becoming the Church of the Millennium in 1974, the Foundation Faith of the Millennium in 1976, the Foundation Faith of God in 1978, and finally the Best Friends Animal Sanctuary in 1984. In its last incarnation, the Church became an animal rights group with no discernible link to religion except for perhaps a strained interpretation of paganism (see Bainbridge 2015). By most accounts, the Process Church was dissolved by transmutation.

7. Split and Splinter

Religions may also split or splinter, developing schisms. The original group may become defunct as the new schisms essentially replace the original. Erica Baffelli has followed the demise of Aum Shinrikyo after the arrest of Asahara Shōkō and other top leaders. Aum was officially banned in the wake of the sarin gas attacks in the Tokyo subway station. The residual members formed two groups, Aleph and Hikari no Wa. Both groups claim significant theological differences from Aum, but were born of the crisis of the "Aum Affair" (Baffelli 2012, this volume; Baffelli and Reader 2012).

The Holy Order of MANS (HOOM) was founded by Earl Blighton in the 1960s and combined Theosophical, Gnostic, Rosicrucian, yogic, and traditional Roman Catholic elements into a uniquely blended religious belief system (Lucas 1995). Blighton died in 1974 and Vincent Rossi assumed leadership of HOOM. Under Rossi, the church was rebranded as Christ the Savior Brotherhood, achieving communion with the Orthodox Church in 1988. A splinter group formed, The Brotherhood of Christ under Father Peter Bowes, but was short-lived. It was later united with another splinter group, the Holy Order of Sophia led by Mother Clare Watts (Linda Cozzolino). The newly formed group was subsequently named the Order of Christ Sophia (Lewis and Levine 2009). Bowes left in 2012 to found the Ruach Center; Watts died in 2017 and the group was renamed the Order of the Mystical Christ/Sophia Wisdom Centers under the leadership of Isabella Tures (Cusack 2019b: 2). In the cases described, the original religious group produced splinter groups which replaced the progenitor and became something entirely different.

Exogenous Forces of Demise

8. Organized Opposition and Mobilization

Research suggests that state control of minority religions has been increasing in recent decades (Finke, Mataic, and Fox 2017; Kirkham 2013). Minority religions are often cast as a threat to the public and even to their own members. This can be seen vividly in the efforts by well-organized, transnational anticult networks that seek to stigmatize groups such as "cults," making sweeping claims about destructive practices (brainwashing, mass suicide, sexual abuse, involuntary labor, stockpiling weapons, etc.) and pressuring government authorities to take actions (Richardson 2004; Shupe and Darnell 2006). Wright and Palmer (2016, 2018) have documented a sharp increase in state raids on minority religions starting in the 1990s. They gathered data on 149 state raids in nineteen different countries in North America, Europe, Australia, South America, Japan, and Israel. The data cover raids over a seven-decade period beginning shortly after the Second World War. From the 1990s there was an exponential increase in raids; they found that almost 81 percent of government raids on NRMs have taken place since 1990 ($N = 120$). Richardson (1985) has suggested that one long-term impact of state control of minority faiths is the "deformation of NRMs." The use of mass raids on NRMs can have numerous debilitating effects, including sensationalistic news coverage labeling a group as a "destructive cult," the creation of a hostile local climate, costly legal fees to mount a legal defense against charges, and adverse financial and business impacts.

Some minority religions have not been merely debilitated but thoroughly decimated. Wright (this volume) documents seven cases in which government raids resulted in the dissolution or complete destruction of the religious communities. These seven cases do not include other instances where actions by the state drove groups underground or out of the country altogether (Wright and Palmer 2016, 239–40). In some instances, groups such as Horus (aka International Center for Parapsychology and Scientific Research of the New Age) and the Center for Teaching of Biodynamism, both in France, were forced to close their doors and even banned. Any review of religious demise stemming from external forces must consider the role played by aggressive or repressive state actions of control.

9. Religiocide and Religious Cleansing

When emphasizing the agency of native elites (old or new) in the process of the establishment of new religious identities, we have dealt with them as instances of transmutation and replacement (see above). The category of religiocide refers to the same effect—a total or almost total change in religious identity in a population—but the agency lies here with intruding forces, typically missionaries who collaborate with economic and political powers. Religiocide or religious cleansing refers to the planned destruction of a competing religious tradition by violent means; these means can range from physical acts like killing, imprisonment, physical punishment, and destruction or sacrilege of religious and ritual objects, to threats, denial of access to sacred sites to other means like re-education, denial of social or legal recognition, where the latter can also take the form of denying the religious character of traditions. In the case of the Lule Sami (Lapps), an authoritative study has found that it was "the threats, punishments and sacrileges, more than anything else, that decultured the Lule Sami from their indigenous religious customs" (Rydving 1995: 165). The expression "more than anything else" indicates that in most historical cases change was not violently enforced on all people. The most tragic contemporary example of a religiocide or religious cleansing is the actions by ISIS against Christians and Yezidis, but we may also recall the anti-Muslim Bosnian genocide.

The Roman Catholic Church under Pope Innocent III organized a crusading army to destroy the Cathars of Southern France in 1209. The Cathars rejected the authority of the Church and its priesthood, labeling the Pope and the hierarch corrupt and unworthy. Offering indulgences similar to those in the Crusades, as many as 10,000 crusaders marched against the Cathars. After the victorious crusaders had leveled town after town, the Albigensian Crusade in southern France came to an end in 1229 (Power 2013: 1061). Yet the heresy of Catharism continued for almost a century after this military victory, being ended only by the Inquisition led by Jacques Fournier, Bishop of Pamiers, from 1318 to 1325, in which the last Cathar perfect, Guillaume Bélibaste, was burned at the stake in 1321 (Given 1997: 90).

The US Calvary's massacre of the Lakota Sioux ghost dancers at Wounded Knee, South Dakota, in 1890 is also an example of official conquest and genocide. Roxanne Dunbar-Ortiz, in her brilliant history of indigenous peoples in America (2014), has documented untold cases of US government military actions in the form of conquests, raids, and massacres targeting Native American tribes and their "heathen" beliefs. Space does not permit an exhaustive account of these kinds of incidents. But we can be sure there are countless examples of Western colonization leading to religious demise among indigenous peoples.

Concluding Thoughts

In offering an outline delineating categories of demise, we acknowledge that endogenous and exogenous forces are often intertwined and not mutually exclusive. Similarly, few historical and empirical cases will fit one of our nine categories/trajectories exclusively. The cases we describe above are meant to illustrate these categories for heuristic purposes, not to exhaust their empirical analysis. For example, leadership and organizational issues will pervade most cases of demise, even where leadership issues did not trigger the chain of events. When considering the cases discussed in the subsequent chapters of this book, we sought to identify evidence where one category appeared to be the best fit for the data.

To provide a simplified roadmap for the following chapters, Table 1 provides a matrix of our nine factors/trajectories applied to the cases discussed in this volume.

This matrix illustrates the logistical complexity of our collective endeavor while attempting to account for multiple factors and influences on religious demise. Though we employ case studies in the following chapters to carve out some pathways to understanding religious demise, we have a larger purpose in mind. It is our hope that this volume provides a compass or template for a more theoretical approach to religious demise and that others may build on what we have modestly achieved in this exploratory work.

Table 1 Matrix of factors affecting religious demise

Factors	Chapters								
	2	3	4	5	6	7	8	9	10
Leadership		x	x	x	x	x	x		
Economic resources					x		x		
Intergenerational transmission				x	x				
Violent self-annihilation									x
Cognitive disconfirmation			x		x				
Transmutation	x								
Split/splinter		x							
Organized opposition		x	x			x	x	x	
Religiocide								x	

References

Ashcraft, W. M. (2018), *A Historical Introduction to the Study of New Religious Movements*. London and New York: Routledge.

Atuhaire, B. (2003), *The Ugandan Cult Tragedy: A Private Investigation*. Cambridge: Janus Publishing Company.

Baffelli, E. (2012), "Hikari no Wa: A New Religion Recovering from Disaster," *Japanese Journal of Religious Studies*, 39 (1): 29–49.

Baffelli, E. and I. Reader (2012), "Impact and Ramifications: The Aftermath of the Aum Affair in the Japanese Religious Context," *Japanese Journal of Religious Studies*, 39 (1): 1–28.

Bainbridge, W. S. (2015), "The Paganization Process," *Interdisciplinary Journal of Research on Religion*, 11: 1–26.

Ben-Yehuda, N. (2014), "The Sicarii Suicide on Masada and the Foundation of a National Myth," in J. R. Lewis and C. M. Cusack (eds.), *Sacred Suicide*, 11–28. Farnham and Burlington, VT: Ashgate.

Berger, P., G. Davie, and E. Fokas (2008), *Religious America, Secular Europe? A Theme and Variations*. Burlington, VT: Ashgate.

Bruce, S. (2011), *Secularization: In Defence of an Unfashionable Theory*. Oxford: Oxford University Press.

Bullivant, S. S. (2019), *Mass Exodus: Catholic Disaffiliation in Britain and America since Vatican II*. Oxford: Oxford University Press.

Chaves, M. (1994), "Secularization as Declining Religious Authority," *Social Forces*, 72 (3): 749–74.

Chidester, D. (1988), *Salvation and Suicide: An Interpretation of Jim Jones, Peoples Temple, and Jonestown*. Bloomington: Indiana University Press.

Cusack, C. M. (2019a), "Both Outside and Inside: 'Ex-Members' of New Religions and Spiritualities and the Maintenance of Community and Identity on the Internet," in G. Chryssides and S. Gregg (eds.), *The Insider/Outsider Debate: New Perspectives in the Study of Religion*, 393–415. Sheffield: Equinox.

Cusack, C. M. (2019b), "The Elusive and Multiple Demises of New Religious and Spiritual Groups," unpublished seminar paper.

Dawson, L. (2011), "Prophetic Failure in Millennial Movements," in C. Wessinger (ed.), *The Oxford Handbook of Millennialism*. Oxford: Oxford University Press. Available online: https://www.oxfordhandbooks.com/view/10.1093/oxfordhb/9780195301052.001.0001/oxfordhb-9780195301052-e-8

De Jong, A. (2018), "The Disintegration and Death of Religions," in M. Stausberg and S. Engler (eds.), *Oxford Handbooks Online*, 1–23. Oxford: Oxford University Press.

Dunbar-Ortiz, R. (2014), *An Indigenous People's History of the United States*. Boston: Beacon Press.

Festinger, L., H. Riecken and S. Schachter (2009 [1956]), *When Prophecy Fails*. London: Pinter & Martin Ltd.

Finke, R., D. Mataic, and J. Fox (2017), "Assessing the Impact of Religious Registration," *Journal for the Scientific Study of Religion*, 56 (4): 720–36.

Firth, R. (2011), *Rank and Religion in Tikopia: A Study in Polynesian Paganism and Conversion to Christianity*. London: Routledge.

Frankfurter, D. (2018). *Christianizing Egypt: Syncretism and Local Worlds in Late Antiquity*. Princeton: Princeton University Press.

Frisk, L. and S. J. Palmer (2015), "The Life Story of Helge Fossmo, Former Pastor of Knutby Filadelfia, as Told in Prison: A Narrative Analysis Approach," *International Journal for the Study of New Religions*, 6 (1): 51–73.

Given, J. B. (1997), *Inquisition and Medieval Society: Power, Discipline and Resistance in Languedoc*. Ithaca, NY and London: Cornell University Press.

Hall, J. R. (1989), *Gone from the Promised Land: Jonestown in American Cultural History*. London: Transaction.

Hall, J. R. (1995), "Public Narratives and the Apocalyptic Sect: From Jonestown to Mt. Carmel," in S. A. Wright (ed.), *Armageddon in Waco: Critical Perspectives on the Branch Davidian Conflict*, 205–35. Chicago, IL: University of Chicago Press.

Hall, J. R., P. Schuyler, and S. Trinh (2000), *Apocalypse Observed: Religious Movements and Violence in North America, Europe and Japan*. London: Routledge.

Janzen, R. (2001), *The Rise and Fall of Synanon: A California Utopia*. Baltimore, MD and London: Johns Hopkins University Press.

Kirkham, D. M. (2013), *State Responses to Minority Religions*. London: Ashgate.

LeWarne, C. P. (2009), *The Love Israel Family*. Seattle, WA: University of Washington Press.

Lewis, J. R. and N. Levine (2009), *The Children of Jesus and Mary: The Order of Christ Sophia*. New York: Oxford.

Lucas, P. C. (1995), *The Odyssey of a New Religion: The Holy Order of MANS from New Age to Orthodoxy*. Bloomington: Indiana University Press.

Melton, J. G. (1991), "Introduction. When Prophets Die: The Succession Crisis in New Religions," in T. Miller (ed.), *When Prophets Die: The Postcharismatic Fate of New Religious Movements*, 1–12. Albany, NY: State University of New York Press.

Miller, T. (2010), "The Evolution of American Spiritual Communities, 1965–2009," *Nova Religio: The Journal of Alternative and Emergent Religions*, 13 (3): 14–33.

Ofshe, R. (1980), "The Social Development of the Synanon Cult: The Managerial Strategy of Organizational Transformation," *Sociological Analysis*, 41 (2): 109–27.

Palmer, S. J. and C. Hardman (1999), *Children in New Religions*. New Brunswick, NJ: Rutgers.

Palmer, S. J. and N. Finn (1992), "Coping with the Apocalypse in Canada; Experiences of Endtime in La Mission de l'Esprit Saint and the Institute of Applied Physics," *Sociological Analysis*, 53: 397–415.

Power, D. (2013), "Who Went on the Albigensian Crusade?" *English Historical Review*, CXXVIII (534): 1047–85.

Richardson, J. T. (1985), "The Deformation of New Religions: Impacts of Societal and Organizational Factors," in T. Robbins, W. Shepherd, and J. McBride (eds.), *Cults, Culture, and the Law*, 163–75. Chico, CA: Scholars Press.

Richardson, J. T. (2004), *Regulating Religion: Case Studies from Around the Globe*, New York: Kluber.

Robbins, J. (2014), "How Do Religions End? Theorizing Religious Traditions from the Point of View of How They Disappear," *Cambridge Anthropology*, 32 (2): 2–15.

Robbins, T. (1986), "Religious Mass Suicide before Jonestown: The Russian Old Believers," *Sociological Analysis*, 47 (1): 1–20.

Rydving, H. (1995), *The End of Drum-Time: Religious Change among the Lule Saami, 1670s–1740s*, Stockholm: Uppsala University; Almqvist & Wiksell International.

Shupe, A. D. and S. Darnell (2006), *Agents of Discord: Deprogramming, Pseudoscience, and the American Anticult Movement*. New Brunswick, NJ: Transaction.

Stark, R. (ed). (1985), *Religious Movements: Genesis, Exodus, and Numbers*, ed. Rodney Stark. New York: Paragon House.

Stark, R. (2012), *The Triumph of Christianity: How the Jesus Movement Became the World's Largest Religion*. New York: HarperCollins.

Stark, R. and W. S. Bainbridge (1985), *The Future of Religion*, Berkeley, CA: University of California.

Tuzin, D. (1997), *The Cassowary's Revenge: The Life and Death of Masculinity in a New Guinea Society*. Chicago, IL: University of Chicago Press.

Wessinger, C. (2000), *How the Millennium Comes Violently: From Jonestown to Heaven's Gate*. London: Seven Bridges.

Wilson, B. R. (1987), "Factors in the Failure of the New Religious Movements", in D. G. Bromley and P. E. Hammond (eds.), *The Future of New Religious Movements*, 30–45. Macon, GA: Mercer University Press.

Wright, S. A. (1983), "Defection from New Religious Movements: A Test of Some Theoretical Propositions," in D. G. Bromley and J. T. Richardson (eds.), *The Deprogramming/Brainwashing Controversy: Sociological, Psychological, Legal and Historical Perspectives*, 106–21. New York: Edwin Mellen.

Wright, S. A. (1984), "Post-Involvement Attitudes of Voluntary Defectors from Controversial New Religious Movements," *Journal for the Scientific Study of Religion*, 23 (2): 172–82.

Wright, S. A. (1987), *Leaving Cults: The Dynamics of Defection*, Washington, DC: Society for the Scientific Study of Religion. Monograph Series.

Wright, S. A. (1988), "Leaving New Religious Movements: Issues, Theory and Research," in D. G. Bromley (ed.), *Falling From the Faith: The Causes and Consequences of Religious Apostasy*, 143–65. Beverly Hills, CA: Sage.

Wright, S. A. (2014), "Disengagement and Apostasy in New Religious Movements," in L. Rambo and C. Farkadian (eds.), *Oxford Handbook on Religious Conversion*, 706–35. New York: Oxford University Press.

Wright, S. A. and A. L. Greil (2011), "Failed Prophecy and Group Demise: The Case of Chen Tao," in D. Tuminia and W. Swatos (eds.), *How Prophecy Lives*, 153–72. London: Brill.

Wright, S. A. and H. R. Ebaugh (1993), "Leaving New Religions," in D. G. Bromley and J. K. Hadden (eds.), *Handbook of Cults and Sects in America*, 117–38. Greenwich: JAI Press.

Wright, S. A. and S. J. Palmer (2016), *Storming Zion: Government Raids on Religious Communities*. New York: Oxford University Press.

Wright, S. A. and S. J. Palmer (2018), "Countermovement Mobilization and State Raids on Minority Religious Communities," *Journal for the Scientific Study of Religion*, 57 (3): 616–33.

Yadin, Y. (1966), *Masada: Herod's Fortress and the Zealots' Last Stand*, New York: Random House.

2

When Does a Sacrifice Become "Just Meat"? A Sketch for a Theory of How Religions Stop Working

Joel Robbins

How can we tell when a religion has met its demise? We may think we know the end of a religion when we see one, but determining a definitive expiration date can be difficult. The workings of human memory and the vagaries of individual practice mean that a largely dead religion can hang on as a matter of stories of its heyday, or of small-scale revivals of bits and pieces of its ritual life, long after it might make sense to read last rites over the faith from an analytic point of view. Just as Elvis and Jimmy Hendrix keep releasing records for years after they are gone, in the realms of culture and social life more generally it seems no breaks are completely clean ones. It is this fact that motivates my opening query: how do we know when it makes sense to declare a religion officially dead?

I want to suggest one answer to this question here. I do not propose it as the only answer, but it is one that works for the case of religious demise I know best, and I hope it might work for others as well. My answer hinges on showing that we can determine fairly securely when the surviving bits of an old religion no longer do the work they once did: when healing rituals no longer heal or protect, rites of passage no longer confer new social roles, rituals of fertility no longer produce abundance, etc., and when discussions from memory therefore no longer feed into workable plans for action. In order to understand how we can determine when a religion stops working, we will need to know something about what makes a working religion work, and thus looking at how religions cease to function can give us an interesting vantage point on that issue. I therefore hope this argument may be of some worth for wider debates about what we can learn about religions more generally by studying the ways they pass on (a topic I take up in different terms in Robbins (2014)).

The primary theoretical resource I am going to draw on to illuminate how religions work and stop working is John Searle's (1995) account of the nature of what he calls "institutional facts." This theory is, in my experience, much more compelling when one uses it to solve a concrete problem than it is when presented in strictly abstract terms. For that reason, I first discuss my research with the Urapmin of Papua New Guinea and the complexities that surround the demise of their indigenous religion, and only then do I turn to exploring how Searle's account of the nature of institutional facts can help understand why it makes sense to claim that this demise has in fact been complete, despite some evidence that might be taken to point to a contrary conclusion.

On the Passing of an Indigenous Religion

The Urapmin are a language group of approximately 400 people living in the West Sepik Province of Papua New Guinea (PNG). Even by PNG standards, the Urapmin are remote. They have no electricity, roads, or airstrip, hardly participate in the cash economy, and live at six hours arduous walk from any of their nearest neighbors. They were not colonized until after the Second World War, and even when the Australian colonists reached their region the Urapmin were largely left on their own, their small population and the difficulties of accessing them making them mostly an afterthought for the rather bare-bones colonial government the Australians put in place. The same is pretty much true of the Australian Baptist Missionaries who set up shop among their neighbors to the East and West in the 1950s. They too rarely sent emissaries to Urapmin. In terms of outsiders directly pushing the Urapmin to adopt radically new ways of living, they have for the most part been left alone.

In the early 1990s, when I carried out fieldwork among the Urapmin, people complained regularly about government neglect, but there was little they could do about it. When it came to mission neglect, however, the Urapmin had found a way to address their concerns. In the 1960s, when their neighbors among whom missionaries were living were converting to Christianity and abandoning the regional religious system in which the Urapmin held exalted specialist roles, the Urapmin sent many young people, mostly boys but also some girls, to live at the mission station to their East and study at the mission schools. These young Urapmin were eager students and they learned with great success the missionaries' version of the Baptist faith. Many learned it so well that the mission employed them as evangelists to groups even more remote than the Urapmin themselves, but others went home to Urapmin and taught their relatives about Christianity. The efforts of these young teachers were in some respects remarkably successful; they taught all younger people to read the Papua New Guinea *lingua franca* (Tok Pisin) so they could read the Bible and they taught elder people many key Bible stories and the rudiments of the Christian tradition. They did not, however, make many converts. Thus, from the late 1960s through the mid-1970s, Urapmin was a community with a good deal of Christian knowledge, but very little Christian practice beyond private prayer offered by individuals who had converted at the mission school.

This picture changed radically in 1977. In the mid-1970s, a charismatic revival movement that had begun in New Zealand and later found its way to PNG began to move through much of the country, carried from place to place by local people. It was in 1977 that the revival made it to the Urapmin area. Several Urapmin who had witnessed the revival in other parts of the region brought news of it home. Very quickly, people began to be, as they put it, "kicked" by the Holy Spirit. They reported feeling hot, deeply convinced of their own sinful nature, and confident that the Christian God really existed. Over the course of months, many Urapmin adults and young people had these experiences, and those who did not witnessed their relatives having them. In response, more and more people converted. By the end of the year, the entire community defined itself as Christian, and working individually and collectively toward Christian salvation has been at the center of Urapmin life ever since.

In a piece about a different topic, I would go on to write more about the nature of Urapmin Christianity. I would point out how sophisticated it is, and how closely it follows patterns of thought and worship found in charismatic and Pentecostal churches around the world (see Robbins 2004a). Here, however, my primary concern is what happened to traditional Urapmin religion (what they call "the ways of our ancestors") in the wake of their conversion. That religion was primarily focused on prospering the gardens that provide the bulk of the

Urapmin diet and on growing boys into strong warriors. An elaborate men's cult featured a roughly twenty-year cycle of male initiation and fertility rituals aimed at these goals. Furthermore, as is often the case, at least in Melanesia, these rituals were linked to a very elaborate system of taboos that regulated contact between men and women and between older and younger men. People in these different social categories could not eat the same foods or, in the case of men and women, even walk on the same paths through Urapmin territory. Assuring that contact was minimized, women and children slept and ate in "women's houses" that formed a horseshoe pattern around a central "men's house" in which men slept. Two much larger men's houses which women were prohibited from entering were located on separate sides of the Urapmin territory and were the focal point of male ritual life, where initiations were in part held and where sacrifices of meat were offered to the bones of ancestors.

As the Urapmin understand their history, as the revival gathered steam and more and more people converted, the community completely abandoned their traditional religion—or, as they like to put it, they "threw it away." They removed the most important ancestral bones to the forest, desacralized the now empty main men's houses, disposed of personal ritual paraphernalia and burned various magical objects. Moreover, they stopped observing almost all the taboos that once governed so much of daily life. "God made everything," they say, and "he wants everyone to use all that he made." Men and women of all ages began to eat together and partake of the same foods. And men moved into women's houses, the village men's houses falling into disrepair and disappearing. By the time I arrived in Urapmin in the beginning of the 1990s, almost all vestiges of traditional religion were gone from the landscape, and the ways of life shaped by that religion, and well attested both in Urapmin memory and in pre-conversion ethnographies of the neighbors, were gone (e.g., Barth 1975; Jorgensen 1981). Christian concerns and rituals dominated the scene (see Robbins [2004a; 2014] for more detailed accounts of the process of abandoning traditional religion).

It is important to note that this account is not primarily my own construction. This is how Urapmin narrated their own recent history to me. Crucial to them was the observation that after God "came and got us," everything changed. As far as they were concerned, their old religion was wholly a thing of the past. As they liked to put it: "Before is before, and now is now." If I pushed hard, I could get people to talk a bit about traditional religion, but it almost never came up spontaneously and it is fair to say that it had virtually no grip on people's hearts and minds. What was most important to the Urapmin in the early 1990s was that they were Christian, working on being taken to heaven when Jesus returned. Despite what was at that time a strong anthropological tendency to downplay religious change and search diligently for evidence that past patterns of belief still governed the way people lived at least their religious lives, I could not disagree with them (Robbins 2007). Anthropologically speaking, it made no sense to try to understand the Urapmin as anything but very committed Christians, and that is how I have written about them since concluding my fieldwork.

A Dead Religion and Its Afterlives

In spite of Urapmin claims to have abandoned their traditional religion, on very rare occasions one could witness bits of past kinds of religious thought and action float by on the passing stream of community life. In the rest of this section, I want to document some of those passing bits of traditional religion as a prelude to arguing that we should not see them as evidence for the claim that *that* religion is in some sense still alive. As I have done thus far, I will start with the ethnography, building from what strikes me as smaller to larger instances of traditional religion rearing its head. That ethnography in place, I will turn to my main argument that these instances did not "work" in religious terms and therefore do not trouble the claim that Urapmin traditional religion has in fact met its demise.

I begin with a very minor example of a reappearance of a traditional religious theme, one that passed so quickly that it hardly caused a ripple on the surface of Urapmin life. It involves a young man who himself was only tenuously integrated in the community. His father had been the first Urapmin man appointed as a representative of the then new colonial government in the 1950s. This man was charged with enforcing the few rules the government insisted that everyone, no matter how remote and otherwise neglected, needed to follow (e.g., ending cannibalism and open air tree burial). By the early 1990s he was remembered as an outsize figure—someone who did a lot to "civilize" the Urapmin, but who was also harsh and not afraid to jail people who did not comply with his orders. He also died young, and his sons, having been raised in a unique household without a model of traditional Urapmin subsistence masculinity, and without a father when they came of age, became to various extents lost souls. The young man in question, who was in his twenties during my fieldwork, was the most lost of all. In a move that was unusual for most Urapmin, he was frequently away from the community, presumably living in a squatter settlement in the major mining town five days walk to the north. He only drifted into Urapmin short periods at any given time before leaving again.

During one of his returns, he brought with him a Rastafarian dreadlock wig from the mining town. As part of one of the major male initiations, older teenage boys wore large wigs. When asked why he was sitting on the verandah of his family house most of the day for several days wearing his Rasta wig, this young man announced that he was initiating himself. One could imagine that from a personal point of view this was a deeply meaningful act by which a young man who was having great difficulty finding a way to achieve successful Urapmin adulthood attempted to bootstrap himself over the barrier he had been having so much trouble crossing. But despite my hopes that his personal ritual might get people talking in more vivid ways about the old initiation system I was eager to learn about, his actions left people nonplussed and generated very little interest. After a few days, he drifted out of the community again. I rarely saw him after that.

During the second year of my fieldwork, two brief events related to traditional religion transpired in quick succession. Compared to the wig-wearing case, these galvanized the wider community much more intensely. One involved the coming of an English film crew to Urapmin to make a few minutes of a multi-part documentary about dogs around the world. The director of the film had contacted me by letter to ask about filming a segment on the use of magic with dogs to help them succeed in the hunt. He offered to pay the community a substantial sum by local standards for their time and participation. But his plan was complicated by the fact that the Urapmin no longer practiced hunting magic. That was something thrown out during the revival and replaced by prayers to God for assistance in the hunt. There would, then, be nothing for the film crew to see.

Given this difficulty, I was inclined to drop the whole matter of the documentary. But some Urapmin leaders came up with a neat solution. There was a singular character in Urapmin named Kinimnok. I have written about him at length elsewhere, so here I will only mention that he was the most notoriously deviant character in the community (Robbins 2018). Though he, like all Urapmin, attended church, he was also the only active polygamist left in the community, and he was histrionic in ways that violated the tenets of ideal Urapmin comportment. He was also a great hunter, and people reckoned he probably still knew some hunting magic and would be willing to perform it for the camera. He confirmed this and so the film crew came to Urapmin.

When the day came to film the hunt, Kinimnok, some kin, a dog, the director, a cameraman, and I set off for the forest around noon. Everything was wrong with this plan. The marsupials the Urapmin hunt are nocturnal, so hunting occurs at night. But the camera needed daylight. Hunters also have to be nearly silent to avoid alerting their prey to their presence. Urapmin hunters, and their dogs, are skilled at moving almost silently through the forest. But as I had already proven in my few inept attempts to accompany hunts in the past, foreigners are not good at this—much less those carrying heavy equipment. Capturing Kinimnok doing the magic with the dog went fine, but after hours of all of us tramping around in the high forest produced not a single sighting or smelling of a marsupial by man or dog, Kinimnok and his kin became very agitated. They wanted us to go back to the village and promised that if we did, they would carry on into the night and catch a live marsupial (not usual practice, but not unheard of) and bring it back to the village where the film crew were staying. In the morning, the dog could run it up a tree in the forest just outside the village, Kinimnok could shoot it with his arrow, and they would have their footage. In the end, this was agreed and the plan went off without a hitch.

What is most interesting for present purposes is not, however, the events I have recounted so far. For as we visitors were leaving, I could hear the Urapmin talking about how performing traditional hunting magic had probably been a bad idea. Then I heard them praying repentantly to God to forgive their backsliding and bless them and the dog so they could find a marsupial. Even as extreme outside inducements had led some Urapmin to allow their greatest deviant to practice a bit of traditional magic, in the end the Urapmin saw this as a failure (in religious terms, and in hunting ones as well) and they immediately made up for it with a return to more usual Christian practice.

Around the same time the filming of the documentary was being planned and then carried out, another sequence of events involving traditional kinds of religious practice was taking shape. In Urapmin, all adult deaths are caused by sorcery. One Urapmin village saw a number of deaths in fairly rapid succession over the last few years, and it was assumed that a sorcerer must have a vendetta against it. Christian ritual specialists had planted small crosses around the village and prayed to God to block the sorcerers, but another death had occurred. In the wake of this most recent attack, someone mentioned that they knew that a group living far to the West of Urapmin—a group the Urapmin saw as less "modern" and less fully Christianized than themselves—had a traditional ritual that would put a village plagued by death "in the dark" so that the sorcerers could not "see" their victims. He noted that some people still knew how to practice this ritual and could come and perform it for this village. This suggestion was controversial as many thought of this ritual as a huge step in a backsliding direction. But people in Urapmin constantly bemoan their tiny population, and the village did seem under siege. During the period the filmmakers were in Urapmin, public opinion shifted, and arrangements were made to have the foreign ritual specialists come after they had left.

The days before and the day of the ritual were from my point of view quite uncanny. Before doing the ritual, people had to observe a few days of food taboos (and taboos on sexual contact) of the kind they had abandoned in 1977. As an anthropologist who had not known the Urapmin were Christian when I set out to live with them, I have to confess my heart leapt. This felt like a glimpse of the kind of Urapmin religious life I had expected to find on the basis of the earlier ethnographies I had read. But the rite did not lead to any nostalgic discussion on people's part of a world they had lost, and perhaps this should have been predictable as this was not, after all, a traditional ritual of their own. In the event, the main ritual action involved building a large, roofless arbor-like structure at the edge of the forest around the village, blocking the view of the village from the direction it was thought the sorcerer came and thereby, as noted, putting the village in the dark. This imagery struck me as perhaps a bit too suited to the larger frame around this ritual, since Urapmin, like so many others, see Christianity as bringing a "light" that overcomes a prior darkness. As far as I know, no Urapmin picked up on this resonance, but for many the whole series of events had been unpleasant. It came as no surprise then when the morning after the ritual I awoke to find that a giant cross the height of the arbor, as well as a smaller one of the kind Urapmin had formerly placed around the village during the Christian anti-sorcery ritual, had been erected in front of it (Figure 1). As with the hunting magic, people quickly went back to praying to the Christian God for protection against sorcerers, and no one ever spoke about the ritual again, at least to me.

The three events I have described thus far need to be counted as very minor tears in the fabric of Urapmin Christian life, and as ones that people quickly used the needle and thread of repentance and Christian prayer to patch up. The last somewhat traditional religious practice I want to mention is different. It is, like the others, contested, but it is also recurrent. It has much greater claim to be part of Urapmin contemporary religion.

The practice in question is the sacrifice of young pigs to nature spirits who are making children sick. Most illnesses of any duration in Urapmin are caused by nature spirits, who clutch their victims tightly and must be forced or persuaded to let go if their victim is to recover. These nature spirits are traditional figures in the Urapmin landscape. They once overran all of Urapmin territory. In terms of their traditional religion, however, the ancestor who created the Urapmin and their neighbors, a singular woman named Afek, banished these nature spirits from the villages in which she placed the people she created, but gave them the rest of the land and the animals it housed as their own property. Until their conversion, the Urapmin had to respect these spirits by observing taboos they put in place. Only by doing so could they safely use the resources the spirits "owned." If they failed to observe the taboos, some of which, like being very quiet when outside the village so as not to disturb the nature spirits, were hard to follow consistently. When Urapmin broke these taboos, the spirits grabbed them and made them sick.

In the wake of their conversion, the Urapmin say that God owns everything and gives it to them freely—no resources now or, despite people's earlier misunderstandings, ever did legitimately belong to the nature spirits. Yet like many Pentecostal and charismatic Christians around the world, the Urapmin do not doubt that these spirits still exist and have power; they have simply been redefined as wholly evil (Meyer 1999; Robbins 2004b). Thus, Urapmin pray regularly to God to protect them from the nature spirits, and when they are sick, they engage in prayer rituals asking God to tear these spirits from them

Figure 1 Crosses erected in front of arbor built at edge of village for anti-sorcery ritual. Photograph by Joel Robbins.

and bind them somewhere far from Urapmin territory. This is the primary Urapmin way of dealing with illness. There is, though, one peculiar thing about the power of nature spirits. This power enables them to make adults sick, but not to kill them. As noted, all adults die from sorcery. But nature spirits are powerful enough to kill children, and it is when children have sicknesses that linger even after several prayer rituals have been practiced for them that people resort to an older way of dealing with them: they sacrifice a pig to the offending spirit, entreating it to take the "smell" of the roasting meat and let go of the child.

These sacrifices are both rare and controversial. They are called for by the Christian ritual specialists who first try to heal the sick by soliciting the help of the Holy Spirit in entreating God to cure them. When these rites have failed to cure sick children, they begin to claim that the Holy Spirit has now told them that it is time to sacrifice a pig to the offending spirit. Many people are opposed to these sacrifices, which they and everyone else recognize as a return to a traditional kind of practice. Whenever a sacrifice is called for, opponents vocally raise the possibility that it may have been an evil spirit posing as the Holy Spirit who has told the ritual specialist to suggest that the rite be held. But no one wants to see a child die when all options for a cure have not been exhausted, and so on rare occasions these sacrifices do take place.

Key to my argument here is the way those who conduct sacrifices frame them in Christian terms. As I've already noted, it is Christian ritual specialists, claiming inspiration by the Holy Spirit, who determine when to perform them. More than this, the rites begin with long and detailed prayers by a Christian Pastor. Having presented one of these prayers in its entirety elsewhere, I will just mention that their core theme is that it is God, and not the sacrifice itself, that performs the healing (Robbins 2009). It is the key moment in one such prayer that gives this essay its title, and it is a moment that makes my point with great clarity. It comes when the Pastor, near the end of his prayer before the piglet is shot with a lethal arrow, proclaims:

> Jesus, you were a good lamb that died to bring our lives back to us. That's what you did and we too bring a young piglet and kill it and do a ritual about this. This is what we will do and so God you look at us. God send down only your strength. It is just meat, so we will kill it and eat it and so God send down only your strength and holiness and heal this child.

Please, I have said this and God, you! God you are merciful, you are peaceful, you are happy and so I pray to you. Please look carefully at this child and heal her. Chop off the hands and feet of the poison snake spirit, the dog spirit, the cassowary spirit, the echidna spirit, whatever kind of spirit-like things, residents of the trees, any kind of man [a way of referring to spirits], any kind of man, snake spirits, any kind of man, send him away to his own house. You take him and step on him and crush him and, please, heal this child.

After some repetition, the Pastor reiterates his core point in conclusion:

We … are just men, so Jesus please you yourself [must do this]. Jesus, I send her to you. I have said enough and it is true [this is the formulaic conclusion used with most prayers].

The sacrifice is "just meat," those performing it are "just men." For these reasons, the sacrificial rite itself cannot heal the sick child. This is why the Pastor, in a prayer that is fully part of the rite itself, must call on God and Jesus to do the actual work of healing.

My suggestion is that the Pastor's prayer reveals the truth for the Urapmin of the other cases as well. Wearing the wig, doing the dog magic, and erecting the arbor are, like the sacrifice of the pig, rituals that no longer work. In all but the wig case, they require accompanying Christian rites if human goals are to be achieved. As for the wig case, that one was simply hopeless and its practitioner left again after trying it. Now, the time has come to face the question of how rituals and religions in general work and what has to happen to render them, like these rites, no longer effective.

On Broken Religion and the Passing of Institutional Facts

As I noted in the introduction, the theory I will deploy to explain why it makes sense to see the fragments of traditional religious thought or practice that occasionally make an appearance in Urapmin as no longer constituting "working" religion, or even still-working parts of a broken religion, is philosopher John Searle's account of the nature of institutional facts. I was introduced to this theory many years ago by my late, much missed colleague Roy D'Andrade. For many years after that initial introduction, I felt that Searle's theory was too minimal to do all of the work that he asserted that it could do. But still I could never shake the sense that there was something to the theory, and when I began to take up the question of how a religion stops working—a question that came to me most forcefully when reading Jonathan Lear's (2006) wonderful book *Radical Hope* about cultural change among the Native American Crow—I realized I had finally found a context in which Searle's theory was just the right tool to use. I've provided this brief bit of personal intellectual history primarily as a warning. You, like me, might at first feel that the theory I'm about to present is too "small" or simple to do the big job of helping us pinpoint the moment at which a religion expires, but I urge you to let the argument I make with Searle's help sit for a while before rejecting it on these grounds.

That admonition in place, here is the core of Searle's argument. Its foundation is a distinction Searle (1995) makes between "brute facts" and "institutional facts." As he explains, "Brute facts exist independently of any human institutions; institutional facts can exist only within human institutions" (Searle 1995: 27). An example of a brute fact is that water boils when heated to 100 degrees centigrade. An institutional fact, to use one of Searle's favorite examples, is that pieces of specific kinds of paper printed with specific patterns count as money. Water would keep boiling at 100 degrees centigrade even if no human beings knew that it did so. Paper currency, by contrast, would stop being money if no human beings knew that it was or were prepared to treat it as such. The same is true, Searle asserts, for all of the institutional facts that make social life possible and give it its shape.

Having distinguished between brute and institutional facts and argued for the foundational role the latter play in social life, Searle (1995: 28) offers a schematic definition of institutional facts as sets of "constitutive rules" that take the following form: "'X counts as Y in context C.'" Thus, for example, certain bits of paper count as currency in the United States because there are shared rules in that country that take the form of a statement like "properly patterned bits of green paper (X) count as money (Y) wherever U.S. currency is recognized (C)." As long as the people involved in a transaction accept this institutional fact, these bits of paper will count as currency.

Although he does not make this point at any length, Searle (1995: 27) does acknowledge that his model of institutional fact grows out of his work on speech acts (Searle 1969). That work, in turn, draws heavily on J. L. Austin's

(1962) well-known account of the nature of performative utterances that do not point to things in the world, but rather do things and in many cases even create things that did not exist in the world before they were performed. Indeed, it is possible to consider speech acts as paradigmatic examples of institutional facts in Searle's sense and his model may be easier to understand when illustrated by way of an account of how a particular speech act works. In this spirit, consider the making of a promise. The accepted way to make a promise, at least in the linguistic culture of the United States that I know best, is to say "I promise Z." If I say "I promise to call you tomorrow," I have in fact created something new in the world, a new promise. I may not in the end fulfill my promise, but in that case I will be responsible for my failure to do so, suffering the consequences in terms of our relationship and my general reputation. I will suffer these consequences because once I make my promise by saying "I promise to call you tomorrow," that promise exists in the world independently of me and obligates me in a way I cannot make disappear. It exists, in turn, because those in the United States' linguistic culture I am describing hold to a constitutive rule that states that "saying 'I promise Z' (X) counts as making a promise (Y) in the context of this United States' linguistic culture (C)." If I were to say "I hope to call you tomorrow" or "I will do my very best to call you tomorrow," my speech would not be the right kind of statement to count as making a promise, and I would not have made one. You might still be disappointed if I fail to call tomorrow, but I would not suffer the same consequences for my failure as I would if I had said that "I promise to call." It is the existence of the X counts as Y in context C rule that makes promising possible, and it defines the form in which promises must be given in order to come to exist. Once that rule is in place, any time one says "I promise" in the right conditions, a promise is automatically created.

Along with helping illustrate how institutional facts depend on constitutive rules of the X counts as Y in C type, speech act theory also brings us back to the issue of religions and how a religion can cease to function. It brings us back to religion because of the important role that theory has played in anthropological approaches to understanding ritual. From Finnegan (1969), Tambiah (1985), and La Fontaine (1977), on to Rappaport's (1999) influential theory of ritual, ideas drawn from speech act theory have been crucial building blocks of many seminal discussions of the nature religious rites. I want to suggest that we can extend those discussions with the help of Searle's later elaboration of the core planks of speech act theory as a theory of institutional facts. In this framework, rituals, like speech acts, would be kinds of institutional facts because they are based on constitutive rules of the X counts as Y in C type. Thus in Urapmin sacrificing marsupials to ancestral bones (X) could in the past prosper gardens and grow young men into warriors (Y) if done during phases of several of the initiation rituals that took place in one of the main men's houses (C). The sacrificial ritual was effective precisely because doing those actions in that context counted as making that outcome occur. This analysis is fully in keeping with the earlier work on ritual cited just above, but Searle's discussion has the advantage of revealing the mechanism that makes rituals effective by defining their performance (X) as counting as doing whatever it is they aim to do (Y) if they are done in the right time, place, and manner (C).

If, and this is the claim I have been building toward, it is constitutive rules of the X counts as Y in C type that make rituals work, then they will stop working when the constitutive rules that make them effective cease to apply. This is what has happened in Urapmin. You can certainly wear a wig and claim to be initiating yourself, but you cannot make yourself a man in this way because being initiated no longer counts as being a man among the Urapmin. Likewise, you can perform dog magic, or an anti-sorcery rite, or a pig sacrifice to heal a child, but these too are not effective: they no longer count as the way to achieve the goals at which they aim. Various types of Christian prayer and ritual now count as the way of reaching those ends, and that is why the performance of each of these rites is followed by or in the case of sacrifice framed by prayer and often professions of repentance. It is because these "counts as" relationships are gone that these shreds and patches of traditional ritual that occasionally make an appearance in Urapmin life do not challenge either my own or Urapmin people's insistence that their traditional religion is over—they can do no work of their own and therefore do not succeed as kinds of religious action that can challenge the role Christianity plays in Urapmin life.

I need to make two quick observations before closing. First, you may have noticed that I had been talking about ritual and then made a quick jump to religion in the last paragraph. I do not have space to justify that leap here, but put schematically I would note that for Searle, religions would be made up largely of institutional facts, and not all of these would be ritual facts (see Stausberg

2010: 365–9). Thus, for example, in traditional religion, Afek (X) counted as the most important ancestor and creator spirit (Y) in the context of that religion (C). Now Urapmin say she was just a normal person who misled people about her powers, which in truth belong to God. Afek and the other ancestors who were at the center of traditional Urapmin religion no longer "count as" ancestors, and thus one can no longer orient religious life around them, even if one can still remember and tell stories about how people used to do so.

Second, in explaining how a religion stops working, I have focused on the breakdown of the "counts as" relation that is part of the formula for constitutive rules. But one might also imagine that elements of a religion could break when the contextual part of the rule falls away. For example, when the Urapmin emptied their men's houses, the context in which to do major parts of their initiations disappeared, and this is perhaps another reason initiations are no longer institutional facts among the Urapmin. I think it would in the future be worth investigating breakdowns in contextual requirements as well as the collapse of "counts as" relations when thinking about the different ways religions end.

Conclusion

Anthropologists and other scholars of religion need a theory of when religions end precisely because so much of their disciplinary histories, tied up as they are with notions of tradition and deep and persistent cultural and social patterns, lead them to downplay change (de Jong 2016; Robbins 2007). Their first impulse is most often to see any hints of traditional religious ideas or practices as proof that old structures still govern the shape of people's lives. I've tried to provide a theoretical vantage point from which to identify cases in which this is not going on—cases, that is, in which however messy the break between the old and the new we can still say with some assurance that a religion has met its demise precisely because it can no longer do the work it once did.

But my argument has been about more than how anthropologists and others can get past their commitment to finding cultural continuity in order to recognize that religions do end. As I noted in my introduction, I have meant to look backward from the nature of religious demise to ask what it can tell us about how religions stay alive. On the basis of the argument I have made here, central to the persistence of any religion is that it remains rooted in still functioning X counts as Y in C type constitutive rules. Preventing a breakdown of such rules is what keeps a religion vital. To be sure, this point does not offer a complete theory of religion or even of religious demise. For one thing, it is focused on identifying the moment of religious death, not on considering all the processes that can lead to that moment (see Robbins 2014). But I hope that it has made at least one small, narrowly aimed contribution to the emerging study of how religions end.

References

Austin, J. L. (1962), *How to Do Things with Words*, ed. J. O. Urmson and Marina Sbisá. Cambridge, MA: Harvard University Press.

Austin, J. L. (1975), *How to Do Things with Words*. Cambridge: Harvard University Press.

Barth, F. (1975), *Ritual and Knowledge among the Baktaman of New Guinea*, New Haven, CT: Yale University Press.

De Jong, A. (2016), "The Disintegration and Death of Religions," in M. Stausberg and S. Engler (eds.), *The Oxford Handbook of the Study of Religion*, 646–64. Oxford: University of Oxford Press.

Finnegan, R. (1969), "How to Do Things with Words: Performative Utterances among the Limba of Sierra Leone," *Man* (n.s.), 4 (4): 537–52.

Jorgensen, D. (1981), "Taro and Arrows: Order, Entropy, and Religion among the Telefolmin," Ph.D. dissertation. University of British Columbia.

La Fontaine, J. (1977), "The Power of Rights," *Man* (n.s.), 12: 421–37.

Lear, J. (2006), *Radical Hope: Ethics in the Face of Cultural Devastation*. Cambridge, MA: Harvard University Press.

Meyer, B. (1999), *Translating the Devil: Religion and Modernity among the Ewe in Ghana*. Trenton, NJ: Africa World Press.

Rappaport, R. A. (1999), *Ritual and Religion in the Making of Humanity*. Cambridge: Cambridge University Press.

Robbins, J. (2004a), *Becoming Sinners: Christianity and Moral Torment in a Papua New Guinea Society*. Berkeley, CA: University of California Press.

Robbins, J. (2004b), "The Globalization of Pentecostal and Charismatic Christianity," *Annual Review of Anthropology*, 33: 117–43.

Robbins, J. (2007), "Continuity Thinking and the Problem of Christian Culture: Belief, Time and the Anthropology of Christianity," *Current Anthropology*, 48 (1): 5–38.

Robbins, J. (2009), "Conversion, Hierarchy, and Cultural Change: Value and Syncretism in the Globalization of Pentecostal and Charismatic Christianity," in K. M. Rio and O. H. Smedal (eds.), *Hierarchy: Persistence and Transformation in Social Formations*, 65–88. New York: Berghahn.

Robbins, J. (2014), "How Do Religions End? Theorizing Religious Traditions from the Point of View of How They Disappear," *Cambridge Anthropology*, 32 (2): 2–15.

Robbins, J. (2018), "Where in the World Are Values? Exemplarity, Morality and Social Process," in J. Laidlaw, B. Bodenhorn, and M. Holbraad (eds.), *Recovering the Human Subject: Freedom, Creativity and Decision*, 174–92. Cambridge: Cambridge University Press.

Searle, J. R. (1969), *Speech Acts*, Cambridge: Cambridge University Press.

Searle, J. R. (1995), *The Construction of Social Reality*. London: Penguin Books.

Stausberg, M. (2010), "Distinctions, Differentiations, Ontology, and Non-humans in Theories of Religion," *Method and Theory in the Study of Religion*, 22: 354–74.

Tambiah, S. J. (1985), *Culture, Thought, and Social Action: An Anthropological Perspective*. Cambridge: Cambridge University Press.

3

Did Aum Shinrikyō Really End?

Erica Baffelli

The execution of thirteen members of Aum Shinrikyō (Aum Supreme Truth, hereafter Aum) in July 2018[1] revived media attention for the group founded by Asahara Shōkō (born Matsumoto Chizuo, 1955–2018) that became notorious in 1995 when some of its members perpetrated a sarin gas attack in the Tokyo subway. Started as a small yoga center in 1984, in the span of a decade Aum developed into a hierarchical organization that encouraged members to become renunciants (*shukkesha*) and live communally. Its teachings, influenced by Buddhist doctrine, extreme ascetic practices, and catastrophic end-of-time thoughts resulted in visions of a cosmic struggle with evil forces, manufacture of chemical and biological weapons, and violent crimes toward perceived enemies and the larger society. In the weeks following the Tokyo sarin gas attack on March 20, 1995, the police raided Aum facilities throughout the country and arrested hundreds of members. On May 16, Asahara was arrested at the group's compound in Kamikuishiki, a village near Mt. Fuji. The group's assets were frozen, weapons seized, material and documents confiscated, and the organization put under strict surveillance not only by the police, but also by citizen organizations and the media. In October of the same year, Aum lost its status as a registered religious organization under the Religious Juridical Persons Law (*shūkyō hōjin hō*) and in early 1996 Aum was declared bankrupt. In the months following the sarin gas attack in 1995, when facilities and private houses were searched, members interrogated and arrested and several criminal charges were laid against the group, many members defected. From around 10,000 members living communally before March 1995, the membership decreased to about 500 renunciants by April 1998 (Maekawa 2001: 181). The group was therefore severely weakened after 1995, a process that resulted in Aum dropping its name in 1999.

The aim of this chapter is to contribute to a discussion about the demise of religion and about *how* and *when* religious groups dissolve (de Jong 2018; Robbins 2014), by asking the question of *what does it mean for a religion to end* when a religion or a religious organization ends as a consequence of a traumatic experience, in this case violent acts perpetrated by members of the organization itself. This article does not discuss the demise of a tradition as a whole, but it focuses on a relatively small and short-lived new religion, whose actions, however, had a profound and long-lasting impact in Japan (Baffelli and Reader 2012; Reader 2000; Kisala and Mullins 2001). Despite the limited years of activities of the organization and the relatively small membership, this chapter argues that in order to fully address the question "What did it mean for Aum to end?" several perspectives need to be taken into consideration and that the question cannot be fully answered without also understanding what is still lingering.

Relatively little information and few academic studies were available on Aum before 1995, but after its crime became evident the group has received extensive and continuous media attention and coverage (Baffelli 2016; Gardner 2001; Hardacre 2007). It has also been investigated by several academic publications, looking in detail at its organizational structure, teachings and activities (Reader 2000; Inoue and RIRC 2011, 2015; Shimazono 1995, 1997), the consequence and aftermath of the Aum Affair (Baffelli and Reader 2012; Kisala and Mullins 2001; Wilkinson 2009), and its memorialization (Pendleton 2011; Ushiyama 2016). Previous publications (Baffelli 2012, 2016; Maekawa 2001) have also discussed the attempts by ex-Aum members to continue as a group after 1995 by either staying in Aleph (the new name of Aum since 2000) or joining a new organization called Hikari no Wa (literally "Circle of Light") established in 2007 by a small group of members led by Jōyū Fumihiro, ex-spokesperson of Aum and ex-representative of Aleph. This chapter offers a new perspective on Aum by looking at its demise and dissolution after 1995.

Examples of Decline and Demise of "New Religions" in Japan

To date the study of Japanese "new religions" (*shinshūkyō*) has focused mainly on rapid growth and expansion rather than on decline or demise, in order to emphasize narratives of religious innovation.[2] However, while numerous new organizations were established in the postwar period, following the promulgation of the Religious Corporation Law (*Shūkyō hōjin hō*) in 1951, which defined the rights of religious institutions as juridical persons and granted them tax breaks, several groups only lasted a few years and quickly disappeared. For example, in one of the first studies in English on new religions McFarland (1967) mentioned the cases of short-lived groups such as Denshinkyō or Boseikyō. Other organizations lasted for longer periods, but eventually declined and (almost) disappeared often due to a combination of both internal dynamics, such as leadership crisis, schisms, or organizational failures, and tensions with the larger society, that is, in other words, a combination of "endogenous" and "exogenous" factors (Stausberg, Wright, and Cusack, this volume). These dynamics have been identified in a few studies. For example, the dissolution or erosion of new religions in the Japanese context has been investigated in relation to conflicts with the media or the State, as in the case of a short-lived group called Renmonkyō. Established by Shimamura Mitsu (1831–1904) in 1883, in the late nineteenth century, Renmonkyō became one of the largest new religious organizations. In 1894 Renmonkyō and its leader became the object of a defamatory campaign by *Yorozu Chōhō*, a popular newspaper. The conflicts with the press and subsequently criticism the group attracted resulted in a decline in membership, and activities were slowly discontinued (Dorman 2012; Sawada 2004; Takeda 1991). Another example is provided by a small organization established in the 1940s, Jiu and its leader Jikoson (nee Nagaoka Nagako, 1903–1983). As discussed in details by Dorman (2012), in this case the group did not survive pressures from the authorities and intensive media scrutiny, also due to the presence of high-profile celebrities in its membership, such as the *go* (Japanese chess) master Go Seigen and the sumo champion Futabayama. While celebrities helped the group to access audiences, it was also exposed to an incredible amount of media attention. In 1947 the police raided Jiu headquarters in Kanazawa and arrested Futabayama. National newspapers widely reported on the arrest, attacked (and ridiculed) the "strange" religious organization, and accused Jikoson of being mentally unstable. Futabayama eventually left the organization and issued an apology for his behavior. A further example is provided by Murguia (2011) who documented how the death of the leader Chino Yuko resulted in the restructuring of leadership in the group Chiho Shōkō (Chiho True Law, also known as Panawēbu Kenkyūjo or Pana-Wave Laboratory), a small organization established in 1977 which received intense media and public scrutiny in 2002–3 due to escalating tensions with residents and authorities in Gifu and Fukui prefectures. This resulted in the group being labeled as potentially dangerous (Baffelli and Reader 2012: 13) and its facilities being raided by the police (Dorman 2005). These events, combined with the leader's death and lack of financial resources, caused a sharp decline in membership. According to Murguia (2001:108) after Chino's death the number of resident researchers has been reduced to only ten and made the future of the organization uncertain. Failures and setbacks, however, do not necessarily lead to the dissipation of the organization. It is not uncommon for new religious movements to face criticism and scrutiny, especially in their early stage of development and these pressures may make a group very fragile and potentially lead to outbursts of violence (Davis 2000; Dawson 2002; Reader 2011, 2000). The case of Kōfuku no Kagaku, a religious organization established in 1986 by Ōkawa Ryūhō, however, shows how a group can survive significant setbacks and failures that could potentially threaten its survival. In particular, disappointing results during elections and the rejection of the application to establish a university are explained in Kōfuku no Kagaku by reinterpreting failures as temporary setbacks on a longer-term plan of building Utopia on earth (Baffelli 2020) and by diverting the attention on success stories.

Recent studies (Baffelli and Reader 2018a) have also looked at erosion as a slow process occurring over several years, rather than a sudden dismantling or dissipation. This process could be accelerated by the dead or aging of the leader resulting in the aging of the group itself that is unable to attract new members and to maintain its relevance for existing followers. An example of this process could be seen in Agonshū, a Buddhist organization established in the 1970s, which after the death of the charismatic founder in 2016 has been confronted with a sharp decline of membership and lower attendance at events, raising questions about the potential survival of the group in the longer term. The case of Aum Shinrikyō, however, presents a distinctive case due to the violent event of March 1995 followed by sudden and abrupt changes in the organization.

Ending Aum

In the case of Aum, it is undeniable that the sarin gas attack and subsequent events had a tremendous impact on the future of the organization, but the discussion about the end of Aum and, more precisely, about *what* has ended also requires taking into consideration different levels, such as institutional, organizational, and individual (in particular the members), and considering how different actors understand the end of Aum. By doing this it becomes evident that discussing the end or endings of Aum is also crucial in order to understand how ex-Aum members are still perceived in Japan and how Japanese society is still dealing with the aftermath of 1995.

Before discussing how different actors are elaborating the end of Aum, a brief note is necessary about the interviews with ex-members that have been collected for this chapter about their experiences with Aum.[3] As pointed out in studies on affiliation and disaffiliation or defection from new religious movements,[4] ex-members' narratives change over time and they should be understood as part of a process that could last for months or even years (Frisk and Palmer 2015; Wright 1987). The separation from Aum for many members was due to a precipitating event; that is, the sarin gas attack that resulted in disillusionment toward Aum beliefs and practices, disaffection and disaffiliation. In a similar way to other case studies (Bromley 2006; Chryssides 2019; Wright 2014), the strategies and process of disengagement varied across members. While for some of them the disengagement happened rapidly after the 1995 event, for others the process lasted for several years. As interviews collected for this research have been carried out more than twenty years after the events, the analysis of the members' accounts should also take into consideration how their stories have been shaped by other narratives about Aum—produced and circulated by the media, scholars, victims, anti-cult activists, anti-death penalty and human rights activists, and ex-members[5]—as well as their "temporal variability" (Wright 2014); that is the fact that interviewees have now been removed from their experiences for several years and they are reconstructing "their biographies in light of what has happened to them in the interim" (Wright 2014: 721). The period when the interviews were conducted, however, is particularly significant for the discussion about the *end* of Aum. When the first interviews were conducted in 2016, the twentieth anniversary of the sarin gas attack the year before had attracted a renewed public and media attention toward Aum and its (ex)members with interviews appearing in magazines and several TV programs and documentaries being produced. This had prompted ex-members to reflect on their experience with Aum. At the same time the last trials involving Aum members were coming to an end. When follow-up interviews were conducted in late 2017 and early 2018, all the trials and appeals had ended, making it legally possible that the executions of members on death row could now take place at any moment.⁶ Therefore the sense that something was about to end in a definitive way—and how the forthcoming event produced ambivalent and divergent feelings in ex-members—was implicitly present in our conversations, even when the potential executions of Asahara and other members were not directly addressed in the interviews. Asahara and six members on death row were eventually executed on July 6, 2018, followed by the remaining six members three weeks later, on July 26. The timing of the simultaneous executions also suggested that the event represented significant closure not only for the victims, the group itself and its members, but for the entire country. The year 2018 represented the thirtieth and final year of the Heisei era in Japan, according to the calendar based on imperial eras, further to the request of Emperor Akihito to abdicate. A new era, named Reiwa, started in May 2019 with the enthronement of the new Emperor Naruhito. Executing Asahara and other Aum members before the beginning of the new era could then be seen as a way to close the previous one by ending one of its most painful chapters (Baffelli and Reader 2018b).

Aum Did Not End

It could be argued, however, that Aum Shinrikyō did not end in 1995, when it lost its official registration, nor in 1999, when it lost its name, because its members have continued their activities in some form, mainly through two groups that are still currently active. In January, 2000 the name of Aum Shinrikyō was changed to Aleph (Baffelli 2012, 2018) and the group is still operating under this name nowadays, although the spelling was slightly changed in Japanese in 2003. Aleph has continued teaching about liberation (*gedatsu*) and enlightenment (*satori*), two central concepts in Aum doctrine, while still focusing its activities around yoga and austerities, although the group appears to have dropped the most extreme ascetic training.

In March 2007, a splinter group from Aleph was established, called Hikari no Wa (officially, the Circle of Rainbow Light) led by former Aum spokesperson Jōyū Fumihiro. Contrary to Aleph, Hikari no Wa publicly rejected Asahara as a leader and Aum teachings and introduced new practices, rituals, and activities (Baffelli 2012).

Current membership in both organizations is rather difficult to assess. The annual report by the Public Security Intelligence Agency (PSIA)[7] maintains that both groups are still active and potentially dangerous and it indicates an increase in membership for Aleph especially in some locations.[8] Members, however, have informally contested that these figures do not include the people leaving the organization or joining only for a very limited period of time. As far as Hikari no Wa is concerned, it appears that the group membership is decreasing and from about thirty members living communal lives in 2011 (Baffelli 2012: 35), the group currently declares that only twelve members live together and some of them are elderly and with illness.[9] Most of them reside in Tokyo (six people) and, according to the group itself, only a quarter of members who left Aleph and joined Hikari no Wa in 2007 are still in the organization. The group, however, is continuing its activities mainly consisting of yoga and qìgōng classes, public talks, Buddhist sermons, and pilgrimages to religious sites around Japan, as well as critically attacking Aleph in order to persuade its members to disaffiliate.

Therefore it could be argued that Aum, although with a significantly reduced membership, was able to overcome the events of 1995 and restructure itself in order to continue its activities by maintaining some of the previous practices or, in the case of Hikari no Wa, attempting a more radical, and not necessarily successful nor uncontested, re-definition of its own identity (Baffelli 2012).

Furthermore, both organizations are still subjected to two new laws introduced in 1999, the Victims Compensation Law (*Higaisha kyūsai-hō*) and the Organizational Control Law (*Dantai kisei-hō*, full name *Musabetsu tairyō satsujin kōi o okonatta dantai no kisei ni kansuru hōritsu*, Act for the Control of Organizations which Committed Indiscriminate Mass Murder). Both laws work together to strictly control Aleph (and since 2007 Hikari no Wa) by inspecting their facilities and requiring the groups to submit a list of assets and of membership roles every three months. The Laws were initially approved for three years and in 2018 they were renewed for the sixth time, despite Hikari no Wa had filed an action for the laws to be revoked. The renewal of the special laws and continuous strict surveillance of Aleph and Hikari no Wa indicate that, from an institutional and legal point of view, Aum has not ended. According to the PSIA the surveillance is still necessary because, despite the change of name and the rejection of violent practices, members are still continuing Aum activities as based on Asahara's teachings.

Aum Did End

It could also be argued that Aum *as such* collapsed 1995, following a process that culminated with the sarin gas attack, but that had already started in the years preceding it. The erosion of the organization had already started before the tragic event of 1995. Aum was failing in attracting new members and for this and other reasons it was intensifying its attempt to recruit while members were pressured to join the communal life (Reader 2011). It is now also clear that in March 1995 a massive raid was being planned by the Tokyo Metropolitan Police with local police departments (Wilkinson 2009: 76) after conspicuous evidence of Aum members' involvement in several violent crimes had been gathered. Therefore, although the sarin gas attack triggered the "end of Aum," the group was already facing crucial challenges for its survival.

At the institutional level, closure was imposed on the group by the sarin gas attack and the arrests, and later executions, of the leader and members. Aum, now Aleph, and Hikari no Wa are no longer allowed to register under the Religious Corporation Law and their activities are now strictly monitored (Baffelli 2018, 2012; Wilkinson 2009: 98). The police raids also resulted in the erasure of Aum material infrastructure. In particular, the main facilities in Kamikushiki village (Yamanashi prefecture), including the notorious Satyam 7 where the lethal gas was produced (Ushiyama 2016: 147–8), were dismantled in the years following the sarin attack. Since 2006 the village itself doesn't exist anymore, but it has been split into two parts and merged with two different towns.[10]

Following the 1995 events, all Aum activities, such as shops they ran around the country, were also discontinued. As a consequence, books, magazines, and other items produced and sold by the group were rapidly removed from shop shelves or destroyed by members. A lay member I interviewed during my fieldwork explained to me that, although they didn't leave the organization, when the responsibilities of the sarin gas attack and other crimes became clear, they hastily burned all the items and books they had at home for fear of a police search.

More significantly, Aum was also dismantled from the point of view of its embodied practices and relationship between members and the leader. The loss of the leader is central to this process, as Asahara effectively disappeared after March 1995 and his interaction with the outside world became more and more fragmented and, at the end, unintelligible. During the trials he refused to provide any explanation of the group's actions and did not admit any responsibilities for the crimes, leaving the members who were not involved in the violent acts struggling to understand what happened and why the group they joined and committed their lives to ended up committing such atrocities.

Aum practices, based on individualized ascetic austerities and secretly transmitted teachings, depended on a strong bond with the leader and therefore could not be continued in the same way without his physical presence. One of the central issues was that ranks in Aum were determined by performances in austerities. When a member was recognized by the leader to have achieved a particular spiritual level through ascetic training (*shugyō*), she/he would receive a holy name and they would thereafter be called by the new name inside the organization. Receiving a holy name indicated a new social status, and consequently exemplary behavior was expected by high-ranked members, as in the case of the "clear" level in Scientology discussed by Bainbridge and Stark (1980:128). Furthermore, holy names were also a proof of ability to reach higher spiritual status through austerities, and therefore members receiving them would become role models for other followers to aspire to. After 1995 not only the community of members was dismantled, but the leader was unable to bestow holy names resulting in the collapse of the *shugyō* system. The inability to perform austerities, both from a point of view of absence of physical place and absence of the leader,[11] implied for the members still at a lower level in the hierarchy the impossibility to advance in their spiritual path and for the ones at a higher level the loss of recognition of their roles and of the authority they gained inside Aum. For members who left the organization when they moved back to a lay society and stopped using their holy names, or when confronted with people from outside, not only the "Aum language" connected to austerities and holy names was not understood, but frowned upon, after testimonies and documents showed that members who were chosen for committing violent acts and murders were considered to have achieved superior spiritual levels (Reader 2009: 149).

The imposed process of structural eradication of Aum was therefore concurrent with a process of active disengagement performed by the (ex) members themselves, either by rejecting Aum and its teachings, as in the case of members of Hikari no Wa (Jōyū 2012; Munakata 2010), or by a more individualized process of active termination of their own connection with Aum *as they knew it* by discontinuing the use of holy names and stop performing austerities. The three levels (institutional, practices, leader/community) have been dismantled after 1995 and members' narratives focus on the idea that "nothing is how it was before" reinforced the perception that Aum had indeed ended. However there is something that is still lingering at the micro-level of individual (ex)members' narratives who declare that they are still struggling to end Aum and to break the connection with it and it is to this third aspect that we will turn now.

The Impossibility of Ending Aum

The discussion about ex-Aum members and their past experience is inevitably a discussion about loss: first of all of a *way of life*, that is the communal lives with other members—a life that one of the interviewees defined as "without responsibilities" (*musekinin*)—but also the loss of their (younger and stronger) ascetic bodies and the power associated with the ability of performing ascetic training. The physical loss of human lives is also, unavoidably, a constant presence in members' narratives, emerging in discussions about or allusions to the victims of Aum's violence, including first of all victims of sarin gas attacks and murders perpetrated by members; but also members killed by other members or who died during extreme austerities; and members who were executed. Therefore the sense of loss, in particular, of embodied practices and emotional community provides an interesting point of view to trace what *doesn't end*, what it is still lingering when the organization seems to have collapsed or it is eroding.

As mentioned previously, the dismantling of Aum after the sarin gas attack resulted in some members' decision to actively abandon and question their beliefs by creating an organization, Hikari no Wa, which constructed itself in opposition to Aum (Baffelli 2012). By rejecting all teachings and practices considered dangerous, however, Hikari no Wa ended up facing an identity crisis and members struggled to clearly explain what the group is and what it wants to be. Some members decided to leave the organization completely, but in doing so they were confronted with significant loss, in terms of both loss of what empowered them (austerities) and loss of communal links with other (ex)members. Some members, such as Hirano Akiko,[12] who left Aleph in 2007 to join Hikari no Wa, describe this loss in positive term, as a painful but necessary process, while others, such Ueda Naoko, who left shortly after the 1995 events, still think that if the violence hadn't happened, they would have continued their life in the organization.

To actively dismantle Aum ex-members have to renounce both austerities and the Aum community. The two elements are strongly connected in Aum, where both individualized practices and communal life were emphasized, but they are also the most difficult bonds for members to sever because they gave them both a status and an identity as members of a like-minded community. It also gave them an escape from a life they didn't want and a possibility to have extraordinary experiences.

For these reasons, some ex-members feel that they cannot get closure with Aum because they cannot openly talk about it, especially they cannot openly talk about their positive experience in the organization. This is due to both a taboo surrounding discussion about Aum (e.g., they feel they cannot talk about it with their families) and their awareness that external people would not understand them anyway. This reinforces the idea, already present in Aum before 1995, that members are an elite of special people that society and other people don't/cannot understand. The acceptance of not being an "elite" is also crucial to understand the process of members who are attempting to distant themselves from Aum, as in the case of Hikari no Wa (Baffelli 2012). Because of the impossibility to talk about their experience with "outsiders," ex-members mainly communicate in close circles, often through online communities, that tend to reinforce internal narratives that serve as the filter through which they reinterpret their past experience. And this doesn't allow them to "restart the clock" of their life and finally *end* Aum. It could also be argued, as Yamamoto Nozomi affirmed in her interview, that "Aum cannot end" and that even for (ex-)members who have consciously distanced themselves from it, the feeling of being (or having been) part of something special as well as the strong connection between asceticism and fear of ending up in hell seem to stick around and make it difficult for members to accept a compromise or "to find a conclusion" (to quote another interviewee). According to another interviewee, Watanabe Eriko, who joined Aum in her late teens and was also part of Aleph for a few years, Aum cannot end for members who were renunciants, even after the execution of the leader, because the karmic connection (*goen*) with him cannot be broken. Even without an organization or a physical center the connection is still there and Asahara's consciousness (*ishiki*) may one day reincarnate. To put it in the work of Ueda Naoko, "None of us has been able to successfully end Aum" (… *minna umaku oumu o owaru koto ga dekiteinai*).

Conclusion

Earlier in this chapter I have argued that Aum *as such* ended in 1995 and that the organization was already eroding before the tragic event of March 1995. A few members during interviews hinted at the possibility that going out in a spectacular way was deliberate and that Asahara was aware that Aum's days were numbered. The leader, they claim, was aware of the impending police raids and was convinced that the government was conspiring against Aum. Although this may have been possible, and it is not unlikely that some members were aware that Aum was under investigation (Reader 2011), these comments are rather speculative and the people who could possibly shed light on these assumptions, in particular Asahara, are no longer alive. However it is undeniable that the memory of Aum will surely not disappear and, from this point of view, the violent acts perpetrated by the organization counteracted failure and made sure that the group will be remembered.

As pointed out by Ian Reader, the subway attack was an "act of performance violence of global significance" (2011: 315) and through that Aum entered into the history books, similarly to other groups that were involved in violence such as the Peoples Temple led by Jim Jones in Jonestown, or David Koresh and the Branch Davidians in Waco Texas. In contrast, groups like Jiu mentioned at the beginning of this chapter, that peacefully dismantle, will rarely be remembered and their memory will fade away.

The memory of Aum is still present nowadays in Japan. Despite the executions in 2018, it appears that ex-members, victims' families, and society at large are still struggling to come to terms with the events of the 1990s and therefore Aum cannot completely end. This makes us wonder whether Aum would truly end only when all people speaking and understanding its language (and practices) will be gone.

Notes

1 Asahara Shōkō and six members—Hayakawa Kiyohide, Inoue Yoshihiro, Niimi Tomomitsu, Tsuchiya Masami, Nakagawa Tomomasa, and Endo Seiichi—were executed on July 6 while the remaining members on death row—Miyamae (Okazaki) Kazuaki, Yokoyama Masato, Hashimoto Satoru, Koike (Hayashi) Yasuo, Toyoda Toru, and Hirose Ken'ichi—on July 26. All Japanese names follow the standard Japanese order of family name first followed by given name.

2 According to Cusack and Lewis (this volume) studies on new religious movements in other contexts as well have generally tended to focus on narratives of origin and success, rather than failure and demise. Decline and failure have been investigated from the point of view of failures of leadership (Dawson and Whitsel 2011); leadership crisis and increased tension with society (as discussed by Frisk [2002] in relation to the Rajneesh movement in Oregon in 1980s); and failed prophecy leading to collapse of the group (Wright and Greil 2011).

3 Fieldwork in Japan was supported by grants by the Institute for Gender Studies (Ochanomizu University), The Great Britain Sasakawa Foundation, and the Japan Foundation Endowment Committee.

4 For a discussion on terminology, see Wright (2014).

5 Publications by ex-members include Hayashi (1998), Hayakawa and Kawamura (2005), Jōyū (2012), Munakata (2010), and the two books by Asahara's daughters, Matsumoto Satoka (2010) and Matsumoto Rika (2015).

6 In Japan is it customary not to execute someone on the death row if trials of other cases connected to this person are still pending. In December 2011, all sentences and appeals regarding Aum members were finalized. However, later in the same month Hirata Makoto, one of the three Aum members still on the run, surrendered himself. Few months later, the other two fugitives, Kikuchi Naoko and Takahashi Katsuya, were arrested and the trials and appeals related to their cases were completed in January 2018 (see Baffelli and Reader 2012; Baffelli 2018).

7 The Public Security Intelligence Agency (PSIA, in Japanese *Kōan Chōsachō*) was established in 1952 as part of the Ministry of Justice and charged of implementing the controversial Anti-subversive Activities Law (*Habōhō*).

8 An English version of the report is available at http://www.moj.go.jp/psia/english_aum_shinrikyo (accessed January 8, 2020). The PSIA also argues that a third splinter group exists and is called Yamadara no Shudan (Group Led by Yamada). According to the report the small group separated from Aleph in 2015, but very little information is provided on their activities.

9   See http://www.joyu.jp/hikarinowa/overview/ (accessed January 8, 2020).
10 The northern part of Kamikuishiki was merged with the town of Kōfu, while the southern part with the town of Fujikawaguchiko. While merger of villages is not uncommon in nowadays Japan, due to population decline and resulting economic constraints, the reputation of the village was undoubtedly tainted by Aum's notoriety (Ushiyama 2016: 148).
11 On the idea of feeling community and embodied practices in Aum female ex-members' narrative, see Baffelli (forthcoming).
12 Names and identifying details have been changed to maintain confidentiality.

References

Baffelli, E. (2012), "Hikari no Wa: A New Religion Recovering from Disaster," *Japanese Journal of Religious Studies*, 39 (1): 29–49.

Baffelli, E. (2016), *Media and New Religions in Japan*. New York and London: Routledge.

Baffelli, E. (2018), "Aum Shinrikyō," in L. Pokorny and F. Winter (eds.), *Handbook of East Asian New Religious Movements*, 193–210. Leiden: Brill.

Baffelli, E. (2020), "Failures and Successes: A Japanese New Religion's Reactions to Uncertainty," in K. Knott and M. Francis (eds.), *Minority Religion and Uncertainty*, 56–69. London: Routledge.

Baffelli, E. (forthcoming), "Living Aum: Austerities, Emotion, and the Feeling Community of Former Aum Members," *Nova Religio*.

Baffelli, E. and I. Reader (2012), "Impact and Ramifications: The Aftermath of the Aum Affair in the Japanese Religious Context," *Japanese Journal of Religious Studies*, 39 (1): 1–28.

Baffelli, E. and I. Reader (2018a), *Dynamism and the Ageing of a Japanese "New" Religion: Transformations and the Founder*. London: Bloomsbury.

Baffelli, E. and I. Reader (2018b), "The Aum Shinrikyō Executions: Why Now?" *Fair Observer*, July 13. Available online: https://www.fairobserver.com/region/asia_pacific/aum-shinrikyo-asahara-shoko-execution-tokyo-subway-attack-japan-news-71111/

Bainbridge, W. S. and R. Stark (1980), "Scientology: To Be Perfectly Clear," *Sociological Analysis*, 41 (2): 128–36.

Bromley, D. G. (2006), "Affiliation and Disaffiliation Careers in New Religious Movements," in E. V. Gallagher and W. M. Ashcraft (eds.), *Introduction to New and Alternative Religions in America*, vol. 1, 42–64. Westport, CT: Greenwood Press.

Chryssides, G. D. (2019), "Moving Out: Disengagement and Ex-Membership in New Religious Movements," in G. D. Chryssides and S. E. Gregg (eds.), *The Insider Outsider Debate: New Perspectives in the Study of Religion*, 317–92. Sheffield and Bristol: Equinox.

Davis, W. (2000), "Heaven's Gate: A Study of Religious Obedience," *Nova Religio: The Journal of Alternative and Emergent Religions*, 3 (2): 41–67.

Dawson, L. L. (2002), "Crises of Charismatic Legitimacy and Violent Behavior in New Religious Movements," in D. G. Bromley and G. Melton (eds.), *Cults, Religion, and Violence*, 80–101. Cambridge: Cambridge University Press.

Dawson, L. L. and B. C. Whitsel (2011) "Leadership and the Impact of Failed Prophecies on New Religious Movements: The Case of the Church Universal and Triumphant," in D. G. Tumminia and W. K. Swatos (eds), *How Prophecy Lives*, 115–51. Leiden and Boston: Brill.

De Jong, A. (2018), "The Disintegration and Death of Religions," in M. Stausberg and S. Engler (eds.), *The Oxford Handbook of the Study of Religion*, 1–23. New York: Oxford University Press.

Dorman, B. (2005), "Pana Wave: The New Aum Shinrikyō or Another Moral Panic?" *Nova Religio: The Journal of Alternative and Emergent Religions*, 8: 83–103.

Dorman, B. (2012), *Celebrity Gods: New Religions, Media, and Authority in Occupied Japan*, Honolulu: University of Hawai'i Press.

Frisk, L. (2002), "The Satsang Network: A Growing Post-Osho Phenomenon," *Nova Religio: The Journal of Alternative and Emergent Religions*, 6 (1): 64–85.

Frisk, L. and S. J. Palmer (2015), "The Life Story of Helge Fossmo, Former Pastor or Knutby Filadefia, as Told in Prison: A Narrative Analysis Approach," *International Journal for the Study of New Religions*, 6 (1): 51–73.

Gardner, R. A. (2001), "Aum and the Media: Lost in the Cosmos and the Need to Know," in R. J. Kisala and M. R. Mullins (eds.), *Religion and Social Crisis in Japan: Understanding Japanese Society through the Aum Affair*, 133–62. New York: Palgrave.

Hardacre, H. (2007), "Aum Shinrikyō and the Japanese Media: The Pied Piper Meets the Lamb of God," *History of Religion*, 47 (2/3): 171–204.

Hayakawa, K. and K. Kawamura (2005), *Watashi ni totte Oumu towa nandattanoka*. Tokyo: Popurasha.

Hayashi, I. (1998), *Oumu to watashi*, Tokyo: Bungei Shunjū.

Inoue, N. and S. J. Risāchi Sentā (eds.) (2011), *Jōhō jidai no Ōmu Shinrikyō*. Tōkyō: Shunjūsha.

Inoue, N. and S. J. Risāchi Sentā (eds.) (2015), *Ōmu Shinrikyō o kenshō suru*. Tokyo: Shunjūsha.

Jōyū, F. (2012), *Oumu jiken 17-nenme no kokuhaku*. Tokyo: Fusōsha.

Kisala, R. and M. R. Mullins (eds.) (2001), *Religion and Social Crisis in Japan: Understanding Japanese Society through the Aum Affair*. New York: Palgrave.

Maekawa, M. (2001), "When Prophecy Fails: The Response of Aum Members to the Crisis," in R. J. Kisala and M. R. Mullins (eds.), *Religion and Social Crisis in Japan: Understanding Japanese Society through the Aum Affair*, 179–210. New York: Palgrave.

Matsumoto, R. (2015), *Tomatta tokei*. Tokyo: Kōdansha.

Matsumoto, S. (2010), *Watashi wa naze Asahara Shōkō no musume ni umareteshimatta noka*. Tokyo: Tokuma.

McFarland, H. N. (1967), *The Rush Hour of the Gods: A Study of New Religious Movements in Japan*. New York: Macmillan.

Munakata, M. (2010), *20 sai kara no 20 nenkan: "Oumu no seishun" to iu makyō o koete*. Tokyo: Sangokan.

Murguia, J. S. (2011), "When Prophets Fail to Fail: A Case Study of Yuko Chino, Chino Shoho, and the Pana-Wave Laboratory," in D. Tumminia and W. H. Swatos (eds.), *How Prophecy Lives*, 99–113. Leiden: Brill.

Pendleton, M. (2011), "Subway to Street: Spaces of Traumatic Memory, Countermemory and Recovery in post-Aum Tokyo," *Japanese Studies*, 31 (3): 359–71.

Reader, I. (2000), *Religious Violence in Contemporary Japan: The Case of Aum Shinrikyō*. Honolulu: University of Hawai'i Press.

Reader, I. (2009), "Bodily Punishments and the Spiritually Transcendent Dimensions of Violence: A Zen Buddhist Example," in A.-R. Madawi and M. Shterin (eds.), *Dying for Faith: Religiously Motivated Violence in the Contemporary World*, 139–51. London: I.B. Tauris.

Reader, I. (2011), "The Transformation of Failure and Spiritualization of Violence," in A. R. Murphy (ed.), *The Blackwell Companion to Religion and Violence*, 304–19. New York and Oxford: John Wiley & Sons Ltd.

Robbins, J. (2014), "How Do Religions End? Theorizing Religious Traditions from the Point of View of How They Disappear," *Cambridge Anthropology*, 32 (2): 2–15.

Sawada, J. (2004), *Practical Pursuits: Religion, Politics, and Personal Cultivation in Nineteenth-Century Japan*. Honolulu: University of Hawai'i Press.

Shimazono, S. (1995), "In the Wake of Aum: The Formation and Transformation of a Universe of Belief," *Japanese Journal of Religious Studies*, 22 (3–4): 382–415.

Shimazono, S. (1997), *Gendai shūkyō no kanōsei: Ōmu Shinrikyō to bōryoku*. Tokyo: Iwanami shoten.

Takeda, Dōshō (1991) "The Fall of Renmonkyō, and Its Place in the History of Meiji-Period Religions," in N. Inoue (ed.), *New Religions: Contemporary Papers in Japanese Religion 2*, trans. Norman Havens, pp. 25–57. Tokyo: Kokugakuin University.

Ushiyama, R. (2016) "Memory Struggles: Narrating and Commemorating the Aum Affair in Contemporary Japan, 1994–2015," PhD dissertation, University of Cambridge, Cambridge.

Wilkinson, G. (2009), "The Next Aum: Religious Violence and New Religious Movements in Twenty-First Century Japan," PhD dissertation, University of Iowa.

Wright, S. A. (1987), *Leaving Cults: The Dynamics of Defection*. Washington, DC: Society for the Scientific Study of Religion.

Wright, S. A. (2014), "Disengagement and Apostasy in New Religious Movements," in L. Rambo and C. Farkadian (eds.), *Oxford Handbook on Religious Conversion*, 706–35. New York: Oxford University Press.

Wright, S. A. and A. L. Greil (2011), "Failed Prophecy and Group Demise: The Case of Chen Tao," in D. G. Tumminia and W. H. Swatos (eds.), *How Prophecy Lives*, 153–72. Leiden: Brill.

4

The Dissolution of a Religious Community: The Case of Knutby Filadelfia in Sweden

Liselotte Frisk

Knutby Filadelfia, a religious community in Sweden with Pentecostal roots, came under the spotlight in 2004 when a murder and a murder attempt took place in the group. The 23-year-old wife of the Pastor Helge Fossmo was shot dead and a male member was seriously wounded. Helge Fossmo was found guilty of conspiracy to murder and was sentenced to life in prison. Sara Svensson, one of the Pastor's mistresses, was convicted as the perpetrator. She had carried out the crimes under the influence of the Pastor, as he had been sending anonymous text messages to her phone urging her to perform the deed. The young girl believed the messages came from God. She was later committed to psychiatric care.

The community survived the 2004 murder, lawsuit, and media siege which followed these events. However, several years later, in autumn 2016, the group faced another crisis and gradually all members defected. In May 2018, Knutby Filadelfia ceased to exist legally and officially. Nearly all the members were long-term engaged and had been members for twenty years or more. Some of the younger members were born and raised in the group. The dissolution of the group generated hard feelings, and three of the people in leading positions were reported to the police by former members for physical violence and sexual abuse. The court case took place in January 2020.

Based on the preliminary enquirer report (PER 2019) prepared for the court case, as well as interviews and informal conversations with former members between 2017 and 2019, this study aims to explore the reasons for the demise of Knutby Filadelfia. The author has been researching the group since 2011 and has conducted many interviews as well as periods of participant observation during the years the group was fully functioning.

The method of the interviews and informal talks for this chapter utilize a narrative approach, basically giving the interviewees freedom to construct their own narratives about the demise of the congregation, with the interviewer probing and asking clarifying questions. The demise of the group, a process which started in September 2016, was very difficult for most of the members. Many ex-members are still (as of December 2019) in therapy to treat their traumas and several have been on sick leave for longer periods of time. For ethical reasons, no formal interviews were performed until March 2018 when some time had passed since the crisis. Up to that point only informal conversations were conducted. After each informal conversation the interviewer took down as many detailed notes as possible. Between March 2018 and December 2019, five formal interviews with seven informants were conducted with former members holding different positions and statuses in the group; however, all in a sense belonged to the central strata and not to the periphery of the group. For reasons of confidentiality, the former members who were primary sources for this study are not presented with any details, to eliminate the risk that they could be identified. All of them have consented to be interviewed for this project and have been informed of their rights not to reply to certain questions and withdraw from the project at any time. To avoid the risk of identification, the interviews were not recorded but detailed notes taken. The project is a continuation of a former project about children in different new religions, where engagement and disengagement in the groups were one theme, and for which ethical permission was obtained.

All the material was carefully read through several times, with the question about the reasons for the demise of this group in mind, until patterns emerged and different themes appeared. The themes which emerged most strongly, and on which the analysis is based, were disappointment in leaders' behavior, constant stress and overwork in the lifestyle of the group, failure of prophecy, isolation of the charismatic leader from the group, and, lastly, therapist intervention.

Before these themes will be analyzed, the history and ideology of the group will be briefly described. For this purpose, previous academic research about the group has been used as source material. The most important contribution here is a doctoral dissertation by Sanja Nilsson, published in March 2019, as well as a couple of articles written or co-written by the author. Interviews conducted with members and leaders before 2016 are also used, and not anonymized if they have been used in non-anonymized forms in published articles before as well as informal conversations in rare cases.

History and Ideology of Knutby Filadelfia

Knutby Filadelfia was founded in 1921 as a quite ordinary Pentecostal congregation (Peste 2011: 218). Its early history is described in detail in the dissertation by Nilsson (2019: 72–4). In 1985, Kim Wincent became the head Pastor (Lundgren 2008: 54–6). At this time, a fertile Christian milieu with influences from several orientations was significant in Sweden. The most important Faith Movement church in Sweden, Word of Life, was established in 1983 by a former state church priest in Sweden, Ulf Ekman (Coleman 2000: 89–90). Wincent attended a Bible school arranged by the Word of Life and was inspired by the experience. Nilsson remarks that Ekman's teachings were characterized by elements of evil spirits and spiritual battles that were later to play an important role in the Knutby Filadelfia congregation (Nilsson 2019: 73).

In 1992, Åsa Waldau (b. 1965), a former popular and controversial youth pastor in the Pentecostal congregation of Uppsala and the future charismatic leader of Knutby Filadelfia, moved to Knutby (Nilsson 2019: 74). Waldau, who was the granddaughter of one of the leading figures of the early Pentecostal Movement in Sweden, Willis Säfve,[1] had grown up in a secular home but had a salvation experience at the age of sixteen. In Knutby, she started to work mainly with music and with children. During this time, she also traveled to different parts of Sweden as a traveling evangelist and attracted a lot of attention. Many considered Waldau to have direct contact with God. Several of the people she met during these travels later moved to Knutby. Among these were Helge Fossmo and Sara Svensson, who later came to play important roles in the history of Knutby Filadelfia (interview 1). Also Pastor X,[2] one of the accused key persons in the court case in 2020, came to Knutby around the year 2000 (interview 2).

Knutby Filadelfia started a Bible School in 1997 (Nilsson 2019: 75). Within a few years, the membership doubled to around 100 members (interview 1). The new community consisted of mainly young and enthusiastic people with a family background in the Pentecostal Movement (Lundgren 2008: 59). Knutby Filadelfia gradually developed a belief system which was partly unique for the group. Around the year 2000 there was a strong expectancy that Jesus would return very soon to usher in the millennium. Many of the members believed that Knutby Filadelfia would have a special role in the coming global events, and the most special role was reserved for Åsa Waldau (informal conversations 1). At the end of the 1990s, some members began to speculate that the concept of the Bride of Christ could refer to a human person, and soon Åsa Waldau was placed in the role of the future wife of Jesus. Later she became known in the media as "the Bride of Christ" (Nilsson 2019: 81). In December 1999, the first wife of the Pastor Helge Fossmo was found dead in the bathtub in their house, a death which was at the time considered to be a tragic accident.[3] The unexpected death of a young person was a shock to the community, and it was close at hand for the members to think that God's kingdom would soon come and that they would meet their close friend again. Many people in the congregation had a deep longing for this to happen. The members of Knutby Filadelfia prayed for the imminent return of Jesus (informal conversation 1) and talked in this context about "coming home" and "being taken home." This sentiment was later criticized as possibly referring to death as something positive, providing a context of rationalization for what later became a charge of murder (Peste 2011: 217).

Prophecies, visions, and demons played a major role in the community's theology, as in classic Pentecostal congregations (Lundgren 2008: 61–3; Peste 2011: 219). Many members had dreams and visions about Åsa Waldau as the Bride of Christ (interview 5, informal conversation 2). Additionally, it was believed that Waldau and Fossmo, as well as other members of the congregation, were under attack by demons. Fossmo was believed to be in frequent battles with the Devil, and he initiated a secret sexual relationship with Sara Svensson, claiming this would increase his power to fight the Devil. Evidently, Fossmo also had other secret extramarital relationships in the congregation (Nilsson 2019: 77).

The murder in 2004 created tremendous attention in Swedish media, which lasted for several years. Knutby Filadelfia was excluded from the Swedish Pentecostal Movement due to "unorthodox beliefs" (Frisk 2018). In

2008, Waldau withdrew from official leadership in the group, allegedly due to overwork and to prepare for the impending return of Jesus (interview 5). During the next years, she worked as an artist, musician, and designer. Although she was not any more present in the everyday life of the community, her music and paintings were (Frisk 2018).

Reasons for the Demise of Knutby Filadelfia

Disappointment in Leaders' Behavior

In March 2016, a seventeen-year-old girl in the congregation told a few adults that one Pastor—who held a special position as a guide and leader for Åsa Waldau and who was seen as a spokesman for Jesus (PER 2019: 53: 277, 2019: 51: 135)—had sexual relations with her (PER 2019: 50: 14).[4] According to the girl, he had started by holding her hand stating that this action gave him spiritual power, which contributed to keeping Åsa Waldau in peace. This, in turn, was important to hasten the return of Jesus (PER 2019: 56: 5). After that, their meetings became more and more intimate until the relationship was consummated (PER 2019: 56: 11–12).

This event was the first of a series of disappointments in a leader for the small group of members in leading positions who were informed about it. It would fall into the category of what Stuart Wright calls "disillusionment," which he attributes to the moral failure of leaders becoming a catalyst for defection (Wright 2014). Bryan Wilson suggests that one significant factor which may lead to dissolution of religious groups is failure or success of the leadership to live up to the members' expectations (1987: 32–41). A sexual relationship with this young girl was not what was expected from the Pastor.

Another disappointment for the core group was the disclosure that the Pastor (who was married with two children) had sexual relationships with several other women in the congregation as well (PER 2019: 50: 14). The core group then went to Åsa Waldau to inform her and get advice as to how to handle the matter. However, Waldau—who, in her own words in the preliminary enquirer report, felt a close bond to the Pastor, from which she could not break free until half a year later—said that the Pastor was seduced by the women and that the core group should help him (PER 2019: 53: 278). She also said, however, that the Pastor had to apologize (PER 2019: 50: 14). Evidently, Waldau seems to have interpreted this event in the context of evil spirits, which she thought were trying to overpower the Pastor. According to one informant, someone close to Waldau saw in a vision black claws attacking the Pastor (interview 5).

During the next few months, the core group kept the knowledge about the abuse to itself. Seeds of doubt and disappointment had, however, been sown. One informant said that one of the consequences of this event was that some people in the core group started speaking with each other in a more honest way, particularly about things in the group which did not work well. The patterns of violence and stress in the group had risen to new levels (see next section), and one informant expressed that he could see that the fruits of what was happening in the group were not good. Some people felt really bad and the informant could see that the discipline in the group had become too rigid (interview 6).

In September 2016, some in the core group confronted Waldau over issues of the failing Pastor, as well as alleged violent incidents toward a woman in the group (PER 2019: 52: 221). The confrontation with Waldau seems to have occurred gradually over a period of several days. Pressing Waldau, it was disclosed that she also had an intimate relationship with the Pastor (PER 2019: 51: 121). Waldau herself says in the preliminary enquirer report that she believed the Pastor would lead her to Jesus and that she obeyed when he said she should give her body to him (PER 2019: 53: 277). This seems to have been the death knell for the core group to the idea that Waldau was the Bride of Christ (PER 2019: 51: 121).

The information about the failing Pastor was disclosed to everyone at a congregational meeting, and in October 2016 he was expelled from the congregation (PER 2019: 56: 23). There was still hope that the congregation could continue, but sometime later the relationship between Waldau and the Pastor was made public by the core group. Waldau was expelled in December (PER 2019: 50: 80). One informant expressed that it was the male Pastor who failed and fell. However, Waldau was knocked down in the fall as well (interview 6).

Constant Stress and Overwork in the Group's Lifestyle

From around 2008, according to one of the women, Waldau started to be physically violent toward her (PER 2019: 50: 20). This pattern of violent behavior in the group spread, especially from Waldau but also among the others in the core group, starting around 2011–12 (PER 2019: 53: 250) and then gradually escalated. It reached its peak around 2013–15 (PER 2009: 51: 92). One of the members explains that Waldau acted as she did to save the members from evil spirits (PER 2019: 51: 115). Waldau herself explains that it was of utmost importance that the members would not lose their eternal life and that everyone had to be ready when Jesus returned, which could happen any minute. When Waldau thought that someone lied, for instance, she became very worried and tried to stop them from committing sin (PER 2019: 53: 244–6). When she spoke with someone and felt there was a spiritual obstacle, then she interpreted the source as evil. In these situations she describes that sometimes she would slap the member to wake him up, to make him take command of the situation himself (PER 2019: 53: 248–9). Waldau also explains that she used what she calls symbolic acts like putting her foot on people, or pressing them against a wall (PER 2019: 53: 265–6). Other acts of violence might happen when the women closest to her became physically too close, and she felt that they were invading her space and did not move when she asked them to (PER 2019: 53: 255).

Waldau claims that there was an agreement in the group that mild violence was a way to fight evil spiritual powers (PER 2019: 53: 263). It was believed that if Waldau had to use violence, it was the member's own fault (PER 2019: 51: 117) and that the members should be thankful for the correction (PER 2019: 50: 31). This also meant that they should not resist the punishment as this was the way to forgiveness by God. After some time, a culture developed that the members of the core group should punish each other, to spare Waldau from having to punish them herself (PER 2019: 50: 77). The third Pastor accused in the police investigation, who reported himself regarding one violent incident, explains in the preliminary enquirer report that he thought that the exposed member wanted to do something which he could not because of the intervention of evil powers and that the Pastor therefore had to drag him by force (PER 2019: 52: 223).

Because of the increase of violence, the stress in the group escalated during the last two years of its existence. This was not, however, the only reason. There was also a practice that members of the core group, for spiritual reasons, were isolated from the congregation and Waldau if the latter perceived that they were open to evil powers. It was called "to stand wrong" or "to be out of grace."

Informants describe the desperation they felt when faced with the possibility that they would not be among the chosen when Jesus returned (Frisk 2019: 328). It was believed that members in this predicament could pay off the perceived debt to God. Some worked day and night, and others paid large amounts of money or bought expensive gifts for Waldau (Frisk 2019: 337–8). Also, the sexual relations between the women and the accused Pastor could possibly be explained in this light (Frisk 2019: 338), as women were made to understand that agreeing to this relationship might precipitate the second coming (PER 2019: 56: 5).

There were other trials for some core group members, which also increased during the last two years. Some who worked in building enterprises labored day and night to build new projects in Knutby, initiated by Waldau, and became mentally and physically exhausted (interview 3). One Pastor reports that in the autumn of 2016, they had twenty-one building projects that they worked on (informal conversation 3). Although it was not clearly expressed that Jesus would live in Knutby when he returned, it seems it was the belief of some members (Nilsson 2019: 83). Some members were asked to leave their own homes, to sleep on a floor in some other house (PER 2019: 50: 45) or even outside (PER 2019: 51: 92). This continued for months. Several of the married members were also told that they should not have intimate relations with each other (PER 2019: 51: 88), which didn't sit well when it became known that the accused Pastor and Waldau were in a sexual relationship.

Failure of Prophecy

Another factor which might lead to the dissolution of religious groups, suggested by Bryan Wilson, is related to failure of confirmation of ideological beliefs (1987: 32–41). Disconfirmation of beliefs is in some cases expressed as failure of prophecy (Festinger, Riecken, and Schachter 1956). Although Festinger's thesis as a whole—that failed prophecy leads to intensified proselytism—has been tested by many, with mixed results, cognitive dissonance (experiences of inconsistencies in our attitudes or between our attitudes and our behaviors) is an important factor to take into account regarding the failure and dissolution of religious groups (Tumminia 2011). Cognitive dissonance arises when beliefs, values, or opinions individuals hold come into conflict with their experience of reality (Stone 2011).

Regarding failure of prophecy in Knutby Filadelfia, the group—and not least Waldau herself—had been waiting for almost twenty years for Jesus to return. Waldau expressed in the preliminary enquirer report that the main problem for her was that as time passed, the imminent return of Christ failed to materialize, challenging her faith (PER 2019: 53: 250). One informant said in the interview that every day when Waldau woke up, and Jesus had still not come, was a failure for her. This situation led to frustration and sadness, which in turn seemed to engender more physical and mental violence (interview 6). Another member expressed in the preliminary enquirer report that violence escalated during the last few years because Waldau was in poor mental health due to frustration (PER 2019: 51: 133).

It is possible that, had not other factors like disappointment in leadership as well as stress and overwork in the group been present, the group might instead have developed in the direction of effective dissonance management. In the words of J. Gordon Melton, whenever a prophecy fails, groups usually engage in reconceptualizing the prophecy in such a way that the element of "failure" is eliminated. The ultimate reconceptualization is most frequently accomplished through a process of "spiritualization," which means that the prophesied event is reinterpreted in such a way that it is seen as having occurred as predicted, but on a spiritual plane (Melton 2000). However, due to other factors present in the situation, this did not happen in Knutby Filadelfia.

Isolation of the Charismatic Leader from the Group

In 2008 Waldau ceased actively working in the congregation as a Pastor and started to live a secluded life in her house. According to one informant, it had happened before that for extended times Waldau lived in seclusion. During the years before the murder in 2004, for example, it was believed that her seclusion had contributed to things going wrong in the group (interview 2).

Thus from 2008, Waldau became quite isolated from other congregation members in the core group. Her seclusion was based on several reasons. One reason was that she had worked feverishly since the murder in 2004 to support the congregation during the media storms, and that this work finally became too much for her. She felt that she had to create a distance between herself and people needing her help. She was also disappointed, both with certain ex-members who had been very critical toward her in the media (interview 1) and with certain members which she felt were not serious about their mission (interview 5).

In the preliminary enquirer report, Waldau said the idea that she should stop working came from other people in the core group, and that she was very sad about that and saw it as a trial. She believed her mission forward would be to just rest and receive love and joy (PER 2019: 53: 239). According to one informant, this was also a step toward precipitating the return of Jesus. Waldau would just focus on being ready for her future role. With this understanding, some people started to serve her—cleaning and managing her household, so that she could rest (interview 5). However, with this arrangement she also received very limited information about what was occurring in the community. Potentially negative information was kept from her because it was believed that it might disturb her peace of mind (interview 5).

According to one informant, through her isolation Waldau lost the connection that was most meaningful to her: preaching (interview 5). One of the members of the core group said in the preliminary enquirer report that Waldau's isolation increased her frustration, which was another factor contributing to her physical violence (PER 2019: 51: 130).

Therapist Invention

Early in the process of the demise of Knutby Filadelfia, when the members started to understand that they had lived in an illusion for many years, several of them came into contact with therapists. Some of them claim that through contacts with their therapists, their memories about events of abuse returned to them (PER 2019: 50: 29, 2019: 50: 48). The contact with the therapists also seems to have sometimes been contributing to the interpretation of the ex-members' experiences as manipulation and brainwashing (interview 5).

Especially three therapists seem to have been important in the members' subsequent interpretation of the events, two of them being well known in the anticult network in Sweden. According to the preliminary enquirer report, it was after contacts with the third therapist by several of the members that they decided to report the incidents of abuse to the police (PER 2019: 56: 36–7). Also other friends of the members used concepts like manipulation and abuse in communications with the members (PER 2019: 52: 175).

Discussion

The demise of a religious group may have several sources or causes. In the case of Knutby Filadelfia many factors interacted and reinforced each other. Disappointment/disillusionment in the leaders was a triggering factor. Had not the multiple sexual relationships of the Pastor occurred or been discovered, the fate of Knutby Filadelfia might have developed in a completely different way. And had not the sexual relationship between Waldau and the Pastor occurred or been disclosed, her exaltation as the Bride of Christ might still have seemed plausible. Another important factor was failed prophecy. The frustration on the part of the charismatic leader to failed prophecy contributed to her handling the community members in harsh ways, which had adverse effects on the believers. Exacerbating Waldau's frustration was her isolation from the congregation (partly self-imposed, but in the hope that Jesus would soon come), and her forfeiture of preaching, the activity most meaningful to her. Finally, the ex-members' subsequent interpretation of their experiences in the group through therapy was important for the eventual outcome. Most of the ex-members stopped short of the interpretation that they had been manipulated and abused. But without the contact with these therapists, who initiated and encouraged this abuse/manipulation narrative, the direction or disposition of the group might still have developed in other ways.

Below I want to discuss two crucial factors more in detail: the role of Waldau in the congregation, and the relationship between theology and sexuality.

The Role of Åsa Waldau

Åsa Waldau was unquestionably the ultimate charismatic leader in Knutby Filadelfia, with a special role partly due to her function as the Bride of Christ, but also due to the charismatic qualities which the members of Knutby Filadelfia perceived that she had (interview 2) long before the idea of her as the Bride of Christ dawned. In spite of Waldau's indubitable charisma, it is clear from the interviews that several people were involved in constructing this worldview (interview 4). The idea that she was the Bride of Christ came from Helge Fossmo and not from her (Waldau 2007: 237–44), and many people reinforced this belief through visions and prophecies (interview 5; informal conversation 2). Waldau tried to live up to the role which was created for her, the repercussions of which created an unhealthy power relationship and also paved the way for abuse (interviews 5 and 6).

Many informants agree that the accused Pastor, who was seen as the spokesman for Jesus and the spiritual guide for Waldau, actually accrued more power and impact with time (interviews 2, 5, and 6). As the years passed, he developed a set of unique teachings about things such as inventive ways to repay spiritual debts and forms of punishment and lamentation. It remains unclear if Waldau was aware of these teachings (interviews 2 and 5). Some informants indicate that the isolation of Waldau may also have contributed to the Pastor's intention to acquire more power and authority (interview 4). As Waldau's mission was to focus on the coming of Jesus, she ceased to engage in the matters of the congregation as before (interview 5). Evidently, some members took advantage of Waldau's absence (interviews 2 and 3). Certain sources report that a few people close to her either reinterpreted or miscommunicated what Waldau had said or handled matters according to their own ideas (interview 5). Two informants indicated that they were irritated by some who played the "victim role," when they were perpetrators as well and failed to take responsibility for their own actions (interviews 2 and 3).

Crucial for the sequence of events, and pertinent to the question of the significance of the presence of the charismatic leader in the community, was that Waldau was absent during the days when the accused Pastor was confronted by some of the people in the core group in the Fall of 2016 (interview 2). One informant said that with Waldau present, this confrontation would have been impossible, as she would have had the power to stop it, as she had already done in spring the same year (interview 6). With Waldau on another continent, there was space for the members to start thinking more independently (interview 2).

Summarily, the role of Waldau was strong; however, there also seems to have been other power centers in the congregation where members played a part in the sequence of events as well.

The Relationship between Theology and Sexuality

An intriguing factor is that the sexual behavior of Pastor X is so similar to the sexual behavior of Pastor Helge Fossmo just before 2004. Both were married and had several nonmarital relations with the theological motivation that they were fighting evil spiritual powers through these relationships. Especially enigmatic is how the second Pastor could initiate such a behavior, as he must have been aware of what Fossmo did a few years before and the connection in 2004 between the extramarital relationships to abuse and even murder.

It might be informative to look at the theology of Knutby Filadelfia for clues to theological interpretations of sexuality. Basically, the worldview legitimated a positive reading of sexuality within marriage. As in mainstream Pentecostalism, the teaching in Knutby Filadelfia was that sex belonged within marriage (Frisk 2018), and most members were not aware of any exceptions.[5] However, there was a teaching that since Jesus had never married or experienced sexual relations, there was a special love waiting for him in the form of his Bride. According to the teaching in the community, Jesus was longing for his Bride, both spiritually and physically. One informant observed that this teaching could have justified this novel belief. In effect, the accused Pastor, as the spokesman for Jesus, was supposed to feel as Jesus felt, and convey this to Waldau to make her feel loved. At one time he had, for instance, written a love song for her, which supposedly came from Jesus (interview 5). It seems that this role could be interpreted by other male members of the congregation as appropriate, following the lead of Pastor Helge Fossmo (PER 2019: 51: 84). In this way, feelings of sexual arousal were open to be interpreted as coming from God. Such feelings could be easily transferred to other women and be given a spiritual meaning from the perspective of the two Pastors (interview 5). The teaching of fighting evil spirits was already in play and could quite easily be invoked to justify the extramarital sexual relationships. It is still, however, an enigma that the second Pastor seems to have acted with little regard for the dreadful outcome that befell the first Pastor.

Conclusion

The demise of Knutby Filadelfia was the result of the confluence of several factors: disillusionment in the leaders; failed prophecy leading to frustration on the part of the charismatic leader, leading to stress and fatigue of the members; the isolation of the charismatic leader from the community; and the intervention of therapists at the very end of the community's existence.

Although there is a marked responsibility for the wrongdoings in the community on the part of the charismatic leader and the accused Pastor, there is a shared culpability on the part of the larger religious community. The isolation of the charismatic leader opened up opportunities for action by other core members that were not always constructive for the general membership and the community.

Finally, the teaching about the Bride of Christ and the implicit physical relationship between Jesus and his Bride led to several male members to adopt the mission to show the Bride how loved she was by Jesus. While this behavior was largely symbolic, at least with the second Pastor, the relationship was literally consummated which was one of the key disappointments with the leadership that led to the demise of the Knutby Filadelfia community.

Notes

1. See Nilsson (2019: 70).
2. His name is not disclosed in this article, as he has not (yet) been charged with any crime.
3. In 2004, Helge Fossmo was also tried for murder of his first wife, but was not convicted as the judge decided that there was not sufficient evidence (Peste 2011: 218).
4. The legal age of consent in Sweden is fifteen. This relationship was, however, considered morally wrong since sexual relationships were approved only within marriage by the church. Also, the girl was in a dependent position in relation to the pastor.
5. There was, however, one exception of which a handful of members were aware. It concerns the husband of Åsa Waldau, who since around the year 2000 had a relationship with another woman, with the knowledge and blessing of Waldau, as she was waiting for Jesus. They are currently married (interview 6).

References

Coleman, S. (2000), *The Globalisation of Charismatic Christianity: Spreading the Gospel of Prosperity*. Cambridge: Cambridge University Press.

Dawson, L. L. and B. C. Whitsel (2011), "Leadership and the Impact of Failed Prophecies on New Religious Movements: The Case of the Church Universal and Triumphant," in D. G. Tumminia and W. H. Swatos Jr. (eds.), *How Prophecy Lives*, 115–52. Boston: Brill.

Festinger, L., H. W. Riecken, and S. Schachter (1956), *When Prophecy Fails*. Minneapolis: University of Minnesota Press.

Frisk, L. (2018), "Knutby Filadelfia: A Schismatic New Religious Movement within the Pentecostal Context," in J. Moberg and J. Skjoldli (eds.), *Charismatic Christianity in Finland, Norway and Sweden: Case Studies of Historical and Contemporary Developments*, 137–58. Cham, Switzerland: Palgrave Macmillan.

Frisk, L. (2019), "Spiritual Shunning: Its Significance for the Murder in Knutby Filadelfia," *Journal of Religion and Violence*, 328–45. January 10, 2019. Available online: http://www.pdcnet.org/jrv/onlinefirst.

Lundgren, E. (2008), *Knutbykoden*, Stockholm: Modernista.

Melton, J. G. (2000), "Spiritualization and Reaffirmation," in J. R. Stone (ed.), *Expecting Armageddon: Essential Readings in Failed Prophecy*, 145–58. New York and London: Routledge.

Nilsson, S. (2019), *Performing Perfectly: Presentations of Childhood in Knutby Filadelfia before and after the Dissolution of the Congregation*. Göteborg: University of Gothenburg.

PER (2019), *Förundersökningsprotokoll Uppsala TR B 6654-17*.

Peste, J. (2011), "Murder in Knutby: Charisma, Eroticism, and Violence in a Swedish Pentecostal Community," in J. R. Lewis (ed.), *Violence and New Religious Movements*, 217–29. Oxford: Oxford University Press.

Stone, J. R. (2011), "The Festinger Theory on Failed Prophecy and Dissonance: A Survey and Critique," in D. G. Tumminia and W. H. Swatos Jr. (eds.), *How Prophecy Lives*, 41–68. Leiden, Boston: Brill.

Tumminia, D. G. (2011), "Introduction: How Failure Succeeds," in D. G. Tumminia and W. H. Swatos Jr. (eds.), *How Prophecy Lives*, 1–8. Leiden, Boston: Brill.

Waldau, Å. M. (2007), *Kristi brud—vem kan man lita på?* Skara: Heja Sverige ABM.

Wilson, B. R. (1987), "Factors in the Failure of the New Religious Movements," in D. G. Bromley and P. E. Hammond (eds.), *The Future of New Religious Movements*, 30–45. Macon GA: Mercer University Press.

Wright, S. A. (2014), "Disengagement and Apostasy in New Religious Movements," in L. R. Rambo and C. E. Farhadian (eds.), *The Oxford Handbook of Religious Conversion*, 706–35. Oxford: Oxford University Press.

Interviews and Informal Conversations

Interview 1. Interview with Åsa Waldau, May 28, 2014.
Interview 2 (two informants). March 24, 2018.
Interview 3. September 24, 2018.

Interview 4. September 26, 2018.
Interview 5. November 11, 2019.
Interview 6 (two informants). December 16, 2019.
Informal conversation 1 with Pastor Peter Gembäck 2011–15. Notes were taken and the content has been checked with the Pastor.
Informal conversation 2. August 14, 2018.
Informal conversation 3 (four informants). April 1, 2017.

5

Demise and Persistence: Religion after the Loss of "Direct Divine Control" in the Panacea Society

Alastair Lockhart

On March 13, 1919, Mabel Barltrop (1866–1934), a 53-year-old widow with four grown children, received a divine message that she should gather twelve followers, equivalent to the twelve disciples of Christ, and that they would soon "go forth in power and no man shall withstand you" (Fox c. 1921: 269). Barltrop was a follower of the late-eighteenth/early-nineteenth-century prophet, Joanna Southcott (1750–1814), and was part of a network of women in Bedford, a town in the English Midlands, who followed Southcottian teachings. They were engaged in practices of channeling messages regarded as coming from transcendent sources and had been expecting the arrival of a new Messiah for several years. Joanna Southcott had left a sealed box of prophecies, which was still in the possession of her followers, and which she had instructed could not be opened except by bishops of the Church of England. Campaigning for the box to be opened was one of the core activities of the network, and this was linked to their expectation of a messianic moment (Shaw 2011: 275–92). A month before Barltrop had received the message that she was to "go forth in power," the group had discerned that she was in fact the Messiah—at which point she took on the name "Octavia"—and with the command to gather followers she began to establish a religious group centred on her home in Bedford. The group formed into a small residential community as members moved to the small town and bought houses nearby (Fox 1927: 79–104). In the 1920s, the group discovered a divine method of physical healing, which they began to advertise and distribute by post. Responding to advertisements in newspapers and magazines, inquirers would be sent a small piece of blessed linen and instructions on how to dip it in water to drink and bathe in it in order to cure physical ailments. Over time, the healing had more than 100,000 applications from more than 100 countries (Lockhart 2019).

By March 1920, the community obtained through a divine communication a set of "Ordinances and Doctrines" "which all who are pledged to a Communal life shall embrace" (Fox 1927: 119). These included the proposition that the idea of a "Kingdom of God" referred to an earthly kingdom and not to a heaven elsewhere, that "as the Godhead manifested in Man, so will the Godhead manifest in Woman," and that members should expect immortality on earth—among other tenets (Fox 1927: 120). In 1926, the group was registered as an official charity and the Society flourished and grew for several years, including surviving the death of Octavia in 1934—when her second in command, Emily Goodwin (1858–1943), who was also believed to have the power to receive communications from a divine being, took over the leadership. Goodwin's death within ten years—in the middle of the Second World War—caused consternation, but did not precipitate the collapse of the Society which continued for a further seventy years.[1] Alongside the day-to-day business of developing a perfect community life, transacting with the godhead, and preparing for the return of Christ, the primary activities of the Society were campaigning for the bishops to open Southcott's box, the promotion and distribution of their system of divine healing, and the sale of their literature and publications. While the Society persisted for decades after Goodwin's death in 1943, it began to decline on almost every affiliation metric after that date: new members, residents in the community, and healing applications. The Society had entered a period of steady dissolution, until its eventual closure in 2012 when the last member passed away. This chapter charts the progression and processes of decline in those three key areas of affiliation. A final section discusses aspects of the interpretation of religious demise and persistence in the light of the institutional progression of the Society.

Governance

Despite the disappointment of Octavia's and Goodwin's passing in 1934 and 1943 respectively, in many respects the Society felt secure and functional to the resident members and they developed new ways of managing the day-to-day activities and governance of the institution. The transition to new forms of management and the continuity of practice reflects J. Gordon Melton's assessment of the ways in which the "death of the founder rarely proves fatal or leads to drastic alteration in the group's life" (Melton 1991: 8; Weber 1947: 363–73). With Octavia's death, Goodwin was quick to secure her position and take over full control (Shaw 2011: 317–19, 326–8). The annual report for 1942—reporting the year prior to Goodwin's death, but written after she had passed away on January 22, 1943—referred to her death, and the continuity of the Society's work:

> A year ago or even at the end of 1942 [Goodwin's death] must have seemed, on serious consideration, a quite impossible contingency and one which, did it come to pass, would seem to imply the end of The Society. Nevertheless it has happened and, although the Confidential part of the work and therefore the Sealing must consequently and automatically terminate, The Society otherwise finds itself firmly established and continuing as before.
>
> (The Panacea Society Annual Report 1942: 1)

The following year's report (1943) referred to "the outstanding event of the year [...] the Passing of Mrs. Goodwin" but noted that "work has been carried on and The Society has survived the loss which has, nonetheless, left a blank that it seems cannot be filled and we are very much like a ship without a captain" (The Panacea Society Annual Report 1943: 1). So, the work of the Society continued—with a focus now on the provision of the healing which provided an on-going and purposeful task that may have bonded the community together and at least provided a shared and outward facing purpose.[2] They made administrative changes to continue effective governance: additional trustees were appointed to serve alongside the one trustee who remained (Peter Rasmussen [1875–1961], one of Octavia's oldest and most trusted confidantes), and "all securities and title deeds have been transferred to the new Trustees" (The Panacea Society Annual Report 1943: 2). And, the Society's Council was reconstituted with a new president, chair, and other members (The Panacea Society Annual Report 1943: 2).

Amid the new arrangements and introduction of new personnel into the higher leadership, in the immediate aftermath of Goodwin's death there are indications that the Society saw the continuing healing work as evidence of some kind of prescience by Goodwin and Octavia—in effect a form of continued involvement:

> Although she [Goodwin] has been sorely missed in the Healing Department, the work has continued with a degree of smoothness that could not have seemed possible had the idea of such a contingency been considered before it actually occurred. The value of the training given by Mrs. Goodwin has been increasingly realised and appreciated as have also the marvellous provision and foresight of Octavia's work.
> (The Panacea Society Annual Report 1943: 7)

In 1944, the sense was reinforced:

> It is very noteworthy, notwithstanding that it was never for a moment humanly contemplated that such a contingency would arise as that we would be left without direct Divine Control, yet the Rules and Regulations drawn up by Octavia in 1926 provide absolutely for the position with which we are now confronted, in as much as the Council is constituted, the Governing Body of The Society and full power and authority are vested in it to do anything whatsoever that it considers right and proper.
> (The Panacea Society Annual Report 1944: 1)

In effect, contrary to the common idea that the loss of charismatic leadership is likely to be fatal to the continuation of a religious movement, in the case of the Panacea Society, the loss of the directing personalities understood to be divinely inspired was neatly managed through effective administrative systems (see Melton 1991, discussed above). Effective governance was bolstered by financial security. The Society had a regular financial surplus from tithing payments, and in fact as members passed away they often left substantial legacies to the Society further improving the financial position. For example, the annual report for 1943 records two legacies: £478 16s. 11d. and £558 5s. 2d.

(The Panacea Society Annual Report 1944: 3).[3] In 1945 bequests of £385 19s. 7d. and £1,250 were left to the Society (The Panacea Society Annual Report 1945: 2).[4] The management of the Society continued, it was institutionally secure, and the work went on.

Membership

Full formal membership of the Panacea Society was through a process known as "sealing" which was inaugurated in 1919 (Fox c. 1921: 299, 330). Initially, sealing had been made available to resident members only, but over time it became possible to be sealed and be a resident elsewhere. It was intended that sealed members would ultimately number 144,000 (reflecting the number of "sealed" in the Book of Revelation, see Rev. 7.3), so careful records were kept of their numbers, including the number that withdrew or died (Shaw 2011: 110–11). In any event, sealing seems never to have attracted a great number of individuals; there was a steady progression to 1,285 members around the time of the death of Octavia in 1934 (Shaw 2011: 327). Following Octavia's death, sealing continued under her successor, Emily Goodwin, to a recorded 1,392 members when she died in 1943 (The Panacea Society Annual Report 1943: 5). The death of Goodwin, however, caused a suspension of the ritual work of sealing new members because Goodwin was understood to have been the channel of a divine personality that worked through her uniquely and which could uniquely carry out the transcendent task. The Society noted "the feeling of unreality and the tremendous blank consequent upon this development" in its annual report (The Panacea Society Annual Report 1942: 1).

It was noted that sealing "had to be closed, for the time being" with the passing of Goodwin: "As no further Sealing can take place for the present, there the position must be left, making the total of sealed persons in Companies: 1,392" (The Panacea Society Annual Report 1943: 5). It bears notice that the phrases "for the time being" and "for the present" suggest an emerging adaptation in the Society's theology; perhaps a new expectation that Goodwin or Octavia would be resurrected, or some other inspired individuals would emerge. The details of any such theological revision are not discussed in the Society's annual reports, though Jane Shaw's study of the Society does indicate the kinds of adjustments that took place. Shaw suggests that Octavia's followers "explained her death by believing that she would indeed come again, this time with Christ himself [...] The parallel with Christ was drawn clearly, so that her death could be made explicable" (2011: 322). The death of other faithful members had led to the reinterpretation of a divine message received by Octavia in 1920 to suggest, in Shaw's words, that "members would go, after death, to Uranus and wait for the next Coming of Christ and Octavia" (2011: 325).

This evolution in expectation saw a parallel evolution in the practice of sealing. The sealing process was turned into a ritualized communication between the person being sealed and the departed Goodwin (or the divine entity she had channeled) akin to prayer. Where once individuals had been expected to write to Goodwin to confess their faults, "printed notices were sent to all sealed members and others known to be in correspondence with her notifying them of the position and the necessary cessation of confidential correspondence, with a recommendation to continue to write and voice their confessions to the Divine Mother at their bedsides" (The Panacea Society Annual Report 1943: 7). This was formalized in a notice given to inquirers for the sealing that "the Sealing must now be discontinued, but offering to receive the names of such as expressed a desire to be sealed, their willingness to comply with the required procedure, and wrote to affirm that they had voiced their Life Confession. Such names are recorded in a special register"[5] (The Panacea Society Annual Report 1943: 8). The process of certification was formalized by the Society's Council in the following year:

> A special form of acknowledgement was sanctioned by the Council and has been sent to a few people who were already in correspondence with Mrs. Goodwin, but were too late to have their confessions accepted by her, and others who have expressed an earnest wish that they could be sealed and go on to the next step which they perceive to be indicated by what they have read. This certificate states that the Council accepts their assurance that they have voiced their Confessions to the Divine Mother, has recorded their desire to be Sealed and willingness to comply with all the requirements, and has enrolled their names as desiring to be written in the Book of Life. A register is kept of such candidates.
>
> (The Panacea Society Annual Report 1944: 4)

At Goodwin's death in 1943, 1,392 members had been sealed; following her death, sealing using the new certification system progressed slowly before fading away. A total of 42 people had received the new form of sealing certificate by 1945 (The Panacea Society Annual Report 1945: 4). The 1952 report commented: "During the year the Council's Certificate has been issued to seven persons who duly affirmed that they had made and voiced their confessions. This brings the total of Certificates issued to 76" (The Panacea Society Annual Report 1952: 7). The last reference to certificates being issued in the annual reports appears to be in 1953 when five were sent out, bringing the total to eighty-one (The Panacea Society Annual Report 1953: 5). Annual reports over the years record numbers of "defaulters" in the membership, including a number not replying to inquiries, some withdrawing formally, or others returned undeliverable or deceased. It was assumed, in addition, that many members must have died without the Society being notified.

The Resident Community

Notwithstanding an effective central administration that sustained the Society as an institution then, there was a fading of wider membership numbers as the sealing dissolved, and this was paralleled by a steady decline in the membership of the central management and leadership at the Society's headquarters in Bedford. The peak in resident members came in 1939, when sixty-six individuals lived in Society houses in Bedford. This dropped steadily as residents grew older and passed away or moved into care (aside from a few new recruits to the center, though these were all past middle age) to thirty-eight residents by 1954, twenty-two by 1964, and ten in 1974. At that point numbers collapsed to four members by 1979 and two—perhaps the minimum number needed to regard the center as a functional institution—by 1993. The group appears, then, to be an example of a religion—in Eileen Barker's words—"ageing itself out of existence" (2011: 18).[6] Barker's (2011) discussion is about aging in new religious movements; it reviews the ways in which new religious movements respond to the challenge of growing numbers of older members who are "able to offer only a diminishing contribution to the general weal" and who are increasingly dependent on other members of the group (2011: 20).

While the focus of Barker's study is groups that have *not* met their demise and are facing rather the challenges of maturation, the discussion also refers to groups failing to sustain their membership by producing no children (or by producing children who move away) or by not recruiting younger converts (2011: 6–7)—and the Panacea Society is cited as one example of these. Analysis of the number of members resident in the community and their average ages supports Barker's broad characterization. Based on information available in the Society's institutional archives supplemented from other sources, it is possible to identify a total of 103 core practicing members who were resident in the Society's houses in Bedford and (most of) their birth dates.[7] Sampling at approximately five-year intervals shows a steady increase in average age despite occasional dips alongside a steady decrease in the number of residents. The peak in the number of residents in the sample is in 1938, when sixty-five people had an average age of sixty-four,[8] and the peak in average age is in 2008 when two residents had an average age of eighty-six. The final sample in 2012 has just one resident, aged eighty—who died that year.

The Healing

While the Panacea Society's membership in the Bedford headquarters met its end with the death of the last member, this did not necessarily mean that its ideas and influence came to an end. Elsewhere I have discussed the Society's global influence in its distribution of a system of healing to over 100,000 people all over the world for nearly ninety years (Lockhart 2019). From a peak in 1939 (when more than 8,000 people applied for the healing), healing use steadily declined over the century until, during the last ten years of the Society's existence, 283 people wrote to the healing department—either to apply for healing or to report on the progress of their ailments—the majority from Jamaica, and large proportions from west Africa, the United States, and the UK (Lockhart 2019: 133–4). Assent to particular beliefs was not formally required for people to subscribe to the healing—they were only required to follow particular water-taking practices and report to the Society on their progress at prescribed intervals—it nonetheless carried implicit meanings, was integrated into individual and local belief systems, and some users were also familiar with Panacea theology (Lockhart 2019: 79–80, 108–20). There may have been no sealed members left; the last member of the resident community may have died, but there were still users of the healing when the functions at the religious center closed.[9] On that basis, the institutional core of Panaceaism met its demise before interest in its ideas and practices met theirs. This parallels aspects of Albert de Jong's analysis (discussed below); the extinction of a people does not necessarily cause the utter extinguishing of the religion—there can be some continuation in some other tradition by a syncretic or culture-sharing process (2016: 652).[10] If the few last water-takers who continued the healing can be labeled as "religious"—it might be argued that elements of the religious system have persisted and indeed that, by the same token, to some extent, all religions except the most socially isolated persist in the cultures that knew something of them (something similar might be said of the demise of human individuals). This is one way to understand the wider implication of Robert Bellah's proposal that "nothing is ever lost," and it is explicit in Günter Kehrer's passing observation (which he recognizes has little theoretical usefulness) that to some extent everything ever thought, said, or written leaves a trace in the world (Bellah 2011: 267, cited by de Jong 2016: 661; Kehrer 1986: 222).

In his 1986 study of critical phases in the history of new religions, Kehrer draws attention to definitional questions that pertain in the study of religious demise. Taking a sociological perspective, he defines distinct religious ideas functioning as consciously shared systems of belief for a group of deliberately cooperating people as religions—at least for the purposes of sociological study (Kehrer 1986: 221–2). There is thus a spectrum of religious emergence, from the formation of religious ideas in the minds of individuals, to the deliberate gathering of followers and the forming of groups, to the great transnational world religions. Following Kehrer's supposition, while the Panacea Society persisted as a theological institution, when it was reduced to one resident member around 2008, with a set of disparate and non-communicating wider members, it was sociologically deceased. It might be argued that under Kehrer's conception the Society persisted as a social institution after 2008 as various disparate healing users wrote from time to time to the last remaining resident member—but her death in 2012 brought that remnant social structure to an end as well.

Discussion: Demise and Persistence

J. Gordon Melton's (1991) discussion of the death of prophets in new religions (cited above) refers in the main to groups much larger than the Panacea Society. It appears, in terms of that account, that while the Society had developed sufficiently to overcome the challenge of the end of charismatic leadership in the short term, Octavia's death in 1934 and the death of her immediate successor, Goodwin, a decade later represented a turning point in the Society's fortunes. Membership through sealing/certification slowed significantly after 1943 and halted by 1953, the number of resident members in the Bedford community entered a steep decline around 1943 from which it never recovered, and the number of applications to the healing began a steady decline following a brief recovery after 1945.[11] While the Society had matured further than those cited by Melton that collapsed with the death of their founders (Psychiana and Spirit Fruit Society) and had the advantages of effective administration, well-managed transfer of assets, and financial security referred to by Melton (1991: 9–11), it did not reach the levels of scale and development that are necessary to persist indefinitely.

Overall, then, it is evident that the Panacea Society established itself around 1919, developed prophecy and doctrine, and cultivated members, in the 1920s and 1930s, and then faded slowly to extinction as members died, until the last one passed away in 2012. In a programmatic examination of the "disintegration and death of religions," Albert de Jong identifies the extreme cases of religious demise—genocide and mass conversion—between which a variety of forces and developments are implicated in "continuing processes of change and adaptation that may lead to the disappearance of a particular religion" (2016: 646, from the abstract). While the extinction of the Panacea Society community did not occur with the speed and violence implied by the wars, genocides, conquests, and epidemics which de Jong cites as the external forces causing the demise of communities and thus the mechanisms for the demise of their languages and religions, the effect was nonetheless the same: the end of the community, thus the end of the cultural—including religious—forms it carried[12] (2016: 651–2). To that extent, the end of the Panacea Society is a case of religious demise due to the demise of the members.

Nonetheless, it is pertinent to observe that the institution itself did not come to an end entirely in 2012. At that point all religious functions ceased and the trust managing the group's assets which had originated in 1926 when the Society was first registered as a charity completed a process of modernization, including reorienting its efforts toward good works relieving poverty and sickness in the local area and supporting academic research and public understanding of aspects of religion related to movements like the Panacea Society (the author of this chapter is employed by the Trust as an academic promoting the second of those purposes).[13] The work of preparing the Society for the demise of the last believing member, and reforming and modernizing its functions and structures, including the introduction of trustees who did not subscribe to Panacea beliefs, began while the last two resident members were still present and active. The adjustment that took place in 2012 was in some respects equivalent to the reorganization that took place when Goodwin died in 1943, and which ensured the stability and continuity of the Society at a point of transition. However, the striking point about the 2012 change is that it managed the end of resident members and the establishment of a governing board that did not subscribe to the beliefs of the Society. This might be regarded as an instance of secularization, as the institution persisted but was no longer formally motivated by the religious impulse of its members. This is an echo of the 1943 reorganization which itself had elements of desacralization: not only was direct communication with divine powers understood to have been removed—they referred to it as the removal of direct divine control (The Panacea Society Annual Report 1944: 1)—but a newly formed Council instituted a process of certification for membership making no transcendent claim itself.

The relevance of a broad secularization thesis to the demise of individual religions raises philosophical and analytical problems with the definition and interpretation of the concept of secularization and religion which will not be discussed here.[14] The key point in the debate, presented in David Martin's (1986) study of the application of the secularization thesis to the decline of particular religions, is to "underline the 'ambiguity' in most religious transformations" and to query whether "all transformations can be subsumed and genealogically linked together within one secularization 'story'" (Martin 1986: 313). While the final phase of the Panacea Society might be regarded as a particular secularization—as a secular charitable trust took over the Society's governance—this is insufficient to support a claim that it evidences the effects of any wider secularization in society. The religious motive may have left the institution of the Panacea Society as a social group (so, religious demise, under Kehrer's scheme), but that ensured its persistence as an institution as it enabled the introduction of non-religious management. In effect, the management and governance systems were so effective they outlived the religious impulse that inspired them in the first place. The same is no doubt true of many once religious institutions that continue to function after religious direction is removed; the histories of the older medical hospitals, and the more ancient Oxford and Cambridge colleges are perhaps cases in point (though their antiquity presents different issues in relation to any general thesis of secularization).

Elsewhere, I have referred to the variety of analysis theorizing the existence of a historically continuous, non-official religious space which acts as a repository of pliable and non-mainstream religious ideas. Wouter Hanegraaff, for example, has suggested that the "New Age movement" is an expression of a tradition of esoteric belief with a continuous history going back to the early Renaissance. A strong version of the thesis is presented by Robert Ellwood, who proposes that there is a continuous tradition of alternative spirituality with a history going back to the ancient world (Lockhart 2019: 24–5, citing Ellwood 1992: 59; Hanegraaff 2000: 293–4). While unlikely to fit any "new age" label in itself, the Panacea Society drew on emerging and non-mainstream contemporary movements for membership and ideas operating in the same ecosystem—especially Theosophy, Spiritualism, and Christian Science (Lockhart 2019: 53–6)—and a model of a historical and continuous repository of esoteric spiritual knowledge was explicit in their belief system. They traced their doctrines back to an esoteric strand of thought from Jacob Böhme (1575–1624), Jane Lead (1624–1704), Joanna Southcott (1750–1814), and a string of successor prophets. They also regarded their founder as a new eruption of that divine power (Lockhart 2019: 15–22). They might also be regarded as an essentially Christian breakaway Anglican movement or so departing from the Christian framework as to constitute a new system of belief. The question is complicated by the fact that the Panacea Society regarded Christianity as a failed and mutilated version of their own religion which they regarded as the conserved "true" and "original" religion. What is evident is that the Panacea Society's beliefs were drawn from a diverse range of sources, including the Church of England, a panoply of emerging and non-official forms of religion, and a long tradition of non-mainstream esoteric beliefs. And, the Panacea

Society itself was, for a period of time, a robust social institution within a wider ecosystem of diverse and malleable religious beliefs and practices.

The processes this suggests have a parallel in one model of religious change discussed by Joel Robbins (2014) where he identifies a characteristic of global Pentecostalism: its susceptibility "to the emergence of trends that quickly diffuse around the world and appear to dominate religious life in many places for a brief period, but then just as quickly find themselves displaced by new trends that put them in the shade" (2014: 4). While Robbins does not carry out a detailed analysis of "the processes by which one trend replaces another in Pentecostalism," he draws attention to the potential value of the "pattern of trend formation and dissolution [...] for those interested in the fall of religious complexes and the topic of religious change more generally" (2014: 4). The Panacea Society case study cannot speak to Pentecostalism *per se*; however, Robbins's grammar of religious complexes does contribute to the model of the rise and fall of religious ideas the Panacea Society suggests. The Panacea Society can be understood, in these terms, as the emergence of some core religious ideas from an ill-defined popular conversation about spiritual values and meaning, around which a religious institution began to form—in effect a trend or complex that found currency in a particular social and cultural context—but which ultimately faded and dissolved. This is to suggest that the Panacea Society was a luminous but brief socialization of a set of beliefs and practices that were drawn from a common pliable cultural context, and which is the natural origin— and natural end—of all religious institutions. This is not quite the process of continuity implied by de Jong (2016), which associates continuation with the picking up of motifs in other equivalent religious systems, but it is perhaps a variant: the slipping of beliefs and practices back into a shared vernacular space, or a common discourse of spiritual practice and belief. If the model of human life, death and memory is a valid comparison, it is demise nonetheless.

Acknowledgments

I am grateful to Justin Meggitt, the chair of the Panacea Charitable Trust, and David McLynn, the Trust's Executive Officer, who agreed to be interviewed and provided useful insight into the final years of the Panacea Society.

I am also grateful to Vicki Manners, the Panacea Charitable Trust's archivist, who provided valuable help in identifying relevant documents and other consolidated records in the Trust's archives. Thank you as well to Emma E. Smith who provided kind and patient assistance with the German language source referred to in the chapter.

Notes

1. See Shaw (2011) for a history of the Octavia and the formation of the Society.
2. Rosabeth Kanter (1972) suggested that 1960s communes with community service functions aimed at achieving some transcendent service to society were stronger and more cohesive so less likely to fail (compared to retreat communes which dissolved more easily) (Shepherd and Shepherd 2010: 10–11).
3. Equivalent to a total of nearly £50,000 or US$65,000 today.
4. Equivalent to a total of about £70,000 or US$90,000 today.
5. It was also observed that "so far as is known, no Sealed Member has been killed in an air raid, nor even seriously injured, but many, both Sealed and Water Takers, describe instances of wonderful protection and deliverance not only from injury, but from fear" (The Panacea Society Annual Report 1943: 8).
6. Barker uses the phrase to refer to groups which ultimately made adequate plans to avoid extinction.
7. Birth dates were missing for nineteen individuals in the sample.
8. The peak in resident members was in fact 66 in 1939 (see Shaw 2011: 327).
9. When it closed, the Society's executive officer arranged to send anyone who wrote in for healing a small supply of healing linen sufficient to last them for several years and informed them of the closure of the healing.
10. De Jong gives the example of the belief that "the great goddesses of the Hellenistic Anatolia [...] ultimately go back to Hittite deities" (2016: 652).
11. For healing application patterns, see Lockhart (2019: 44–5).
12. In de Jong's account, this form of religious demise—where a religion expires because its carriers all die—is the minority pathway. "In most cases," de Jong says, "a scenario similar to that of language death," where a population converts to another language/religion, "is much more plausible" (2016: 658). A number of sealed members of the Panacea Society did give up their association and presumably adopted other belief systems.

13 See "The Panacea Charitable Trust." The author is academic co-director at the Centre for the Critical Study of Apocalyptic and Millenarian Movements which is funded by the Panacea Charitable Trust.
14 See Lockhart (2019: 31–44, 125–31) for a discussion of some of these themes in relation to the Panacea Society.

References

Barker, E. (2011), "Ageing in New Religions: The Varieties of Later Experiences," *Diskus*, 12: 1–23.

Bellah, R. N. (2011), *Religion in Human Evolution: From the Paleolithic to the Axial Age*. Cambridge, MA and London: Belknap Press of Harvard University Press.

De Jong, A. (2016), "The Disintegration and Death of Religions," in M. Stausberg and S. Engler (eds.), *The Oxford Handbook of the Study of Religion*, 646–64. Oxford University Press.

Ellwood, R. (1992), "How New Is the New Age?" in J. Lewis and J. G. Melton (eds.), *Perspectives on the New Age*, 59–67. Albany, NY: State University of New York Press.

Fox, R. J. (1927), *The Sufferings and Acts of Shiloh-Jerusalem (a Sequel to "The Finding of Shiloh")*. London: Cecil Palmer.

Fox, R. J. (c. 1921), *The Finding of Shiloh, or the Mystery of God "Finished."* London: Cecil Palmer.

Hanegraaff, W. J. (2000), "New Age Religion and Secularization," *Numen*, 47 (3): 288–312.

Kanter, R. (1972), *Commitment and Community: Communes and Utopia in Sociological Perspective*. Cambridge, MA: Harvard University Press.

Kehrer, G. (1986), "Kritische Phasen in der Geschichte neuer Religionen," in H. Zinser (ed.), *Der Untergang von Religionen*, 221–34. Berlin: Dietrich Reimer Verlag.

Lockhart, A. (2019), *Personal Religion and Spiritual Healing: The Panacea Society in the Twentieth Century*. Albany, NY: State University of New York.

Martin, D. A. (1986), "The Secularisation Thesis—And the Decline of Particular Religions," in H. Zinser (ed.), *Der Untergang von Religionen*, 309–19. Berlin: Dietrich Reimer Verlag.

Melton, J. G. (1991), "Introduction: When Prophets Die: The Succession Crisis in New Religions," in T. Miller (ed.), *When Prophets Die: The Postcharismatic Fate of New Religions*, 1–12. Albany, NY: State University of New York Press.

Robbins, J. (2014), "How Do Religions End? Theorizing Religious Traditions from the Point-of-View of How they Disappear," *Cambridge Anthropology*, 32 (2): 2–15.

Shaw, J. (2011), *Octavia, Daughter of God: The Story of a Female Messiah and Her Followers*. London: Jonathan Cape.

Shepherd, G. and G. Shepherd (2010), "New Religions and Community," *Nova Religio*, 13 (3): 5–13.

Weber, M. (1947), *The Theory of Social and Economic Organization*, ed. T. Parsons and trans. A. M. Henderson and T. Parsons. New York: Oxford University Press.

Panacea Charitable Trust Archive References

Items marked "Panacea Charitable Trust archive" are located at 14 Albany Road, Bedford, MK40 3PH.

"The Panacea Charitable Trust," Charity Commission for England and Wales website: https://apps.charitycommission.gov.uk/Showcharity/RegisterOfCharities/CharityWithPartB.aspx?RegisteredCharityNumber=227530.

"The Panacea Society Annual Report, 1942," TS, Panacea Charitable Trust archive, F.3.2.6.

"The Panacea Society Annual Report, 1943," TS, Panacea Charitable Trust archive, F.3.2.7.

"The Panacea Society Annual Report, 1944," TS, Panacea Charitable Trust archive, F.3.2.7.

"The Panacea Society Annual Report, 1945," TS, Panacea Charitable Trust archive, F.3.2.7.

"The Panacea Society Annual Report, 1952," TS, Panacea Charitable Trust archive, F.3.2.10.

"The Panacea Society Annual Report, 1953," TS, Panacea Charitable Trust archive, F.3.2.10.

6

Denominationalization or Death? Comparing Processes of Change within the Jesus Fellowship Church and the Children of God aka The Family International

Eileen Barker

This is an account of the apparently impending demise of two new religious movements (NRMs) which were part of the Jesus movement that was spreading across North America and western Europe in the late 1960s. Both movements were evangelical in nature; both had a charismatic preacher as its founder; and both believed from their inception in following the lifestyle of the early Christians as described in the Acts of the Apostles.[1] One of the movements began in the small village of Bugbrooke, a few miles southwest of Northampton in the English Midlands; the other began in Huntington Beach, California. The first was to become known, variously, as the Jesus Fellowship Church (JF), the New Creation Christian Community, and the Jesus Army;[2] the second became known, sequentially, as the Children of God (CoG), The Family of Love, The Family, and then, from 2004, The Family International (TFI).[3]

The Jesus Fellowship

Noel Stanton (1926–2009), who had been pastor of the Bugbrooke Baptist Chapel since 1957, had a dramatic spiritual experience in 1969, when "a tide of love broke over him and the Spirit came in power" (Cooper and Farrant 1997: 30). Following this experience, Stanton started to attract a growing number of young people who became "baptised in the Holy Spirit" and found themselves "with fire in their hearts." Although the converts included several young professionals such as doctors and teachers, by 1972 the outreach was focusing in large part on bikers, hippies, Hell's Angels, and acid heads (Kay 2007: 152). As the movement grew, it acquired several properties in the area for communal living, including a nearby farm. It also built up a number of businesses, including wholesale foods, building supplies, and a vehicle repair firm. Some of the members worked outside the community, giving their earnings to the community; others were employed in one or other of the businesses, working on the farm or renovating the movement's properties, where everyone received the same wages, most of which were then donated to "the common purse." Publications included the *Jesus Army Newspaper* and the magazines *Jesus Lifestyle* and *Heartcry*. The Fellowship's House of Goodness Group, selling farm products, health foods, and building supplies, reportedly had an annual turnover of around £15 million and employed about 250 members in the mid-1990s (MacDonald-Smith 1995). By 2003, the Fellowship was reported as having a turnover of about £35 million per annum (Kay 2007: 155).

From its early beginnings, the movement's growth gave rise to a number of criticisms. The local mainstream churches regarded the charismatic movement in general with suspicion. Complaints included the separation of members from their non-member relatives and the social isolation of children within the movement (although the children did attend state schools). Others complained of the noise from the Bugbrooke chapel, and the cars and motorbikes that filled the village, especially on a Sunday evening. Some local firms resented the Fellowship-owned businesses, which were undercutting any competitors by paying low wages, and some local residents resented the Fellowship's rapid purchase of properties in the area (Cooper and Farrant 1997; Hunt 1998). Then, in 1986, the JF was expelled from the Baptist Union of Great Britain on the grounds that the Fellowship's now nation-wide organization and its form of governance could no longer be recognized as a local Baptist church. That same year, the JF was asked to resign from the Evangelical Alliance (which it had joined in 1982) following adverse publicity and what the Fellowship perceived as persecution instigated in large part by a critical letter written by former members and circulated to the press, new members, relatives of members, and other Christians (Cooper and Farrant 1997: 227–9).

Following these attacks, the Fellowship had a period of becoming more defensive, introverted, and withdrawn from the wider society, and there was a continuing loss of membership. However, with the creation in 1987 of the Jesus Army as the campaigning arm of the JF, the movement became more visible. Brightly colored Jesus Army buses and multi-colored camouflage jackets worn by Jesus Army evangelists became a familiar sight in Northampton, London, and elsewhere, declaring war on homelessness, alcoholism, racism, abortion, hate, drug addiction, violence, and crime (Kay 2007: 156). The unemployed and homeless, including those with drug and/or alcohol problems, were offered work and a roof over their heads, thereby making up a substantial proportion of the movement's work force.

At the same time, the JF started seeking greater collaboration and acceptance within other new charismatic and evangelical churches, and by the end of the century it had rejoined the Evangelical Alliance. In 2001 the Jesus Army Charitable Trust (JACT) was registered.[4] This became responsible for running Jesus Centres, described as "places where the love of Jesus is expressed daily through worship, friendship and help for every kind of person."[5] The first Centre opened in 2002 in Coventry; six more were to follow in Northampton, London and other cities. While open to the general public, the Centres were primarily targeted toward the socially and economically disadvantaged, offering a range of services including: information and help for refugees and asylum seekers; information technology and skills training; medical advice; washing and haircutting facilities; counseling; parent and toddler groups; cafes, meetings, and worship groups. The Centres have also acted as gateways to other agencies and other service providers.

Not all converts have been equally committed to the JF, but they could join at (and move between) different levels. Congregational members would attend Sunday meetings; cell group members would attend cell group meetings. Baptized members, having been baptized by total immersion, were considered full members but had not made the "Sevenfold Covenant Commitment" to the Church. Those who made the Covenant Commitment were received as members through the "right hand of fellowship." Style 1 Covenant members attended regular worship services but maintained their own residences; Style 2 Covenant members, in addition to regular attendance, made a regular financial contribution; Style 3 Covenant members belonged to the New Creation

Christian Community, living communally and sharing all resources; while Style 4 members were those who, living some distance from a congregation, were unable to attend regular events.

Life in the communal houses, especially in the early days, has been described as "a Spartan existence" and a "simple lifestyle," with members having few personal possessions (Hunt 2003: 114). In 1991, a list of forty-eight "Precepts" was circulated to Style 3 household leaders by Stanton and Mike Haines (to whom Stanton handed over the leadership prior to his death). Many of the precepts began "We do not …." They included:

> We do not listen to secular music, watch secular TV/video or read secular books;
> We take no part in the celebration of Christmas, Easter or other worldly festivals;
> We do not have hobbies or amusements;
> We maintain a holy separation between the sexes and do not allow flirtation;
> Wives in the community are subject to their believing husbands.
>
> (Haines and Stanton 1991)

Not all members were married. Indeed, those who were most committed took a vow of celibacy. In the words of Stanton, who is said to have frequently preached about the sins of the flesh, "Now we give our genitals to Jesus" (Ironmonger 2019:@4.55/8.07). Less bluntly, a young woman ended a short article on her decision to become celibate and her thoughts during her year's probation before taking her final vow, with the words,

> God! The day has finally arrived—when all will be consecrated to You. I feel a deep peace as I begin this day (still can't believe it's me!—that You have chosen me!) It's your miracle Lord—let Your spirit rise within me, draw me ever close.
>
> (Stockley 2007: 11)

By the beginning of the twenty-first century, the JF seemed to be gathering strength despite complaints from former members and attacks from "anti-cultists." It was proving a growing attraction to a wider spread of the population than most NRMs. Its businesses appeared to be prospering and in 2003 the sociologist Stephen Hunt (2003: 114) was to remark that the

Fellowship's flexible membership, allowing differing levels of commitment, "probably largely explains why the Jesus Fellowship has endured while other similar movements have not survived" (Hunt 2003: 114). By 2007 there were approximately 3,500 members in about twenty-four congregations in various cities and towns of the UK (Kay 2007: 157). But gradually the numbers started dwindling. In 2012 the JF reported having 2,500 members, and, by 2019, the Fellowship had about 1,000 members, 200 of whom were living in communal houses (Lynch 2019b). On May 28, 2019, the following press release appeared on the JF's website:

> On Sunday 26th May, the members of the Jesus Fellowship Church (JFC) voted to revoke the Church's constitution. This means that the national Church, formerly known as the Jesus Army, will cease to exist and the current National Leadership Team will be stepping down from their roles once the winding up of the central Church has been completed.[6]

The Children of God/The Family International

David "Moses" Berg (1919–1994) was another of the many evangelical preachers to be found in the 1960s as part of the burgeoning Jesus movement. Around 1968 he was encouraging young, mainly white, middle-class hippies to devote their lives to Christ and to live with him and his family in their Californian home. Initially called Teens for Christ, the movement was soon to adopt the name Children of God (CoG). Although in many ways like other young "Jesus people," the CoG differed in that they believed not only in the Bible, but also in the interpretation of it promoted by Berg, who they believed was God's Endtime prophet. Inspired by Berg's apocalyptic visions, the CoG became a familiar sight, dressed in sackcloth and carrying placards proclaiming that the Day of Judgement (for America in particular) was nigh.

It was not long before the movement was attracting negative attention, and in 1971 some concerned parents of young converts organized themselves into America's first "anti-cult" organization, FreeCOG, under the leadership of Ted Patrick, who became a renowned deprogrammer, kidnapping and holding converts against their will until they managed to escape or to persuade their captors that they had abandoned their new faith (Patrick and Dulack 1976).

By the mid-1970s, CoG missionaries were living in communities throughout the world. Because of the deprogramming and bad publicity, especially after the Jonestown tragedy in 1978 (see Cusack and Lewis, this volume), they tended to hide their identity. Members communicated with non-members (referred to as "systemites") primarily for purposes of "litnessing" (selling their literature and witnessing (van Zandt 1991: 82–97)) and "procuring" or "provisioning" (persuading people to donate to them, as Christian missionaries, various goods, and services including food, clothing, furniture, airline tickets, and midwifery (Barker 2016: 411)). They did, however, build up many long-term relationships with supporters and trusted friends through these activities, often keeping in touch through providing them with mainstream Christian literature.[7]

Meantime, only Berg's family and a few of his closest followers knew his whereabouts, but he kept in regular contact with his flock through "MO letters,"[8] which consisted of Biblical interpretations, prophecies, and instructions about daily living. In the early days, the expectation was that the Great Apocalypse would come in 1993. As the teaching was that salvation was through faith in Jesus, rather than good deeds, members believed that it was their urgent mission to save as many souls as possible before Jesus's return (May 2013: 159–60).

It was Berg's interpretation of "The Law of Love": "Thou shalt love thy neighbour as thyself"[9] that was to distance the CoG from their fellow Christians. From the early days, the MO letters were indicating that Berg placed a significant emphasis on the importance of love-making and were going into considerable details about how, where, and when it should be performed (Berg 1973, 1976). "Sharing all things" came to include sexual sharing, first within the movement, but then as means of proselytizing and provisioning—a practice that came to be known as Flirty Fishing and which lasted from the mid-1970s to 1987, when it was explicitly banned (Chancellor 2000: 9).[10]

The sexual freedom encouraged within the CoG resulted in a number of cases of child abuse,[11] and between 1978 and 1993 seven different countries instituted a dozen raids, removing over 200 children from the movement. No evidence of sexual abuse was found, however, and eventually all the children were returned (Wright and Palmer 2016: 7, 73–98). Nonetheless, the movement had acquired a reputation as a "sex cult" and one consequence in the early 1990s was a protracted court case in England in which the mother of a member of the movement sought to have custody of her daughter's (as yet unborn) child. The outcome was that the daughter was allowed to keep her child, but, only after the movement, now calling itself The Family, denounced some of Berg's teachings and instituted a number of changes (Ward 1995).

During the court case Berg had died and his widow, Maria Fontaine,[12] and her new partner, Peter Amsterdam,[13] had taken over leadership of the movement and produced a lengthy "Charter," which, rather like the Rule Book of a religious order, laid out in detail the rights and responsibilities relating to the individual members, the homes, and the leadership, as well as procedures and "fundamental family rules" (The Family 1995). The movement also attempted a process of reconciliation with those who had left and had suffered abuse, writing several open letters of apology for past harms.[14]

This was not the first time the movement had undergone radical change. Berg had shown little hesitation in overturning the movement's organization and practices, as is often the wont of a leader wielding charismatic authority. Such changes were referred to as Revolutions. Back in 1978, the "Reorganization Nationalization Revolution" (RNR) had involved Berg's dismissal of over 300 local leaders and the introduction of a more centralized structure. In 1994, Stuart Wright wrote: "It may be argued that the ability of the Children of God/ The Family to adapt to change over time has contributed significantly to its survival into the 1990s" (Wright 1994: 123). Six years later, Gordon and Gary Shepherd, having first sensibly stated that they could not prophesy the future and that new contingencies can always change the situation, wrote:

> But we can modestly say that, at this point in its developmental career, the Family International has successfully instituted organisational forms and mechanisms for sustaining a religious way of life that is likely to persist for generations to come.
>
> (Shepherd and Shepherd 2010: 210)

Before their book went to print, however, the Shepherds had to add an Epilogue mentioning some dramatic changes that Maria and Peter were about to introduce, and about which the Shepherds were to write a further article (Shepherd and Shepherd 2013). The changes, known as the Reboot, were to herald the breaking up of TFI's communal structure and a number of radical innovations that were to result in the movement becoming little more than a virtual community (Borowik 2013, 2018).

What Went Wrong?

Why was it that these two NRMs, both of which had seemed around the turn of the century to be going from strength to strength in their shared mission of witnessing to the love of Jesus, could appear to be on the brink of extinction within a couple of decades? The JF's work for the homeless, unemployed, and aliens had been widely praised, the social services frequently referring people to it, the police asking it to shelter the homeless overnight, and the judiciary sanctioning early releases into the JF's rehabilitation scheme for offenders who had converted to Christianity while in prison.[15] The CoG/TFI had publicly not only renounced but also denounced many of Berg's more controversial beliefs and practices, and they too were being acknowledged for some of the humanitarian work they were doing for the underprivileged in places such as in the African townships where members provided medical assistance, literacy lessons, food they have provisioned for the children, plays warning about HIV in the schools, and help for women infected virus—and much else besides.[16] It is not surprising that scholars might have suspected both movements were casting off some sectarian features in favor of those of a denomination.[17]

Dwindling Memberships

It is common in NRMs for their demographic structure to undergo dramatic changes within a generation. Both movements had reached and passed a peak in their numbers. In 2012 the JF had reported having 2,500 members with over 600 Christian Community members in around seventy houses across the UK, with up to forty persons per household.[18] By the time of the breakup, membership had fallen to 1,000 members, 200 of whom were living in communal houses (Lynch 2019b). TFI's membership had peaked at just over 10,000 (including children) around the turn of the century, but had dropped to below 7,000 by 2009. Following the Reboot in 2010 it fell sharply to 4,500 and thereafter by a further 10 percent each year (Borowik 2018: 65–6). Currently there are around 1,500 members, practically none of whom live in a TFI community, most having their main contact with other members through websites, Facebook groups, or other social media. There are no longer any formal meetings, gathering places, or structures for fellowship.

Both movements could, theoretically, have maintained or increased their numbers through their second generation—had they managed to keep it. Many children born to the JF's married couples during its earlier, most disciplined period, when corporal punishment ("rodding") was accepted as a biblical injunction,[19] had rebelled and left (Cooper and Farrant 1997: 305), but even after that there was a steady stream of departures.

Due to its sexual practices and disapproval of birth control, the CoG were highly successful at producing children,[20] and by the mid-1980s it was claimed the children were outnumbering adults by three to one (Edwards 2018: 28). They were not, however, so successful at retaining their children as they grew up with a regular seepage of second-generation teens and adults, some of whom became among the movement's most vocal opponents. "Trouble makers" had been subjected to punishments that included isolating them for days and beating them with paddles between the late 1980s and early 1990s; "bad apples" were sent on boot-camp-like "Victor Programmes" (Ward: 1995: 162–71). Although others undoubtedly shared much of their parents' beliefs, few wanted to share their lifestyle. By the time the twenty-first century had arrived, of the thousands of children born into the CoG/TFI, the majority had left, leaving an aging population of converts outnumbering second-generation members (Barker 2012).

Beliefs and Finances

Both movements basically shared the beliefs of most fundamentalist Christians.[21] It is unlikely that the JF's beliefs *per se* played a direct role in its demise. Although they doubtless believed in the Second Coming of Jesus, this does not seem to have played a central role in their lives—at least not in the way that it did for the CoG/TFI—where the members lived with an overriding feeling of urgency. During Berg's lifetime, most children grew up not expecting to reach adulthood before Armageddon (Edwards 2018: 44, 68, 81, 119). There was, consequently, little need for anything but the most basic education. The all-consuming mission was to save as many souls as possible. A former member of TFI, writing about her time in the movement, concluded with a quotation attributed to Luther: "Even if I knew that tomorrow the world would go to pieces, I would still plant my apple tree." This, she added, was "quite far removed from the attitude in the TFI ... who, whilst expecting Jesus to come back in their lifetime, simply did not take much stock in preparing for the future" (May 2013: 163).

History is full of millenarian NRMs that have survived the failure of prophecy, early Christianity being but one obvious example. This they have achieved through numerous and different means. The CoG managed to survive the 1993 prediction partly because Father David pointed out that he had never claimed the date was more than a prediction, not a prophecy; no one could know the exact time as "the day of the Lord so cometh as a thief in the night."[22] While some CoG members left because of disillusionment, the majority did not, and when, in 1997, Bainbridge asked over a thousand members "Do you believe that the Endtime has begun or will begin very soon?", 81 percent said "yes, definitely" and another 16 percent answered "yes, probably" (2002: 60).

After the turn of the century, however, the urgency was beginning to diminish. A Board structure was established that was responsible for more long-term planning. It was disclosed that the Lord had instructed the leadership to "begin planning as if we have more time—even 30 to 50 more years" (Amsterdam 2010). The Biblical injunction, "Take therefore no thought for the morrow: for the morrow shall take thought for the things of itself,"[23] no longer seemed such a dependable strategy. While a few elderly members aged sixty-five or over had been accommodated relatively easily in communal homes, it was not clear that an increasing number could be similarly supported. The financial implications of the aging converts would be prohibitive. By 2020, the cost of providing a modest pension of $300 a month to members over sixty-five would be more than 3 million US dollars per annum; five years later, it would be more than 6 million (Barker 2012: 10). There was no way TFI could afford that. Younger converts and second-generation members were encouraged to develop personal plans for their future.

In the CoG's early days, money had come from converts who were expected to "forsake all" handing over any money and valuables that they had and persuading their families to contribute money and supplies to run the communes (Wallenstein 1974: 8–13), but later when any growth in the movement was through births rather than conversions, that source had all but dried up, and members, who were meant to trust that donations would be forthcoming if their faith was strong enough, were not permitted to take outside jobs. The practice of "provisioning" reduced the amount of money that was needed, and clowning, face painting, English lessons, and the sale of literature, books, and videos brought in some cash, 10 percent of which was tithed for the central administration (World Services) and further money needed to be contributed to contingencies funds. As a result, renting rather than buying property, most members were unable to accumulate any assets. There would be little incentive for those who felt wronged to go to court in an attempt to claim reparation.

Conversely, the JF had been "paying heed to the morrow." Its ventures, with plenty of cheap labor, managed to thrive. Profits were plowed back into the businesses which went from strength to strength. According to one report, the entire Jesus Army estate is said to be worth close to £60 million (Lynch 2019c). Even if this figure is exaggerated, it is clear that, unlike TFI, the JF is worth suing.

Curiously enough, it would appear that both the JF's accumulation and the TFI's lack of accumulation of wealth contributed to their respective downfalls.

Child Abuse

Children were neither unwanted nor neglected in either the JF or the CoG. Both movements welcomed them. It could, however, be argued that it was the sexual abuse of children that led to the downfall of both movements, and to some extent this is true. But the manner in which this happened was very different. The official culture of the JF was unambiguously against sexual relations outside marriage. The CoG/TFI, celebrated sexual relations as manifestations of Jesus's love, and, although child abuse was not explicitly advocated, sexual exploration had been unambiguously encouraged from a very early age (Ward, The Right Honourable 1995 Section 5). Repeated apologies had been offered; a rule had been clearly reiterated in The Charter that sexual activity with minors was an excommunicable offense; and relatively effective safeguards had been instituted by the twenty-first century. There can, however, be little doubt that not only a flood of negative books and articles, but also the arrival of the internet and several websites run by disillusioned and/or angry former members (most of whom had been brought up around the Flirty Fishing period)[24] have meant that the movement has continued to be tarnished by its salacious past as a "sex cult." It is, nonetheless, arguable that the abuse was not *directly* responsible for TFI's demise.

The connection between child abuse and the JF's demise is much more direct. There had been stories about Stanton molesting young boys for some time, but these had been treated as rumors by the leadership, and apart from advising him to be more prudent so that his behavior was not open to misinterpretation, little was done. More cogently, the JF's open-door policy and inadequate safeguarding policies resulted in their children becoming vulnerable to sexual predators. Perhaps inevitably, some cases of child abuse came to the attention of the police. In 1993, a multiple child murderer and rapist stayed at JF premises under an assumed name for over a month before he was detected. In 1996, another man with a history of sex offenses against boys, working (also under an assumed identity) as a groundsman, managed to abuse three young boys, for which he received a five-year sentence in 2009. In the wake of such cases, vocal questioning by some former members and outsiders, the growing number of incidents where the Catholic Church was being sued for damages, and changing interpretations of the law on public liability, the JF sought legal advice about whether the Fellowship could be held liable for unauthorized actions by members. This was particularly worrying for community members, who had donated all their assets to the common pot.

Advised to ascertain the extent to which any incidents might have occurred, a letter was circulated by the JF's senior leadership in 2013 to the whole membership, asking for information about any actual or suspected abuse. Over 100 responses were received, most being made by a third party to the incident. These were all handed to the Northampton police. Consequently, a police team under the name "Operation Lifeboat" was established in 2015 to investigate, with the full cooperation of the JF leadership, allegations of physical and sexual abuse. This resulted in the production of further allegations, nearly all of which were dismissed by the police for various reasons. Some were duplicate complaints or proved to be unsupported by the alleged victim; however, most were not criminal offenses but, for example, complaints about bullying. Some cases were, however, taken to court and convictions were secured.[25] Meanwhile, the JF had stepped up its safeguarding policy and commissioned the Churches' Child Protection Advisory Service to conduct a review of its safeguarding (CCPAS 2016). This resulted in the implementation of a far more robust policy.[26]

In July 2017, the JF's five "apostolic" leaders stepped down, pending an investigation of their handling of the abuse allegations. At the same time, some current and former members founded the Jesus Fellowship Survivors Association (JFSA), providing many more allegations and a forum where those affected by past abuse could get professional advice and other assistance. The JFSA now works with lawyers, preparing cases against the JF not only for child abuse, but also for claims of alleged breach of contract, unfair dismissal, unjust enrichment, and mismanagement of funds by Trustees. Furthermore, civil claims can be made when criminal charges are not applicable.[27] The threat of legal proceedings continues, but it is possible that a group action for sexual, physical, and psychological harm could bankrupt the JF Trust.[28] The thousand or so members at the time of the breakup will also be hoping to receive some share of the "common purse" as recompense for their time in the movement. According to the JFSA, the JF trustees may decide to settle all the claims and try to draw a line under them.[29] The new team of JF leaders, having grasped the extent of the financial and other consequences, decided they "did not have the capacity or the desire to continue leading the JF" (Lynch 2019a). They put it to the JF membership, whereupon a majority voted to revoke the Church's constitution.[30]

One significant factor to bear in mind when comparing the two cases is the change in cultural sensitivity to child sexual abuse in the West. In the 1980s, child protection was in its infancy, reporting of abuse was not yet mandatory, and scandals associated with the Catholic Church had yet to flood the media. The relatively visible sexual deviancy of the CoG and the UK court case in the early 1990s meant that the CoG/TFI received widespread publicity at that time but, despite the raids and the continuing attempts by former members to have the movement investigated, the police were relatively uninterested. Then, although there were rumors of abuse occurring within the JF at that time, these tended to be dismissed; JF elders tended to find it difficult to believe that members, especially those whom they respected as men of God, could behave in such a manner. Even when the leadership became concerned about insurance cover, the police were initially only interested in a handful of the 100 or so allegations. But in the wake of the impact of the Jimmy Savile story, the police were becoming increasingly sensitive to allegations of historic abuse.[31] It might also be mentioned that the CoG/TFI never had any insurance, and they had been spread throughout the world, whereas the JF was confined to Britain.

Concluding Remarks

Both the JF and CoG/TFI are leaving in their wake a generation of several thousands of people who dedicated their lives to living for God. TFI calculates that "over 35,000 people have at some point devoted themselves to Christian service with the Family International"[32] and several more thousands have devoted themselves likewise at one time or another to the JF. The two NRMs have shared many beliefs and practices. Both believed strongly in the importance of community and forsaking all for the common purse. At the same time, both viewed their respective movements as activist: one adopting the military metaphor of an army, the other seeing itself as a revolutionary force.

At the time of writing, neither the JF nor TFI has completely disappeared from the religious landscape, and it could be argued that neither has really died. As an entity, the Jesus Fellowship Church exists only insofar as it has to fulfill legal and administrative responsibilities before it formally closes. But all seven Jesus Centres continue to operate as the renamed Jesus Centres Trust with their own local management teams. Some members are attending alternative evangelical churches and living in family accommodation with, perhaps, one or two other erstwhile members, but local JF congregations can continue to exist as independent organizations under their own leadership, no longer affiliated to an umbrella organization (Lynch 2019b). Some members deeply regret the decision of the national leadership team and the circumstances leading up to it, wishing they could remain part of the wider JF community. Others have broken away to begin a new life with memories of their past that range from happy, through regretful, to bitter.

Although the Reboot heralded radical changes, the TFI still exists as "an online Christian network of individuals,"[33] claiming over 1,700 members in nearly eighty countries. But membership has become an ambiguous concept that means little more than to have agreed that one accepts TFI's Statement of Faith and will contribute to its mission to make the world a better place in whatever way one can.[34] Members are expected to tithe a small amount toward the movement's work, which does not necessarily mean the central organization, which now basically consists of Maria and Peter, who play the role of the spiritual and administrative directors and maintain a website to which short homilies are contributed each month, none of which would be likely to raise the eyebrow in most other Christian circles.[35] TFI also has a few other official sites and unofficial blogs where members and interested former members can communicate (Borowik 2018: 63). A few communities continue in various parts of the world,[36] some carrying out truly impressive work of a charitable nature. But there is now a fluidity about membership that makes the once strong boundary between "systemites" and members almost invisible. Some years after the Reboot, Claire Borowik found that members could be uncertain whether their spouse was a member, and not one of the eighty-nine children born to her thirteen first-generation interviewees were members (2018: 70). As with the JF, most erstwhile TFI members now live in nuclear families, possibly attending a local church. Many have taken on paid work, sometimes after going to school to gain the paper qualifications they never got; others have found difficulty in adjusting to a situation in which they have to make their own decisions in an unfamiliar world. There have been some tragic suicides, and stories have circulated about young people having a drug or alcohol dependency (Buck 2017) and/or working in "the adult entertainment business."[37] Most former members, however, would appear to have been slipping into "normal" society with both regrets and happy memories of a past about which they rarely talk. It is unlikely that either Stanton or Berg would recognize their respective movements as fulfilling the visions they once had. But something of their legacy does undoubtedly linger on.

Notes

1 "And all that believed were together, and had all things common" (Acts 2: 44).
2 https://jesus.org.uk/. All websites reference in this chapter were accessed on March 12, 2020.
3 https://www.thefamilyinternational.org/en/
4 Registered Charity Number: 1091912.
5 https://jesuscentre.org.uk/
6 https://jesus.org.uk/
7 It has been estimated that over 10 million copies of *Activated Magazine* have been distributed worldwide. https://activated.org/en/
8 MO letters refer to letters from Moses David Berg to members; he referred to himself as MO.

9   Matthew 22:39.
10 https://media.xfamily.org/docs/fam/ml/ml-501.pdf
11 Sexual relations between an adult and a child were forbidden around 1986 (Ward, The Right Honourable 1995: 112).
12 Karen Zerby.
13 Steve Kelly.
14 http://www.myconclusion.com/category/letters-of-apology
15 https://web.archive.org/web/20170727202822/; http://jesuscentre.org.uk/what-papers-say/press-articles
16 http://thefamilyafrica.blogspot.com/
17 Here "sect" refers to a splinter group from a mainstream religion (Protestant Christianity), and "denomination" to one of many religions that are more accepting of and accepted by society (Niebuhr 1929; Wilson 1970).
18 https://web.archive.org/web/20120814120822/; http://www.newcreation.org.uk/nccc/about_info.shtml
19 Proverbs 13:24.
20 It was not uncommon for mothers to bear a dozen or more children, though not always by the same father.
21 https://web.archive.org/web/20180527205251/; https://jesus.org.uk/about-jesus-fellowship-church/what-we-believe/; https://www.thefamilyinternational.org/en/about/our-beliefs/
22 Thessalonians I 5:2.
23 Matthew 6:34.
24 For example: https://www.xfamily.org/; https://www.movingon.org/; http://www.exfamily.org/
25 https://www.northamptonchron.co.uk/news/former-member-northamptonshires-jesus-army-member-jailed-historic-sex-offences-1035977
26 https://jesuscentre.org.uk/about-jesus-centres/safeguarding-of-children-and-young-people/
27 https://jesusfellowshipsurvivors.org/group-civil-claim-for-ex-community-members/
28 https://jesusfellowshipsurvivors.org/group-civil-claim-for-those-harmed-within-the-jesus-fellowship-jesus-army-under-the-age-of-21/
29 https://jesusfellowshipsurvivors.org/group-civil-claim-for-those-harmed-within-the-jesus-fellowship-jesus-army-under-the-age-of-21/
30 https://jesus.org.uk/
31 Sir Jimmy Savile (1926–2011), a well-known television and radio personality, was exposed as a serial sexual predator of children in an ITV program a year

after his death, leading to the setting up of Operation Yewtree by the London Metropolitan Police, which issued a damning interim report in 2013, concluding that, all too often, children reporting abuse were not taken seriously (Gray and Watt 2013: 24).

32 https://www.thefamilyinternational.org/en/about/membership/
33 https://www.thefamilyinternational.org/en/
34 https://www.thefamilyinternational.org/en/about/membership/
35 https://directors.tfionline.com/
36 https://www.thefamilyinternational.org/en/work/
37 https://culteducation.com/group/918-children-of-god-the-family/6642-cults-sordid-sex-and-secrets.html

References

Amsterdam, P. (2010), "Care of Elderly Family Members: Internal Communication Distributed by The Family International," 30 November.
Bainbridge, W. S. (2002), *The Endtime Family: Children of God*. Albany, NY: State University of New York Press.
Barker, E. (2012), "Ageing in New Religions: The Varieties of Later Experiences," *Diskus: The Journal of the British Association for the Study of Religions*, 12. Available online: http://diskus.basr.ac.uk/index.php/DISKUS/article/view/21/20
Barker, E. (2016), "From The Children of God to The Family International: A Story of Radical Christianity and Deradicalising Transformation," in S. Hunt (ed.), *The Handbook of Contemporary Christianity: Movements, Institutions & Allegiance*, 402–21. Leiden: Brill.
Berg, D. (1973), "Revolutionary Sex," *MO Letter*, March 27. GP No.258.
Berg, D. (1976), "Scriptural, Revolutionary Love-Making, August 1969. No.N-GP," in H. David, R. Atlanta, J. Ashtree, and S. Tribe (eds.), *The MO Letters, Volume I*, vol. 1, 79–82. London: Children of God.
Borowik, C. (2013), "The Family International: Rebooting for the Future," in E. Barker (ed.), *Revisionism and Diversification in New Religious Movements*, 15–30. Farnham: Ashgate.
Borowik, C. (2018), "From Radical Communalism to Virtual Community: The Digital Transformation of The Family International," *Nova Religio*, 22 (1): 59–86.
Buck, S. (2017), "The Hippie Christian Cult That Encouraged Sex with Children Is Still around Today." *Timeline*, 17 January. Available online: https://timeline.com/children-of-god-5245a45f6a2a
CCPAS (2016), *Safeguarding Review for Jesus Fellowship*. Swanley, Kent: CCPAS.

Chancellor, J. D. (2000), *Life in The Family: An Oral History of the Children of God*. Syracuse, NY: Syracuse University Press.

Cooper, S. and M. Farrant (1997), *Fire in Our Hearts: The Story of the Jesus Fellowship/Jesus Army* (1st edition 1991). Nether Heyford, Northampton: Multiply Publications.

Edwards, F. (2018), *Apocalypse Child: A Life in End Times*. Nashville, TN and New York: Turner Publishing.

The Family (1995–8), *The Love Charter*. Zurich: The Family.

Gray, D. and P. Watt (2013), *Giving Victims a Voice: Joint Report into Sexual Allegations Made against Jimmy Savile*. London: Metropolitan Police. Available online: https://www.nspcc.org.uk/globalassets/documents/research-reports/yewtree-report-giving-victims-voice-jimmy-savile.pdf

Haines, M. and N. Stanton (1991) "New Creation Christian Community Precepts, Circular for household leaders of Style 3 Covenant Members," 28 November (typed document).

Hunt, S. J. (1998), "The Radical Kingdom of the Jesus Fellowship," *Pneuma: The Journal of the Society for Pentecostal Studies*, 20 (1): 21–41.

Hunt, S. J. (2003), *Alternative Religions: A Sociological Introduction*, Aldershot: Ashgate.

Ironmonger, J. (2019), "BBC Report on the Jesus Army/Jesus Fellowship," *Victoria Derbyshire Report*, July 19. Available online: https://jesusfellowshipsurvivors.org/bbc-report-on-the-jesus-army-jesus-fellowship/

Kay, W. K. (2007), *Apostolic Networks in Britain*, Milton Keynes: Paternoster.

Lynch, P. (2019a), "Northampton's Jesus Army Votes to Disband in Wake of Historic Abuse Claims," *Northampton Chronicle and Echo*, May 29. Available online: https://www.northamptonchron.co.uk/news/crime/northamptons-jesus-army-votes-disband-wake-historic-abuse-claims-969668

Lynch, P. (2019b), "The Jesus Army Church May be Folding … but Its Centres, Communes and Businesses Will Continue," *Northampton Chronicle and Echo*, May 30. Available online: https://www.northamptonchron.co.uk/news/people/jesus-army-church-may-be-folding-its-centres-communes-and-businesses-will-continue-69963

Lynch, P. (2019c), "Jesus Army Workers Facing Large Pensions Gap Because Church Did Not Pay Their National Insurance," August 8, *Northampton Chronicle and Echo*. Available online: https://web.archive.org/web/20190808223053/ and https://www.northamptonchron.co.uk/news/people/special-report-jesus-army-workers-facing-large-pensions-gap-because-church-did-not-pay-their-national-insurance-1-9027737

MacDonald-Smith, F. (1995), "The Appeal of the Jesus Army to the Young," *Independent*, April 29. Available online: https://www.independent.co.uk/life-style/the-jesus-army-wants-you-1617501.html

May, A. F. (2013), "Living in the Time of the End: A Personal Commentary from My Experiences with the Children of God and the Family International," in S. Harvey and S. Newcombe (eds.), *Prophecy in the New Millennium: When Prophecies Persist*, 155–64. Aldershot: Ashgate.

Niebuhr, H. R. (1929), *The Social Sources of Denominationalism*. New York: Holt.

Patrick, T. with T. Dulack (1976), *Let Our Children Go*. New York: Ballantine.

Shepherd, G. and G. Shepherd (2010), *Talking with the Children of God: Prophecy and Transformation in a Radical Religious Group*. Urbana, Chicago and Springfield, IL: University of Illinois Press.

Shepherd, G. and G. Shepherd (2013), "Reboot of The Family International," *Nova Religio: The Journal of Alternative and Emergent Religions*, 17 (2): 74–98.

Stockley, D. (2007), "Into Unchartered Terrain: Deb Stockley's Journey into Celibacy," *Jesus Life*, 76 (3): 9–11. Available online: https://www.yumpu.com/en/document/read/23653871/slaves-of-all-jesus-army

Van Zandt, D. E. (1991), *Living in the Children of God*, Princeton, NJ: Princeton University Press.

Wallenstein, H. J., Charity Frauds Bureau (1974), "Final Report on the Activities of the Children of God. Report Submitted to Louis J. Lefkowitz, Attorney General of the State of New York," September 30.

Ward, The Right Honourable (1995), "W 42 in the High Court of Justice, Family Division: Principal Registry in the Matter of ST (a Minor) and in the Matter of the Supreme Court Act 1991."

Wilson, B. R. (1970), *Religious Sects: A Sociological Study*, London: Weidenfeld & Nicholson.

Wright, S. A. and S. J. Palmer (2016), *Storming Zion: Government Raids on Religious Communities*. Oxford: Oxford University Press.

Wright, S. A. (1994), "From 'Children of God' to 'The Family': Movement Adaptation and Survival," in J. R. Lewis and J. G. Melton (eds.), *Sex, Slander, and Salvation: Investigating The Family/Children of God*, 121–8. Stanford, CA: Center for Academic Publication.

7

The Fall of Mars Hill Church in Seattle: How Online Counter-Narratives Catalyzed Change

Jessica Johnson

This chapter examines the organizational crisis that led to the demise of Mars Hill Church, an evangelical megachurch in Seattle led by Pastor Mark Driscoll that grew to 13,000 attendees at fifteen locations scattered throughout the Pacific Northwest and beyond, before it collapsed in the midst of administrative and financial scandal at the end of 2014. Before Mars Hill's dissolution, the controversies surrounding Driscoll and the church were rapidly mounting from 2013 to 2014 amid intense turnover in staff as pastors began steadily resigning, and attendance numbers dropped from roughly 13,000 to 7,000 in the summer of 2014.

By August 2014, when a protest organized by former members was held outside Mars Hill's main facility, evidence had surfaced online that supported several accusations against Driscoll, including: plagiarism; the surreptitious use of the marketing firm ResultSource to achieve bestselling author status on a variety of book lists; the misappropriation of "global fund" tithes for churches in Ethiopia and India; and formal charges of bullying and micromanagement lodged by twenty-one ex-pastors (Johnson 2018: 35). In addition, Driscoll's use of social media was becoming increasingly offensive to an ever-larger audience, given his regularly caustic use of Twitter and Facebook (Johnson 2018: 35). In March 2014, Driscoll publicly apologized for his scandalous use of social media in a letter to his congregation that received national coverage. In this message, he said that he would refrain from posting on social media until at least the end of 2014 and give few, if any, media interviews (Johnson 2018: 36).

Weeks later, Mars Hill's Executive Elders (Mark Driscoll, Sutton Turner, and Dave Bruskas) announced a new document retention policy that would destroy all staff emails more than three months old. The plan was dropped only after the group's attorney, Brian Fahling, asked them to preserve electronically stored information that may contain evidence for legal action in which the church, Driscoll, and others in Mars Hill's leadership would be named as defendants in RICO litigation (Racketeer Influenced and Corrupt Organizations Act), Fraud, Conspiracy, Libel, Slander, and Intentional Infliction of Emotional Distress (Johnson 2018: 36). One example of such treatment against a staff member publicly surfaced in late May 2014, when Mars Hill elder Phil Smidt refused to sign a non-compete agreement, which by then had become a common requirement for all departing church employees who wished to receive severance benefits. This contract prevented anyone from serving in a church leadership position within 10 miles of a Mars Hill location. Given the expanse of the church's facilities, this non-compete agreement made it difficult for ex-staff to find pastoral work in western Washington. Non-disclosure agreements were also commonly required, and the threat of legal action invoked distress that haunted leaders long after their employ was terminated (Johnson 2018: 36).

As a result of this negative attention, Pastor Mark resigned from the eldership of Mars Hill Church on October 14, 2014, although he was not deemed disqualified or removed by the board of overseers evaluating his fitness to pastor. Given he left without any judgment of illegal or immoral activity, Driscoll soon established a website under his name through which to release sermons preached at Mars Hill. He also planted a new church within two years of turning in his resignation, The Trinity Church located in Scottsdale, Arizona, which opened its doors in August 2016. Meanwhile, in Driscoll's absence Mars Hill quickly fell apart and officially dissolved as a corporate body on December 31, 2014 (Johnson 2018: 37).

By the time of Driscoll's resignation from leadership a few months before Mars Hill's disbanding, he achieved national influence among young male pastors, particularly within Neo-Calvinist circles, and international attention within Christian and secular media for stirring controversy. This chapter asks, given there was no explicit crime or charge of sexual abuse against Driscoll, what were the social dynamics of dissolution? Why was Driscoll compelled to resign when other authoritarian or abusive religious leaders remained in their pulpits around the United States?

This chapter argues that former members' public testimonies online, as well as other creative uses of social media and archival practices, disrupted Driscoll's charismatic authority and his capacity to control a carefully constructed narrative and strategically revise the history of the church. In turn, this examination considers how the production and circulation of counter-narratives on websites, blogs, and social media, such as Twitter, signaled and catalyzed Mars Hill Church's dissolution and Mark Driscoll's fall. This research is based on a decade of ethnographic fieldwork spent researching Mars Hill from 2006 to 2016, including conversations and interviews with pastors and members before and after the church's disbanding. While some of the material included in this chapter has been analyzed in my book, *Biblical Porn: Affect, Labor, and Pastor Mark Driscoll's Evangelical Empire* (Johnson 2018), I am approaching the following testimonies and blogs written by key actors, as well as the influence that social media had on the church's demise and Driscoll's retirement from leadership, with fresh eyes and new interview material. In this chapter, my critical lens is focused on how the very online technologies used to spread Mars Hill's influence and accrue Driscoll international celebrity became instruments of empowerment, particularly as wielded by two men with distinct leadership positions and perspectives on harmful practices from within the church and by two women who testified to abuses in spiritual authority by turning Driscoll's own words, teachings, and voice publicly against him.

Two Former Pastors' Public Testimonies: Mike Anderson and Jeff Bettger

Among the many confessions and testimonies posted online prior to the demise of Mars Hill Church from 2013 to 2014 that detailed harmful practices perpetrated by administration and leaders on institutional and interpersonal levels, two that had a major impact on audiences within and outside of the church were written by former pastors with distinct roles that provided them with particular authority, insight, and trust—Mike Anderson and Jeff Bettger.

As the former director of the Resurgence, Mars Hill's online networking site for pastors around the world and repository for pastoral teaching content, Mike Anderson was also a frequent traveling companion of Mark Driscoll's, organizing and attending events. In 2013, in a public testimony posted to his blog titled, "Hello, My Name is Mike, I'm a Recovering True Believer," Anderson describes his role working with and for Driscoll as such:

> I spent so much time with him because I was the guy who organized conferences, planned and promoted books, directed the online content, and later worked directly on all of Mark's projects—I was at the center of all of this and I was proud of helping make it bigger. I used to joke that my title should be 'Minister of Propaganda'.
>
> (Anderson 2013)

Anderson recalled heady days of hanging out with ABC News folks, dinner with golfer Bubba Watson, and meeting with "about a thousand 'Christian Celebrities.' I thought we were the supreme blessing to the world" (Anderson 2013). Anderson also relayed a story about having dinner with John Piper and his team at Desiring God that included Timothy Keller, reflecting on how "for me, regularly getting to sit with men like this was the equivalent of a die-hard football fan sitting down with the Super Bowl Champion Seahawks—these were my heroes" (Anderson 2013). Throughout his testimony, Anderson bore witness to the power of celebrity to convict "true believers," including young leaders such as himself, that the "movement" that Mars Hill and Mark Driscoll led was not only blessed by God but "literally the hand of God moving across the world to make it 'better'" (Anderson 2013). Using details concerning his role as marketing director alongside confessional remarks that allude to his own culpability in administrative abuses of authority and power, Anderson presented a compelling testimony that speaks to harms perpetrated by the church that he and his family also fall subject to, using language to not only depict but also enact how this harm came into being and took a persuasive cast such that it became easily justifiable or brushed aside for the sake of the church's multigenerational legacy and perpetual growth.

Anderson began his blog post with a confessional passage that resounds with fascist and nationalist overtones:

> I've seen many friends make bad choices in their 20s. For some, regular partying quickly turned into alcoholism; for others, prescription drugs led them into dark places. For me, it was religion. You see, I'm what they call a True Believer. I really like the idea of changing the world: sacrifice for the cause, single-minded drive for the 'mission,' a charismatic leader. As a 19-year-old I was the kind of guy that was the ideal follower for the crazies of history—the Mussolinis and the Hitlers. Fortunately for the world, the 21st-century version of this extremism isn't hyper-nationalism, it is a megachurch. There's less bloodshed than the 20th-century version, but still a lot of hurt.
>
> (Anderson 2013)

While Anderson distinguished religious true belief in the mission of a megachurch from the conviction in hyper-nationalism evident in the fascist regimes of Mussolini's Italy and Hitler's Germany, his drawing them into relationship was an astute commentary on the authoritarianism of Driscoll's reign as Mars Hill's preaching pastor, as well as the kind of authoritarian charismatic leader that would win the 2016 US Presidential Election and earn over 80 percent of the white evangelical vote. While there was no bloodshed under Driscoll's leadership, his wielding of church and spiritual authority expanded to an alarming degree, as Anderson later notes:

> Some people read the Bible and think about how crazy it was that the people building the Tower of Babel thought they could reach heaven and make a name for themselves. We were trying to do just that. We were trying to build a church so influential, so "pure" that it could change the world—it could be a new reformation … The year before I left staff was rough … the church that I had loved and was committed to started to change in a dramatic fashion … The entire previous executive elder board was broken up and a new executive elder board with massively different values, theology, and ecclesiology was brought in. Long-held beliefs about how a church should be run were secretly changed, fear and intimidation were constant, and power was consolidated even more than it had been. Because I was interested in "tower building," this didn't bother me. When I left, I was actually an advocate for many of the policies that consolidated power. I even co-authored a book with Mark called "Campaigns" about 12 months before leaving staff. The idea behind it was to be able to rally Mars Hill and thousands of other churches behind one pulpit. I am so thankful that this never had the time to get truly implemented.
>
> (Anderson 2013)

As Anderson's testimony continued, he mentioned a shift in leadership that entailed the resignation of one Executive Elder who attempted to keep Driscoll's decision-making power in check, a "shock absorber to help delay bad decisions," and the hiring of a "CFO/COO type" who turned out to be a Driscoll yes-man, "an amplifier and enforcer to any and all decisions Mark would make" (Anderson 2013). Soon after this organizational transition, Anderson realized that he must quit his position at Mars Hill because his "heart was sick" and "the mission had changed and the people making decisions were weak" (Anderson 2013). After leaving the church, Anderson underwent a process during which he did not de-convert *per se*, but began to question what he believed about God, family, and life. His very identity was upended because he spent a decade making decisions based on Driscoll's convictions, rather than his own.

During this period, Anderson recalled reading Eric Hoffer's seminal book *True Believer* (1951) and empathized with a quote by Adolf Hitler in which he described how movements die when they become enterprises akin to corporations, full of posts and offices that attract bureaucrats engaged in preserving the present, rather than molding a new world. After reading Hoffer's study, Anderson concluded, "Mark's desire for control" is what precipitated Mars Hill's demise, as the Resurgence turned into a "giant advertisement" (Anderson 2013). Once this conviction took hold, Anderson began to suffer from "PTSD-like symptoms" and guilt over what he did as a member of Mars Hill leadership, in a church that "represented something profoundly wrong," as a result of believing in a "false gospel" in which Driscoll put himself in the position of Jesus (Anderson 2013). In conclusion, Anderson plainly added, "I'm writing this to tell everyone I ever interacted with that I was wrong to be a part of this." He then begins a series of apologies, including one that states, "I want to apologize to the religious people who I helped enlist in this and similar movements" (Anderson 2013). This blog post was liked 13,000 times on Facebook and received 160 comments. While Anderson was not the first pastor or church member to publicly write about the harms done by Mars Hill administration, his testimony attracted attention due to the high-profile role he played in the church's marketing team and his prominent role in elevating Driscoll's celebrity. His confessional tone displayed a vulnerability and self-awareness that had not previously registered in testimonies by staff who left of their own accord and/or in relatively good standing with the church, without being shunned as a result of dubious disciplinary measures, like the departure of Paul Petry from an eldership role in 2007 (for more information on his firing from a pastoral position and the subsequent exile of his entire family from the church, see joyfulexiles.com).

In 2013, another former Mars Hill staff member who worked for years as a volunteer Lay Elder, Jeff Bettger, penned a blog post on his website *Locus and Honey* about the reasons why he left the church. Bettger's position as an elder was focused on counseling members and working with people on the ground, so his role was less high profile and not as close to Driscoll as Anderson in the Mars Hill hierarchy, but he was respected for his pastoral work and willingness to volunteer at the church despite the financial burden this unpaid time and energy placed on his family. While the theme of running a church like a corporation, and the callousness that this bureaucratic approach breeds, resonates across Bettger's and Anderson's posts, the tone of Bettger's testimony is that of a prayer. After opening with a quote from Ephesians 5:1–21, Bettger wrote:

> Having a mega church background for the last 16 years I have witnessed firsthand the tyranny of injustice done in the name of God. Layoffs during Christmas, weeks after new children are born and first homes purchased. All with the name of God stamped on it, and self-justified because the rest of the business world has those kinds of practices. I am grieved for the state of a church that does not acknowledge and expose the sin of its leaders with love and humility but instead claims it is doing what's best for the body of Christ.
> (Bettger 2013)

This desire to expose truth to the light becomes more urgent as Bettger continues to reflect on the wrongs done when a church is managed more like a business, and pastors are professionalized Christians more concerned about growth metrics and self-preservation as administrators in the organization than spreading the gospel or healing souls for Christ:

> We ought to expose things that lead to division and human arrogance. After all the church should be about familial love NOT BUSINESS. These shady mega church practices are all impure and covetous, and are hidden in the darkness by people calling themselves "Christian professionals" or pastors. They say that it would be unhelpful for the body to know such information.

They say it would be gossip and if you haven't experienced it directly but only heard second hand than it is hearsay and gossip to bring into the light. That is a lie from the pits of hell that gives justification to keep the truth hidden and the ones committing the injustice from true repentance ... Any part of our life that needs to be hidden for whatever reason is not in the light, and should be exposed. Human politics and cunning are not an out-flowing of the Gospel but rather a system built by human hands for human ends. I am the chief of sinners in this way. I have held my cards close to my heart in order for self-preservation. I have been complicit by not speaking out boldly and allowing things to stay hidden. I do not need to do that anymore. I am free to walk in the light even if it takes me into suffering, and chastisement. I Love Jesus and choose Him over a fabricated Americanized version of what we call church. I repent and walk in the light as He is in the light. No more playing politics and calling it church.

(Bettger 2013)

While Bettger's post did not glean as many public comments as Anderson's, its impact was noted by many I spoke with after Mars Hill's disbanding, in part because Bettger had long been involved in Mars Hill Church in some capacity, including work at the all-ages music venue run by the church in the early 2000s called *The Paradox* and as a member of the Mars Hill worship band Team Strikeforce. In effect, Anderson and Bettger publicly testified to a need to repent for their sins as church leaders, offering informed critiques and insightful rebukes of the harm caused by an abusive administration and the pain of following a misleading gospel that could only come from two men with prominent positions within distinct aspects of Mars Hill's ministry.

Two Women's Perspectives: Wendy Alsup on Wives as Their Husbands' Porn Stars and Stephanie Drury @fakedriscoll

Wendy Alsup, a former deacon and leader in women's ministry at Mars Hill, writes a blog called *Practical Theology for Women*. In July 2014, she posted on "The Harmful Teaching of Wives as their Husbands' Porn Stars," revealing how Driscoll's theology of sex encouraged Mars Hill wives to be "sexually free" and "visually generous" (Johnson 2018: 154). Alsup's post stated:

> Mars Hill's teaching on sex has been well exported nationally and even internationally, particularly since 2012 by way of Mark Driscoll's *Real Marriage* book. I believe addressing this might be widely helpful to the many readers of this blog who were previously exposed to this teaching at Mars Hill ... When I got to Mars Hill in Seattle, I valued the pleasure aspect of sex as a good gift from God to married couples ... [but] it's clear from *Real Marriage* that, in Mark's view, sex is the key, central element to a good marriage. And this would be consistent with everything I heard while attending Mars Hill as well ... I felt dissonance in my heart with this teaching. I loved sex and valued pleasure in marriage, but the expectations Mark set up felt crushing—a standard I couldn't live up to. Then my pastor who taught on this subject this summer used a phrase that finally set me free—that pornography sets up a society "with crushing expectations regarding physical appearance and sexual performance." Things clicked in my head at that moment. The weight of crushing expectations that I felt as a result of Mars Hill's teaching on sex wasn't a result of what the Bible said but of the pornographic background from which they stemmed. But was this just me?! Was this just my own personal, prudish reaction?
>
> (Alsup 2014)

Instead of a normative sexuality based on binaries of biblical/sinful practices, Alsup describes an intense sense of expectation. The way in which Driscoll's teaching on biblical masculinity, femininity, and sexuality promotes shame is confirmed in another women's testimony shared on Alsup's blog, which demonstrated how those who had experienced sexual abuse were adversely affected by Driscoll's sermonizing on sex:

> One wife, who came from a background of horrific sexual abuse ... shared how this teaching affected her when she came to Seattle as a newly married 21 year old ... "I felt beaten down and further humiliated by Driscoll's view of women. Some of the things he said that have harmed me: it's the wife's fault if the husband looks at porn if she 'lets herself go' or isn't skilled enough at sex, his obsession with talking about wives giving blow jobs and strip teases, the crass jokes, the frequent references to women being gossips."
>
> (Alsup 2014)

Next, Alsup turns to the story of a man who provides insight into how Driscoll's preaching on porn addiction and the embodiment of sexual freedom adversely affected his marriage:

> I was addicted to pornography for many years which was defiling to me, distorted my view of women, and ultimately defiled my wife. This is (part of) my sin. Mark's teaching in many ways supported this view of women as sexual objects by using the same "construct" of what a porn star, prostitute, or stripper does but applying it to the marriage bed ... The expectation that my wife believed and I readily agreed to was that she was available to me for whatever, no matter what I did, whenever, and if she wasn't *I would probably end up doing worse.* Sex was often empty and emotionally painful. So Mark's recommendation and my sinful silent agreement with the concept of your wife being your personal porn star was apt. Dead, meaningless sex.
>
> (Alsup 2014)

Such perspectives from women and men on Driscoll's teaching on sex and how it emotionally, psychologically, and spiritually harmed them, their marriages, their views of women and men, and their understanding of what a healthy sex life entailed proliferated during the period that Mars Hill began to fall apart. One person who was not a Mars Hill member, but had an insider's perspective on the spiritual abuse perpetrated through Driscoll's teaching on biblical masculinity, femininity, and sexuality, was Stephanie Drury, the real voice behind a Twitter account that gleaned national attention and was attributed with hastening Mars Hill's fall and Driscoll's resignation, @fakedriscoll. In an interview conducted over email with me in September 2019, Drury shared her experiences with Mars Hill and motive for parodying Driscoll on Twitter:

> I never attended Mars Hill Church, but I became familiar with it in the early 2000s because I kept hearing both good and bad things about them. They had billboards everywhere in Seattle and the image-consciousness was obvious. I felt like they were aiming for the lowest-hanging, most financially comfortable fruit—that was the vibe their marketing had. And the fact that they obviously used a marketing team felt like a giant red flag to me. When a church is investing money in marketing instead of putting that money towards people on the margins, my spidey sense starts tingling. We were attending a Presbyterian church on Capitol Hill at the time and it didn't have services during Pride since traffic was so bad, so we decided to visit Mars Hill that day to see what was going on. My main memories of it was how self-conscious it was, how enormous the crowd was, how it felt like a concert and wanted to feel like a concert (they handed out ear plugs at the door because the music was so loud and awesome!), and worst of all, what Mark Driscoll

said from the pulpit that day. He had been meandering around some passage of scripture for about an hour but at least half of what he said were anecdotes to present himself a certain way—he was talking about how much he loves wine, and the crowd was really responding and playing right along—and he inevitably brought it around to sex, and I remember he said, "The wife should always have sex with the lights on if that's what the husband wants." That froze me in my tracks. I had had enough therapy at this point to know that close to half of people in any scenario are survivors of sexual assault. And I was aware enough of spiritual abuse to know how subtle and devastating it is. So when he said that to a crowd filled with so many abuse survivors, I knew how it would impact them and I knew how difficult it would be to reverse that damage, should they ever wake up to what was going on. His statement struck me as purely patriarchal, self-serving, and cruel, and the way it was said was so palatable to the crowd that it gave me chills.

(Drury 2019)

In an interview with *Bust*, Drury defined spiritual abuse as "a form of manipulation in which someone uses threats about what God will either do to you or think about you in order to get you to behave the way they want" (Drury in Whipple 2014). In her interview with me, Drury relayed how she became more intimately aware of the trauma invoked by Driscoll's preaching on biblical femininity, masculinity, and sexuality, as well as Mars Hill's institutional policies concerning the processing of trauma by congregants:

Not long after this I joined a group in which people seeking freedom from trauma shared stories from their pasts … A woman in one of the groups was always shaking with fear when she was there. She said she wasn't supposed to be there because she was a member of Mars Hill Church and had signed a "covenant" to not get outside therapy. The only sort of counseling or therapy she was allowed to seek as a member was that of Mars Hill's sanctioned "counselors." She was very fearful of being caught, but said she felt she had to strive to get away from Mars Hill. She had gotten married to someone she'd met at Mars Hill and the church had pressured her to quit her job and have babies. She had advanced degrees and enjoyed her job but the pressure from the church was such that she did what they said. Now she had several children and was suffering from probable postpartum physiological conditions. She had homicidal and suicidal ideation and when she tried to get help from the Mars Hill counselors, they told her to pray harder and submit to her husband more. This was clearly not working. I thought of her children at home, terrified and trying to fend for themselves as their mother was trying to fend for herself against this system that coerced her into ignoring her intuition and had coerced her husband into dominating her and creating further imbalance between them. I felt completely helpless to do anything but around this time Twitter was taking off. I had a 45-minute commute into work and figured I could pass the time by creating a parody account of Mark Driscoll and possibly expose people to how egregious his teachings were through satire. From reading his tweets I could imitate his voice and friends of mine who had left Mars Hill gave me insider information on what he had said and done. I tweeted as Driscoll asking everyone to pray for his interns who were auditioning stylists for him, I announced men's retreats with Fight Club reenactments, and I asked everyone to please pray for my wife Grace who is working off that baby weight and I'd be weighing her the next morning and we "really covet your prayers." All of these were based on reality that I'd heard from Mark's tweets, his online sermons, and from Mars Hill members.

(Drury 2019)

Specific examples of Drury's tweets parodying Driscoll can be found on @fakedriscoll, which is still in operation, but the *Bust* article also culled several examples, including a few that demonstrate the way that Drury masterfully mimics Driscoll's voice, particularly in language that echoes his patriarchal tone as she mocks his attempts to command spiritual authority: "It's been a tough season for Mars Hill, but God's plan is for you to be inferior to your husband and for your husband to be inferior to me;" "It's not unloving to tell you you'll melt in agony for all eternity. It's unloving that I say this with no proof and total condescension;" "PSA to men: plenty of single women at Mars Hill are dying to submit to you. So if you're church and/or wife shopping, we're all about Jesus" (Drury in Whipple 2014). Finally, in our interview Drury describes pushback from Mars Hill administrators and Driscoll apologists, as well as supportive media attention she received for augmenting @fakedriscoll and the way in which her online community at Stuff Christian Culture Likes (*http://www.stuffchristianculturelikes.com/* and *https://www.facebook.com/stuffchristianculturelikes/*) attracted contributions from survivors of spiritual abuse from Mars Hill:

Within one day of creating @fakedriscoll, I got an email from Mars Hill. I don't know how they got my email, but it was a pretty big email and full of legal-ese. In it they told me "You are allowed to create parody accounts, but it must be clear that the account is fake." So I made that my @fakedriscoll Twitter bio. I was active with the Twitter account for several years. Mark and all Mars Hill accounts and pastors blocked me early on, but people sent me screenshots of their tweets and kept me appraised on what was going on there. My online community Stuff Christian Culture Likes was really active at the time on Facebook and a lot of spiritual abuse survivors were coming forward to talk about their experiences at Mars Hill and in other churches also in the Acts 29 Network (of which Mars Hill was one). The totalitarianism and deep patriarchy wrapped in such a slick package got a lot of people sucked in and once they were in, the damage could easily take root and spread. As I talked to more women who were suffering from the pressure to marry, stay home and breed in the way Mars Hill told them to, with complete submission to their husbands (who appeared to be encouraged to wield this power haphazardly and "like men"), I became more convinced that exposing this darkness was helping people. There was a lot of backlash and I counted it all as joy, as proof I was doing something right. The Seattle Weekly interviewed me for a piece they did on parody Twitter accounts in 2014. That was right before chatroom transcripts surfaced in which Mark Driscoll called women "penis homes." [For information on those transcripts, readers can turn to Warren Throckmorton's website at warrenthrockmorton.com, particularly his post "Mark Driscoll in 2000: 'We Live in a Completely Pussified Nation,' as well as (Johnson 2018)]. That seemed to be the final straw and a week later everything came crashing down and Mark resigned. Suddenly all of the guys I knew who defended Mark Driscoll all along and told me that I was being mean to Mark were distancing themselves from the situation and talking about how bad it all was. I was told by a former pastor who had been in the final meetings at Mars Hill that they said my online presence was a reason they couldn't continue. They said they couldn't withstand the social media onslaught.

(Drury 2019)

While taking different methodological approaches to their critiques of Driscoll's preaching on sex and addressing the spiritual harm that it resulted in, both Alsup and Drury provide theologically intelligent and culturally savvy techniques for speaking truth to power online through participatory forms of Christian community outreach. In Alsup's blog, interview material with women and men provided the necessary gendered perspectives on the relational conflict fomented in marriages and spiritual abuse experienced by individuals through Driscoll's preaching on (supposed) sexual freedom. In Drury's Twitter posts, she parodied Driscoll's voice in a successful gambit to use humor to attract attention within and outside Christian circles to the ridiculous boastfulness and spiritual harm of his assertions of patriarchal authority in a megachurch context. In addition, both Alsup's and Drury's uses of social media elicit contributions, questions, and other forms of participation from those healing from the spiritual abuse that they incurred at Mars Hill, affording online community mechanisms and resources for spiritual growth and health, during and in the aftermath of the church's dissolution.

Conclusion

This chapter has shown how online technologies can be used to challenge the perpetration and effects of spiritual abuse through counter-narratives that enact institutional change and personal healing. In the case of Mars Hill's demise and Driscoll's resignation, former pastors' testimonies and confessions, as well as women's perspectives on Driscoll's preaching on sex, were tantamount to the church's disbanding and Driscoll's fall as an evangelical celebrity. In the end, creative uses of social media and archival practices disrupted Driscoll's charismatic authority and his capacity to control the emotional narrative and strategically revise the history of the church. By demonstrating vulnerability while confessing to their culpability in the harm done by church administration and withstanding criticism to tell their stories former pastors, as well as women who testified to abuses in church and spiritual authority by turning Driscoll's own words, teaching, and voice publicly against him, catalyzed and signaled Mars Hill's demise.

References

Alsup, E. (2014), "The Harmful Teaching of Wives as Their Husbands' Porn Stars," *Practical Theology for Women*, July 28. Available online: https://theologyforwomen.org/2014/07/the-harmful-teaching-of-wives-as-their-husbands-porn-stars.html (accessed August 15, 2014).

Anderson, M. (2013), "Hello, My Name Is Mike, I'm a Recovering True Believer," *Mike Anderson*, n.d. Available online: http://mikeyanderson.com/hello-name-mike-im-recovering-true-believer (accessed July 2, 2014).

Bettger, J. (2013), "Devotional: Ephesians 5: 1-21 Part VI 'Exposed by the Light,'" *Locust and Honey*, December 4. Available online: http://loucstnhoney.com/ (accessed July 9, 2014).

Drury, S. (2019), Interview, September 9.

Hoffer, E. (1951), *The True Believer: Thoughts on the Nature of Mass Movements*. New York: HarperCollins.

Johnson, J. (2018), *Biblical Porn: Affect, Labor, and Pastor Mark Driscoll's Evangelical Empire*. Durham, NC: Duke University Press.

Petry, P. (2012), "Fired Mars Hill Church Pastor Releases History," *Joyful Exiles*, n.d. Available online: https://joyfulexiles.com/ (accessed April 3, 2012).

Throckmorton, W. (2014), "Mark Driscoll in 2000: We Live in a Completely Pussified Nation," *Warren Throckmorton*, July 29. Available online: https://www.wthrockmorton.com/2014/07/29/mark-driscoll-year-2000-we-live-in-a-completely-pussified-nation/ (accessed January 3, 2020).

Whipple, J. (2014), "This Woman Is Battling a Mega-Church, One Tweet at a Time," *Bust*, n.d. Available online: https://bust.com/general/13035-this-woman-is-battling-a-mega-church-one-tweet-at-a-time.html (accessed January 3, 2020).

8

Playing the Religion Card: The Creation and Dissolution of Rajneeshism

Michael Stausberg

For a religion to end there has to be a religion in the first place. In many cases labeling something a religion seems uncontroversial. This is the case, for instance, when the social formation so labeled derives from one of the historical worldviews that are commonly called religions. Several so-called religions comprise established mechanisms of internal differentiation, for example, the establishment of sects, schisms, denominations, schools, or cults (in the sense of organized forms of communal worship). In these cases of derivation, the main protagonists tend to be familiar with the former religious traditions, be it as active participants or as being part of the same cultural and social context. On the other hand, there are cases of cross-cultural and cross-religious inspiration; if somebody who has grown up in a country where Buddhism has no established social presence starts to propagate some "Buddhist" ideas and gets others to do the same, the resulting ensemble would probably still be labeled a religion because Buddhism is generally considered such a thing. This labeling by derivation can impact a phenomenon that by itself is quite remote from practices and semantics we would commonly identify as religious; for example, *yoga* is commonly included in the literature on contemporary religious landscapes. In many cases this is not due to what actually happens in a *yoga* studio, nor based on self-descriptions of what people are doing in there, but is due to the genealogical ties of the notion of *yoga* to India or Hinduism. We can even go so far as to label groups or audiences religious when they themselves have neither invoked the r-word, nor entertain any links to historical traditions generally called religion, as long as they can be likened to what is generally considered a religion by showing some similarities to the prototype.

In this chapter, we will look at a case where the religion-ascriptions have gone through various trajectories. We will encounter a person who made his career by challenging notions of religion, before he became part of a scheme where a religion was created in his name. This episode, however, ended relatively quickly, and this proclaimed end became part of a public posturing. One aspect of his activities that made him prone to religious ascriptions, in both the pre-religion and the post-religion periods, was his choice of stage names that resonated with religious traditions: Bhagwan, which could seem like an appropriate choice for an Indian guru-type; Zorba the Buddha, a hybrid of Greek life-affirmation and Buddhism; Maitreya (the Buddha of the future); and Osho, which could point more into the direction of a Zen-master (while he is said to have explained the word as deriving from "oceanic").

Enlightenment and Provocation

The birth name of our protagonist, Mohan Chandra Jain (1931–1990), hints at his descent from a Jain family from the Western Indian region of Gujarat (India). He grew up with his grandparents and experienced different forms of religious attitudes in his close family. He reports that his father was a pious person, whereas his grandfather was not (Osho 2000: 47). His grandmother felt all religion to be childish (Osho 2000: 10). He grew up in a religiously diverse environment and seems to have visited places from different religious traditions such as churches, mosques, gurudwaras, and Hindu and Jain temples.

At the age of twenty-one, Rajneesh (as he was called from early on) reportedly experienced a nervous breakdown, followed by an extended experience of illumination or "enlightenment." While he refers to the guidance of a *pundit*, who became his "protector," he also states that he "was working without a master," that he "searched but could not find one"—a claim that put him beyond the realm of traditional religions, because "all the religions insist on finding a master" (Osho 2000: 63f). In retrospect he says of his realization that "there is nothing to be done. We are already divine and we are already perfect—as we are. ... God never creates anybody imperfect" (Osho 2000: 66). His statement is ambiguous in terms of its relationship to religion: on the one hand, he invokes "God"—as if he had realized the divine order of things—and he qualified human nature as "divine"—which invokes a religious vocabulary rather than merely perfect. On the other hand, his statement seems to obliviate all religious paths and procedures. He considers this combination of breakdown and breakthrough that he reportedly experienced the nucleus for any potential creation of a religion:

> if I were to make a religion, then this would be a basic thing in it: that anybody who becomes enlightened first will have to go through a nervous breakdown, only then he will have a breakthrough. That is how all the religions are created: individuals imposing their experience on the whole of humanity, without taking into consideration the uniqueness of every individual.
>
> (Osho 2000: 71)

There is the same ambivalence again: his experiences could be turned into the making of a religion, they are germane to religion, but religion is dismissed as something that endangers the expression of individuality.

From 1955 he taught philosophy in a small college in Central India and in 1960 he started to go on lecture tours. Both within his college and beyond Acharya ("teacher," often used for Hindu religious teachers) Rajneeesh, as he was then known, made his name as a provocative and controversial public figure. His iconoclastic anti-authoritarianism was spiced with a great sense of humor. He left his post at the college in 1966. That gave him more independence and he grasped the opportunity to create scandal. For some of his wealthy supporters he arranged meditation retreats and provided counseling. At a lecture series he gave in Bombay in 1968, he praised the psychological and spiritual aspects of sex. He spoke of "the sacredness of sex" (Urban 2015: 81). Apparently inspired by Freud and Reich and tantric texts he praised the coitus as a means to approaching god, and he criticized all major religions for their suppression of the liberating force of human sexuality (Urban 2015: 81f). That created his public perception as the "sex guru." In 1969, the centenary of Mohandas Gandhi, Rajneesh challenged almost every aspect of the Mahatma's message, including, of course, his asceticism and chastity. He held Gandhi accountable for mass poverty and deprivation. In his turn, Rajneesh embraced technology and capitalism. In 1969, he was invited to speak at the Second World Hindu Conference in Patna, where he offended the organizers by criticizing religious practices as futile and priests as thriving on the misery of beggars—all the while pointing toward the Shankarachaya of Puri, one of Hinduism's most reputed authorities who was present on the stage (Bharti 2007; Urban 2015: 34). His bold and direct approach was reported widely in the national press (Bharti 2007).

An Atheist Adopting a Religious Vocabulary

Rajneesh, who after 1971 called himself Bhagwan ("God" or "Blessed One"), eventually settled in an apartment in India's most cosmopolitan metropolis, Bombay. Despite his choice of name, he considered himself an atheist. He explained that calling himself God was meant as a provocation and an invitation for his students to discover their own divine nature (Palmer 1988: 125). In 1985, in retrospect, he speaks of his intention to "hammer religion and try to clean people completely of all this nonsense" (Osho 2000: 107). Thus, in expressing his atheist stance he did not shun an aggressive vocabulary:

> The whole history of religion simply stinks. It is ugly, and it shows the degradation of man, his inhumanity, and all that is evil. And this is not about any one single religion, it is the same story repeated by all the religions of the world: man exploiting man in the name of God. I still feel uneasy being associated with the word religion.
>
> (Osho 2000: 106)

However, he came to realize that in a culture like India, public atheist pronouncements and demeanor made people shy away from him: "Being known as an atheist, irreligious, amoral, became a problem. It was difficult to communicate with people, almost impossible to bridge any kind of relationship with people. In my communing with people, those words—atheist, irreligious, amoral—functioned like impenetrable walls" (Osho 2000: 107). If he wanted to get his message across, he had to adapt his strategy, especially since it turned out that the seekers he was targeting were often involved in religions: "They were the people who would be ready to travel with me to unknown spaces. But they were already involved in some religion, in some sect, in some philosophy; just their thinking of me as irreligious, atheistic, became a barrier. And those were the people I had to seek out" (Osho 2000: 107). As he recounts, this had him adopt a subversive strategy of undermining the basics of religion even though he would appear to engage with religion pro forma; he used the metaphor of play for this non-serious engagement with religion:

> I hate the word religion, ... but I had to talk about religion. But what I was talking about under the cover of religion was not the same as what people understood by religion. Now, this was simply a strategy. I was using their words—God, religion, liberation, moksha—and I was giving them my meanings. In this way I could start finding people, and people started coming to me.
>
> (Osho 2000: 108)

This semantic maneuver could take the following form: "I would speak on God and then tell people that godliness was a far better word. That was a way of disposing of God" (Osho 2000: 110). Maybe the choice of the title Bhagwan (adopted in 1971), which resonates with a traditional semantics, can be seen as part of this strategy. He also donned a long, flowing beard in line with many traditional gurus. And his followers were called *sannyasins*, a traditional name for renouncers even though asceticism in terms of abstention from food and sex was never a requirement.

Apparently, this strategy paid off. Rajneesh was invited to religious conferences and he was able to recruit an increasing number of pupils. He reports that groups were created all over India. He ceased traveling and instead let the people who wished come to him. He reports that he eventually dropped the religious façade he had erected: "Somebody is a Christian, somebody is a Hindu, somebody is a Mohammedan. It is very difficult to find a person who is nobody. I had to find my people from these closed flocks, but to enter their flock I had to talk their language. Slowly, slowly, I dropped their language" (Osho 2000: 113).

The Ashram and a "Religious Minority" Issue

Rajneesh increasingly attracted international followers and he started teaching and publishing in English. In 1974, a follower opened the first Bhagwan meditation center abroad in London. As Rajneesh was suffering from the climate in Bombay, with the backing of some of his wealthy followers, he moved to the more relaxed surroundings of Poona (Pune). In an elite suburb, an ashram was established for him. Bhagwan Shri Rajneesh was the spiritual center and attraction of this institution, and his daily talks were key events for residents and visitors; that these talks were called *darshan* was another instance of his flirtation with a religious vocabulary. In tune with this strategy, buildings in the Ashram were named after Jesus, St. Francis, Meister Eckhart, Krishna, and Buddha. The ashram, which operated like a marketplace for all sorts of experiential activities and a wide range of facilities and therapies, grew rapidly. Bhagwan preached a vision of personal transformation and liberation, for which he engaged a religious vocabulary when he spoke of becoming godlike or even gods, while at the same time being able to enjoy sex, food, wine, and other mundane pleasures (Urban 2015: 91).

The bustling innovative ashram did not operate in reclusion, but affected life in the city, for instance, in terms of public sexual morals. Conservative Hindus felt provoked by the Bhagwan's irreverent attitude. Controversy erupted, Rajneesh was threatened, and there occurred a series of bombings of Rajneesh facilities in Poona. The Rajneesh community tried to voice its concern by once again appealing to religion. The widely circulated English-language weekly news magazine *India Today* (June 30, 1981) cited a spokesman of the Rajneesh foundation as complaining: "This is a clear case of fanatics trying to suppress a minority religion."[1] In addition to problems in Pune, plans of the organization to buy land in order to expand in India proved unsuccessful. Moreover, the financial success of the ashram, which was apparently run as a business, caught the attention of the tax authorities and the charity commissioner, which eventually withdrew the tax-exempt status of the ashram, resulting in enormous amounts of taxes and back taxes to be paid (Urban 2015: 104).

A Religious Commune

The circle of leadership decided to get out of the imbroglio in Pune by relocating the core group out of India and by establishing a new international corporation to which the funds from the Ashram were transferred. Playing on religious tropes, Rajneesh declared himself to be "the messiah America had been waiting for" (Urban 2015: 104). He first settled into a nineteenth-century mansion in Montclair, New Jersey, before his new main secretary, Ma Anand Sheela (or Sheela Silverman, later Birnstiel), on behalf of the corporation purchased a remote ranch in rural Oregon. Establishing a large utopian commune was to be a great social experiment, and Rajneesh and his team managed to entice thousands of typically highly educated, affluent, and ambitious people to move to the new City of Rajneeshpuram, as the settlement was eventually incorporated. This ambitious project was successful on several accounts, and media coverage was initially positive. Smart managers devised a legal structure around the enterprise that comprised several separate but mutually interlocking organizations. The parent organization was called Rajneesh Foundation International (RFI). A November 1984 article from the *Oregon Magazine* cites from the charters of the RFI, according to which it is "organized exclusively for charitable purposes and particularly for the spreading of the religious teachings and messages of Bhagwan Shree Rajneesh" (McCormack 1984). There was also the Rajneesh Neo-Sannyas International Commune ("the Commune"), a corporation incorporated in December 1981. The purpose of the Commune, according to its articles of incorporation, was "to be a religious community where life is, in every respect, guided by the religious teachings of Bhagwan Shree Rajneesh and whose members live a communal life with a common treasury."[2]

Thus, the organizers repeatedly labeled their agenda as "religious"—not the least to obtain benefits, even though Bhagwan retained his ambivalent attitude toward religion. In October 1985, asked whether he was leading a "cult" or a "sect," he responded: "It is simply a movement; neither a cult nor a sect nor a religion but a movement for meditation, an effort to create a science of the inner. It is a science of consciousness. Just as the science is there for the objective world, this movement is preparing a science for the subjective world." Here, he draws on a common opposition between science and religion and locates his "movement" firmly in the camp of science. A little later in the same interview, however, he creates a second distinction, that between religion and religiousness: "So my work is a movement not to create a religion but to create religiousness. I take religiousness as a quality—not as a membership in an organization, but an inner experience of one's being" (Osho 2000: 133). In this sense, the charter was indeed correct to refer to his teachings as "religious."

Religiousness is the positive essence of religions; as he put it in 1986: "It is not a religion, it is pure religiousness, the very essence. Not a flower, but only a fragrance; you cannot catch hold of it" (Osho 2000: 166). Bhagwan's project was to leave religions behind and set its "essence" free, namely religiousness. Becoming religious, in this sense, however also meant to liberate oneself from religion; as he said in 1986: "I have to fight the old traditions, old religions, old orthodoxies, because they will not allow you ever to be healthy and whole" (Osho 2000: 163). Religiousness is something individual; yet, by creating the Rajneesh Foundation International he did not shun institutionalization.

Contrary to a Marxist view of religion that regards religion as the opium of the dispossessed masses, Rajneesh claimed that religion was the ultimate luxury (Osho 2000: 167) craved by those whose other wishes already have been fulfilled:

> When a rich person comes to me, he has money, he has employment, he has a house, he has health—he has everything that one can have. And suddenly he has come to a realization that nothing is fulfilling. Then the search for God starts. Yes, sometimes a poor man can also be religious, but for that very great intelligence is needed. A rich man, if he is not religious, is stupid. A poor man, if he is religious, is tremendously intelligent. If a poor man is not religious, he has to be forgiven. If a rich man is not religious, his sin is unpardonable. I am a rich man's guru. … You are here because you are frustrated with your life. A beggar cannot come because he is not yet frustrated.
>
> (Osho 2000: 146f)

Was this meant as an intellectual provocation, or did Rajneesh also appeal to a sense of social status among his followers? One could also turn it around by saying that poor people could not afford to be admitted to the ashram anyway.

Religion and Religionification: A Problem and a Solution

After an initial period of exceptional growth and relative peace, the relationship of the commune with its neighbors and the authorities in Oregon deteriorated rapidly. Some years after the Jonestown tragedy in 1978, the sudden arrival of thousands of strangers, whose exotic dress and uncommon behavior were unheard of, seems to have caused alarm. Stereotypical fears spread; in 1982 the rumor was reported that the Rajneeshis would sacrifice children, and a local resident wrote to senators, congressmen, and judges to complain about these people who "are not even Christian" but hold "strange ideas and beliefs" (Urban 2015: 116). They certainly met a degree of bigotry and religious intolerance and later defended themselves by presenting themselves as a threatened "religious minority" (Fitzgerald 1987: 258, 337).

In June 1982, one Senator picked up on these rumours and expressed his fears about this "cult" that reportedly practiced all sorts of transgressions (Urban 2015: 116). He also stated that he had "asked the Internal Revenue Service to review the Ranch's non-profit charitable status" (Urban 2015: 119). Tax exemption had already been an issue in Poona, and it threatened to return in the United States. As groups or institutions labeled "religion" can benefit from the waiving of taxes, the status of his "movement" as "a religion" became an important issue. We will return to this as we follow the course of events. Another legal issue concerned Rajneesh's residence permit. He had originally entered the United States on humanitarian grounds and obtained a temporary visa for medical treatment in New York. This was extended for another six months. He then applied for permanent residence in order to be able to carry out his duties as a religious teacher in Oregon. The Immigration and Naturalization Service conducted an interview with Rajneesh and sent officers to Rajneeshpuram. In their opinion, however, Rajneesh and his associates were "charlatans." Accordingly, the agency denied him the desired preferential status as a "religious worker." The IRS argued that Rajneesh's medical issues and his self-imposed silence—already in Pune he had stopped giving public discourses and he initially maintained his public silence in Oregon—would make it impossible for him to act as a religious leader. The commune appealed this decision by putting together a dossier to claim that Rajneesh was a "religious teacher" after all. By appealing to religious mainstream's imagery, Rajneesh was referred to as a "modern-day Christ" and the ideal of "religious freedom" was invoked (Urban 2015: 118f).

It might therefore seem plausible that by claiming the status of "a religion," two problems that were looming over the commune (tax and residency) could be solved. Ma Anand Sheela, Rajneesh's private secretary and *de facto* acting chief of staff, announced in 1983 the creation of "Rajneeshism." Sheela served as the president of the Rajneesh Foundation International, held power of attorney on his behalf, and in 1983 she had announced that Bhagwan would only speak with and through her. Rajneeshism was to be a full-blown religion with sacred texts, rituals, beliefs, feasts, and a clergy. The attempt clearly was to come as close to the reigning prototype of religion as possible. Sheela declared herself to be "the head of a religion" (Palmer 1988: 128). In July 1983, 10,000 copies of the book *Rajneeshism: An Introduction of Bhagwan Shree Rajneesh and His Religion* were published. The slim volume has pictures of Rajneesh at the front and the back. The design was meant to invoke associations with a prayer or psalm book. Some texts are framed like prayers or meditational texts ("I go to the feet of the ultimate truth of the awakened one") and make claims of the salvific necessity of adhering to Rajneesh: "The master is such a magnetic force that your surrender to the master becomes your protection" (p. 5). Under the heading "Why now?" readers are told about the aim of "creating a religion"—namely that it would "accurately reflect" the teachings of the master, contrary to other religions that have been compiled after the death of their respective founders. The text speaks about the "message" of Rajneesh as "a synthesis of traditional Eastern religions and the latest discoveries of Western psychology and science" (p. 13). In the section on "worship," this is not conceived of as praising a deity but "day-to-day living" in abundance and creativity (p. 19). "Rajneeshism's basic and fundamental belief is the freedom of the individual"; the social relevance of this is that "a sannyasin should not be compelled by law to enter the armed forces against his religious decision" (p. 23). In another chapter, the booklet speaks of "Ministers and their functions" and "religious practices," including initiations. The book addresses the process of giving birth and the celebration of marriage—without mentioning any kind of blessing or other potential supernatural intervention. In the "caring for the sick," however, the *mala* is reportedly used as an instrument to "feel Bhagwan's presence" (p. 42). The practices and ideas about death that are reported are devoid of any vocabulary invoking liberation, salvation, resurrection, or the like. The book stipulates that there are annual days of celebration, the first being the day of Bhagwan's "ultimate awakening" (p. 50). Bhagwan is praised as "the institute … the philosophy … the song … the life … the love" (p. 52). As he is still alive, "the creation of his religion is ongoing," so that this book will have future editions (p. 53). Indeed, a second edition was published in November 1983. The text is an attempt to re-describe or re-present the movement as a bona fide religion. In accordance with that, Sheela dressed in flamboyant robes that could seem to recall that of Christian nuns. A recurrent visitor to the commune observed that "in ceremony, costume, and hierarchy, the religious organization had become elaborate, baroque" (Fitzgerald 1987: 356).

Even though not all long-term residents had positive feelings about it (Fitzgerald 1987: 315), the tactics of religionification (or religion-making) could seem to be partly successful. In spring 1984, "after receiving thousands of supporting materials, including letters of recommendation from followers, psychologists, and academics, the INS finally granted Rajneesh preferential status as a 'religious worker'. It did not, however, rule on his residence application" (Urban 2015: 122f). The turn to religion, however, backfired when in October 1983 the Attorney General of Oregon issued a widely publicized fifty-nine-page "advisory issue" in which he came to the conclusion that Rajneeshpuram "violated both state and federal constitutions by failing to separate government and religion" (Richardson 2004: 480). This had the consequence that all state aid to the City of Rajneeshpuram was cut off. Rajneesh reacted to this by saying:

> Just the other day some information came to me: The attorney general of Oregon has declared Rajneeshpuram illegal. The reason that he has given is that here in Rajneeshpuram, religion and state are mixed. Now, in the first place, our religion has nothing to do with any religion that has ever existed on the earth. It is just a legal necessity that we have to declare that we are a religion; otherwise, you cannot find such an irreligious commune in the whole world. What religion is there? No God, no Holy Ghost, no Jesus Christ, no pope, no prayer, nobody concerned at all about death.
>
> (Osho 2000: 251)

His statement admitted that the label "religion" was reclaimed by his movement as a matter of tactics for legal purposes, while it really was no religion at all. While he otherwise operated with the distinction of religion vs. religiosity, he now coins the term "religionless religion"; he also spoke of "the laughing religion" or "religion-ness" (Palmer 1988: 129). He also tried to roll the ball back into the state's court:

> Those people write on their dollar, 'We trust in God.' On the dollar! Who is mixing religion with state? You are mixing religion even with the dirty dollar! In front of the Supreme Court it is written, 'We trust in God.' If

someday I happen to be in the Supreme Court … then I am going to ask them, 'Where is God? And on what authority have you written this? And if at the very gate there is a lie, you cannot ask me to take the oath for the truth'.

(Osho 2000: 252)

In other words: "These people go on mixing religion in every way, but they are legal. … If mixing religion makes a city illegal, then all the cities of the world are illegal because everywhere religion is mixed. This is the only place where religion is not mixed at all. Religion, in fact, does not exist here at all" (Osho 2000: 252). What is generally called American "civil religion" can appear as religious (rather than secular) to outside observers, and many scholars of religion would agree with Rajneesh that religion cannot be unmixed. Yet, it is also true that he actively played the religious game, and his associates turned his negations into a positive entity (a formal religion, Rajneeshism).

In India, Rajneesh had played the religion game in order not to put off those people who would most likely be receptive to his message, and in the United States he played the religion game to get a residence permit and to make his commune flourish. Yet, the legal framework of the United States made the project open to attack insofar as the sannyasins wanted to be a religion and have an incorporated city. The City of Rajneeshpuram had been incorporated in 1982; subsequently, a city council was elected, a city government organized, and a city charter enacted. Following the opinion of the Attorney General, this incorporation was challenged, and in October 1984 the US District Court for the District of Oregon was asked to declare "that the State of Oregon is not required by state law to recognize the municipal status of the City of Rajneeshpuram because to do so would violate the religion clauses of the Oregon and United States Constitutions" and "that the State of Oregon is not required to pay public monies or provide public services to the City of Rajneeshpuram … because to do so would violate the religion clauses of the Oregon and United States Constitutions."[3] The court pointed out that "all of the real property within the City of Rajneeshpuram, the sovereign power exercised by the City is subject to the actual, direct control of an organized religion and its leaders," in particular Ma Anand Sheela who also "has actual control over admission to and expulsion from the Commune, and by virtue of the Commune's dedication to the Bhagwan and the Bhagwan's delegation of power to Ma Anand Sheela, has the power to exercise actual control over the affairs of the Commune." Apart from property, administration, and admission, the court found that for the sannyasins the city was a religious project, and their activities were understood to be religious in nature:

> The followers of the Bhagwan assert that the development of Rajneeshpuram is the fulfillment of a religious vision. Work of every kind is considered a form of worship. Work stations are called 'temples' and various City functions are designated as temples and supervised by the Commune. The primary purpose for establishing the City of Rajneeshpuram was to advance the religion of Rajneeshism. The City was founded to fulfil a religious vision. The City was designed and functions as a spiritual mecca for followers of the Bhagwan worldwide. It serves as a monument to and the residence of the Bhagwan, and as a gathering place for followers at institutions of religious training and at three annual religious festivals.

The State of Oregon had argued in the words of the Court that "recognition of the municipal status of the City of Rajneeshpuram constitutes the establishment of a theocracy that is, the granting of governmental power to a religion." The defendants appealed to the principle of free exercise of religion. The court, however, found "that the potential injury to the anti-establishment principle of the first amendment by the existence and the operation of the City of Rajneeshpuram clearly outweighs the potential harm to defendants' free exercise of religion rights." Furthermore, "to deny defendants the right to operate a city is the only means of achieving a compelling state and federal interest that of avoiding an establishment of religion. If the City of Rajneeshpuram were to cease to exist, defendants would not be precluded from practicing their religion nor from associating with whom they choose in order to do so." Of course, the very issue of avoiding the establishment clause was only put on the table after the conflict between the commune and its neighbors had soured and turned violent.

An Anti-Religious "Bible" and the Public Death of a Religion

This verdict, however, did not inspire the Rajneeshis to give up on doing "religion." In March 1985, *The Rajneesh Bible Volume 1* was published. By all appearance then, the new religion now received its sacred scripture. The book contained thirty discourses held by Rajneesh in late October and November 1984; after three-and-half-year public "silence" he had resumed his talks—immediately after the decision by the Court. Rajneesh continued his paradoxical tactics: on the one hand, by producing nothing less than a "bible" he packed his message in religious terms, while on the other hand criticizing and refuting religion and claiming that his choice of the title bible would serve to demystify "the Bible" as the name just for an ordinary book ("I want it to be clear to the whole world that a bible has nothing to do with holiness" [Osho 1985: 193]). Among the chapters we find discourses with telling titles such as "Godliness Is, but There Is No God," "The Opium Called Religion," "To Be Rebellious Is to Be Religious," "The So-Called Holy Books are Just Religious Pornography," "From Crossianity to Jonestown," "Live Now—Pray Later," "I Am a Gnostic," "The Priest and the Politician—The Mafia of the Soul," "God Is the Greatest Fiction Ever," "Theology—The Jungle of Lies," "I Am Against Religions, but I Am for Religion," "Religion—The Last Luxury." Apparently, the challenge posed by the Court stimulated Rajneesh to reflect on religion and religiosity in more detail; he called his "the first and last religion" (Gordon 1987: 163). Already in June 1985, *The Rajneesh Bible Volume 2* followed, comprising another series of thirty discourses that Rajneesh had delivered at the end of 1984. Again, he addressed religion in talks with programmatic titles including the following: "Pseudo-Religion: The Stick-On Soul"; "Renunciation: Mortgage Today for a Tomorrow That Never Comes"; "God Is Not a Solution but a Problem"; "I Teach a Religionless Religion"; "God—The Nobody That Everybody Knows"; "Faith: The Suicide of Intelligence"; "Society Crowds You Out; Religion Outs Your Crowd"; "They Say Believe; I Say Explore"; "Jesus, the Only Forgotten Son of God"; "One God, One Messenger, One Book—One Big Lie"; "Religion Is Rebellion"; "Jesus—The Only Savior Who Nearly Saved Himself"; "Baptism: Wading for Godot"; "Science Plus Religion—The Dynamic Formula for the Future." This pattern showed no signs of relenting as *The Rajneesh Bible Volume 3* came out in September 1985: it comprised another thirty chapter or talks, several of which deal with religion in similar ways. All three volumes of this work had a print-run of 10,000 copies; their length increased from 753 (vol. 1) to 1,025 pages (vol. 3).

At the time when *The Rajneesh Bible Volume 3* came out, events at Rajneeshpuram took a dramatic turn. Utopian optimism had given way to apocalyptic fears, trust to paranoia, solidarity to power struggles, where voluntary commitment had been exploited, free love was replaced by safer sex, election fraud and bioterrorist attacks had been committed, and an elaborate system of surveillance had been put in place. For it was on September 13, 1985, that Ma Anand Sheela, together with a group of her closest associates, departed from the commune, resigned from all her duties, and fled to Germany. Sheela, "the queen of Rajneeshpuram" (Fitzgerald 1987: 279), served as the "high priestess" of Rajneeshism. Her extreme devotion to Rajneesh, whom she had first met in his Bombay days, had faded and both held each other responsible for the apparent worsening of the state of affairs. Rajneesh, who probably had not thought that Sheela would leave, reacted some days later by unleashing a series of grave accusations, including theft of 55 million US dollars and the attempted murder of Rajneesh's physician.

As part of Rajhneesh's retaliation against Sheela, on September 26, Bhagwan gave permission for his sannyasin to now choose the color of their clothes—red was no longer imposed—and to discard the *mala* they had been expected to wear. "He announced the end of Rajneeshism, saying 'A religion has died'" (Palmer 1988: 131). It seems that he ordered that the book *Rajneeshism* and Sheela's robe as high-priestess of "his" religion to be burned. He is reported to have said that what was burned was the Attorney General of Oregon, "for as there was no religion, so there could be no church-state suit" (Fitzgerald 1987: 363). Footage shown in the documentary *Wild Wild Country* (Netflix, 2018, episode five) shows his followers enthusiastically and cheerfully enacting this public burning at the impressive crematory that had been built before. Sheela's successor as Bhagwan's private secretary (Ma Prem Hasya) proclaims, when disposing of the priestly robe: "This was Sheela's desire to be high-priestess." The comment is met by laughter. When the dress was put on top of the books that are neatly piled up on a stretcher to be placed at the stake, she adds: "And Sheela's desire for popedom. ... And today we're celebrating the fact that Rajneeshism is dead" (37: 30ff). The dissolution of this religion is staged, but the liberation from the supposed darkness of religion is celebrated by adopting a performative vocabulary borrowed from the ways religious authorities have dealt with adversaries and nonconformity in supposedly dark ages: by acts of public burning. We also see the Bhagwan once again adopting his anti-religious stance in one of his trademark statements combining radicalism and the claim to historical relevance: "I'm against all religions. I am not your leader. You are not my followers. I'm destroying everything, so history never repeats again" (36:10). Furthermore, he proclaimed the death of the religion: "For the first time in the whole history of mankind, a religion has died" (37:14). This public closure could seem like a clever strategy to challenge religion, and the accusations against the former "high-priestess" made sense in a scheme where priests were cunning and criminals by nature. On October 1985, he renounced his statement of "guru," saying that he was "merely a friend" of his sannyasins, and the Rajneesh Foundation International was replaced by another organization (Palmer 1988: 132).

Rajneesh claimed that the creation of Rajneeshism had been Sheela's initiative and that she had done so without his permission. Sheela, on the other hand, denied the claims made by her former master and said that "I wouldn't think of such things" (*Wild Wild Country* episode 5 at 39:40). It is impossible to decide who was right: founding a religion was indeed not quite in line with Rajneesh's thinking on these matters, but it also seems unlikely that she could or would have created Rajneeshism against his wishes. At the same time, already in 1984 he had stated in a court deposition: "I am not making anybody head of my religion" (Palmer 1988: 130); here he could seem to have voiced opposition to Sheela's position, but this did not have any consequences. In her autobiography Sheela spelled out the tactical reason for the creation of the religion: "It was important for us to be a religion for immigration purposes. Bhagwan's visa as a religious leader could not be valid unless He had a religion. That is why He created Rajneeshism" (Birnstiel 2012: loc 3205). So, it is not impossible that somebody in the leadership circle came up with this idea, which was then (tacitly) endorsed or endured by Bhagwan who was not averse to appealing to religion when it served his interests.

The project of Rajneeshism was not totally over; however, for in early 1987, 5,000 copies of *The Rajneesh Bible Volume 4* (992 pages) were published. As if ignoring the events of late 1985, it assembled thirty discourses, partly addressing the idea of god (e.g., "Drop God, Drop Guilt—Become Religious"; "God: An Idea Whose Time Has Come—And Gone") that Rajneesh held in late January and February 1985. The public dissolution of the project of religion, however, could not stop the disaggregation of the commune, especially after criminal investigations started following the accusations made by Rajneesh against Sheela. When Rajneesh learned about pending warrants about his own arrest, on October 27, 1985 he attempted to escape and leave the United States in all secrecy. Yet, he was arrested when his jet landed for refueling on its route to the Bahamas. Less than two weeks after his arrest, he was allowed to leave the country, paying fines and prosecution costs of US$400,000. As he had left Rajneeshpuram and could not return, in addition to its managerial leadership (Sheela and her associates) the commune had lost its spiritual center and soon began to fall apart. In 1986 the former major of Rajneeshpuram testified that Bhagwan, Sheela, and the Rajneesh Foundation International had indeed directly controlled the city government. Accordingly, Rajneeshpuram was declared unconstitutional by the District Court Judge (Fitzgerald 1987: 366). The ranch went bankrupt and was left empty in 1987, shortly after *The Rajneesh Bible Volume 4* was published. In 1988, it was sold to an insurance company.

Dead Religions vs. a Living Religiousness (= Zen)

Rajneesh, in the meanwhile, successfully managed to rebrand himself as Maitreya, Zorba, the Buddha and after 1989, "Osho." When no country would admit him, he settled in India and the ashram in Poona was restarted. His tactics of putting the blame on the failure of Rajneeshpuram entirely on Sheela was successful and helped him to save face and his movement (Goldman 2014: 187). The reinvented Ashram in Poona was no longer a social experiment, but functioned more like a luxury resort for affluent spiritual tourists from all over the world. Even in the discourses from his later Poona period, Osho sometimes discussed religion. For example, he said: "There is only one religion, and that is the religion of love. There is only one god, and that is the god of celebration, of life, of rejoicing" (Osho 2000: 270). He returned to his usual criticism of religion: "An organized religion is nothing but a hidden politics, a deep exploitation by the priesthood" (Osho 2000: 276). In retrospect, one cannot help to think of Rajneeshpuram and Rajneeshism here, but Osho does not make this connection. He continued his strategy of contrasting (bad and dead) religion with (good and vibrant) religiosity; the epitome of the latter, which he contrasts with all religions, is now Zen:

> That is the greatest difference between all the religions on one side and Zen on the other side. All religions except Zen are dead. They have become fossilized theologies, systems of philosophies, doctrines, but they have

forgotten the language of the trees. … I call Zen the only living religion because it is not a religion but only a religiousness. It has no dogma, it does not depend on any founder. It has no past; in fact it has nothing to teach you. It is the strangest thing that has happened in the whole history of mankind—strangest because it enjoys in emptiness, it blossoms in nothingness.

(Osho 2000: 274f)

Conclusion: The Death of Religion as Reflexive Performance

The literature on Rajneesh/Bhagwan/Osho during the Oregon period has mostly discussed the conflicts between the commune and its environments, resulting in its eventual dissolution. By contrast, this chapter has focused on one aspect, namely on the founding and dissolution of the religion of Rajneeshism. I have embedded the analysis in the paradoxical ambivalences of Rajneesh toward "religion" throughout his career. While the irreverently self-ironizing playfulness worked well as a discursive approach to attract, entertain, or even illuminate students and followers, when the category religion entered the legal machinery in the United States it first seemed to pay off but eventually backfired, once the state authorities had realized that this could be a way to put the troublesome commune in its place. Once the inner circle of leadership had withdrawn from him, entering the religion game once again—now by officially abandoning it—provided Rajneesh the opportunity to reassert his leadership and to mobilize his followers toward an emancipatory project of ending a religion. Celebrating and staging the "death" of one's own religion was a reflexive performance: performative in the sense of making it happen, felicitous in the sense of effective, and reflexive in the sense of the actors observing themselves as bringing it about. Finally, the death of their religion for them meant contributing to the desired end of religion as such.

Notes

1 https://www.indiatoday.in/magazine/special-report/story/19810630-pall-of-secrecy-and-intrigue-cloud-much-publicised-and-criticised-rajneesh-ashram-773018-2013-11-20

2 https://law.justia.com/cases/federal/district-courts/FSupp/598/1208/1476422/
3 State of Or. v. City of Rajneeshpuram, 598 F. Supp. 1208 (D. Or. 1984), US District Court for the District of Oregon—598 F. Supp. 1208 (D. Or. 1984), October 12, 1984; https://law.justia.com/cases/federal/district-courts/FSupp/598/1208/1476422/ All un-references citations in this para are from this source.

References

Bharti, A. (2007), *Blessed Days with OSHO*, New Delhi: Diamond Books.

Birnstiel, S. (2012), *Don't Kill Him!: The Story of My Life with Bhagwan Rajneesh : a Memoir*, New Delhi: Finger Print.

Fitzgerald, F. (1987), *Cities on a Hill: A Journey through Contemporary American Cultures*. New York [u.a.]: Simon and Schuster.

Goldman, M. S. (2014), "Controversy, Cultural Influence, and the Osho/Rajneesh Movement," in J. R. Lewis and J. A. Petersen (eds.), *Controversial New Religions*, 2nd edition, 176–94. Oxford: Oxford University Press.

Gordon, J. S. (1987), *The Golden Guru: The Strange Journey of Bhagwan Shree Rajneesh*, Lexington, KY: The Stephen Green Press.

McCormack, W. (1984), "Bhagwan's Bottom Line I: Rajneesh's Far-Flung Empire Is More Material than Spiritual," *Oregon Magazine*. Republished: newrepublic.com/article/147894/bhagwans-bottom-line-i (accessed July 28, 2020).

Osho (1985), *From Darkness to Light: Answers to the Seekers on the Path. Talks Given from 28/ 02/85pm to 31/ 03/85pm*. Available online: https://archive.org/stream/selfrealization/FromDarknessToLight_djvu.txt

Osho (2000), *Autobiography of a Spiritually Incorrect Mystic*. New York: St. Martin's Press.

Palmer, S. J. (1988), "Charisma and Abdication: A Study of the Leadership of Bhagwan Shree Rajneesh," *Sociological Analysis*, 49 (2): 119–35.

Richardson, J. T. (2004), "State and Federal Cooperation in Regulating New Religions," in J. T. Richardson (ed.), *Regulating Religion: Case Studies from Around the Globe*, 477–89. New York: Kluwer Academic/Plenum Publishers.

Urban, H. B. (2015), *Zorba the Buddha: Sex, Spirituality, and Capitalism in the Global Osho Movement*. Oakland, CA: University of California Press.

Wild Wild Country (2018), Directed by Maclain Way and Chapman Way, Produced by Juliana Lembi, Duplass Brothers Productions, Stardust Framees Production, Submarine Entertainment, Netflix.

9

State Actions in Western Democracies Leading to the Dissolution of Religious Communities

Stuart A. Wright

One aspect of religious demise that deserves greater attention among scholars involves cases wherein the dissolution of the religious group is a direct result of state actions of social control. I am not referring to cases in authoritarian regimes where religions are forced to register with the state, face government monitoring and surveillance, or risk censorship, arrest, or bans as illegal organizations (e.g., Russia, China, Iran). Rather I am referring here to cases where state actions lead to demise in Western-style democracies that have legislative guarantees and traditions of religious liberty and freedom of belief. Despite these legal and historical protections, minority religions often still face unequal treatment and even state repression (Finke, Mataic and Fox 2017; Grim and Finke 2011; Kirkham 2013; Sarkissian 2015). In some cases, authorities may attempt to circumvent the guarantees of religious liberty by declaring that nontraditional or new religious movements (NRMs) aren't "real" religions. By brandishing the socially threatening label of "cult," actions taken by the state may ignore or trample on religious rights based on the premise that NRMs are pseudo-religions (Anthony and Robbins 1992, 2004; Palmer 2011a: 47). Or the state may be suspicious of "sectarian deviance" seeing groups such as impediments to rational thought and civic ideals (Beckford 2004; Luca 2004: 67). As a consequence, various social control actions by the state may result in what Richardson (1985) calls the "deformation" of religious communities.

Authorities in democratic states may take a range of actions that fall within the rule of law that can weaken, debilitate, or destroy a targeted religious group. These might include measures such as conducting a government audit or launching investigations into alleged financial or tax fraud

(Palmer 2011a: 69–70; Passas 1994; Richardson 1992). Regulatory authorities may decide to probe putative zoning or land-use violations, some involving water and environmental statutes (Cookson 2003; Gordon 1987; Introvigne 2004; Palmer 2010, 2011a). Sometimes authorities will conduct investigations into a religious group's labor and employment practices, particularly in communal groups where members provide unpaid labor in return for housing, food, and healthcare (Gregory 1993; Richardson 1988). In cases where members from foreign countries travel to join a religious community, state officials may use immigration laws as a tool to investigate a group (Gordon 1987). The legal costs associated with any of these kinds of investigations may be substantial, including hiring attorneys, paying court fees, or incurring possible fines for regulatory infractions. The resulting expenses can severely hamper or even bankrupt a modest size group with limited resources. If investigations are picked up by the press, the adverse publicity can have serious repercussions for the group in terms of public relations, damaging the organization's sustainability, even when there is no criminal activity uncovered in the eventual determination of alleged improprieties.

In France, for example, following the tragic mass suicides/homicides by the Order of the Solar Temple in 1994, the French National Assembly voted to establish a commission to investigate the sect phenomenon and soon issued the infamous Guyard List, a blacklist of 173 suspicious *sectes* (Palmer 2011a). Any NRMs appearing on the list were labeled "subversive" and targeted by police who searched their offices, seized computers and files, interrogated staff, and arrested leaders. Groups that previously had congenial relations with their neighbors and communities found themselves disenfranchised and barred from participation in customary public activities. Rental contracts with hotels for conferences were cancelled, NRM-owned businesses boycotted, and service contracts dropped. Professionals and laborers alike lost their jobs or were denied promotions (Wright and Palmer 2018: 626).

Within a few years, the entire French government became engaged in a campaign to combat the *secte* problem. To say this approach was unique in international policy would be an understatement. According to French scholar Etienne Ollion (2013: 122), "only in France would a policy against cults receive a specific and widely used name: *la lutte contre les sectes* (a War on Sects)." With the passage of the About-Picard law in May 2001, the state created new criminal categories, including the "abuse of weakness" (*abus de faibless*), which was used to penalize practices or actions by NRM leaders (*gourous*) toward vulnerable followers. The new law also introduced the concept of mental manipulation (*manipulation mentale*), a French rendition of the discredited, pseudo-scientific notion of "brainwashing."

In some countries, new religions have been prosecuted for alleged "medical fraud" and "psychological abuse." In 1965 the Church of Scientology in Melbourne was raided and members prosecuted for violating the Psychological Practices Act, a law passed specifically targeting the Scientology practice of "auditing," which officials believed was promoting medical fraud (Doherty 2014, 2015). Legislators in Victoria subsequently passed the 1968 Scientology Prohibition Act which banned the practice of Scientology altogether and outlawed possession of its instruments and materials.

In Belgium, a parliamentary inquiry commission was created in 1996 to "work out a policy against sects and the dangers they allegedly pose(d) to people, particularly minors" (Fautre 2004: 114). In April 1997, the Belgian parliamentary commission issued a 660-page report identifying 189 suspect religious sects. The report raised concerns about the alleged illegal practice of medicine (alternative doctrines, practices, and teachings concerning health), tax fraud, alternative or esoteric methods of education, and other potentially harmful sectarian activities.

A particularly effective tactic of state control over new religions has involved investigations of child abuse allegations made by anticult organizations, ex-members, and/or concerned relatives (Palmer 2011b; Palmer and Hardman 1999; Richardson 1999; Wright and Palmer 2016; Wright and Richardson 2011). Researchers have seen the pattern of child abuse allegations increases dramatically in the wake of new child protection laws and policies following what Phillip Jenkins (1998) calls the "Child Abuse Revolution" in the late 1970s and 1980s. Research shows that organized opponents of new or nontraditional religions seized political opportunities and exploited perceived threats of child abuse to effectively mobilize state agents and sympathetic media in a coordinated campaign to assail groups labeled "cults." Claims-making and lobbying efforts by organized opponents exaggerated threats of child abuse in minority religions. Why was this significant? One critical impact of the child abuse revolution was the mandated *state response* to such allegations. Under new state laws, the weight of child protection now fell more heavily to the state. Consequently, even the mere accusation of child abuse was sufficient to impel state action. Anticult organizations and allied opponents seized upon these new political opportunities and threats as NRMs became "soft targets" in new child-saving campaigns. Lacking institutional allies, NRMs faced greater difficulty in defending themselves against charges of child abuse in a politically charged climate of child victimization. According to Richardson (1999: 175), "the new situation … led to a dramatic increase in accusations of child abuse leveled against minority religions."

The narrative of "cult child abuse" was a powerfully resonant trope in the backdrop of a moral panic about "threatened children" (Best 1990; Richardson 1999; Richardson and Introvigne 2007). The state was required to investigate any allegation of child abuse and when combined with the putative threat of a "dangerous cult" resulted in the increased likelihood that a routine investigation by authorities would be elevated to a police raid (Wright and Palmer 2016).

Indeed, in an ongoing study of government raids on minority religious communities in nineteen Western-style democracies over a period of seven-plus decades, Wright and Palmer (2016, 2018) found a select number of cases in which the impact of the state's actions resulted in the demise or dissolution of the religious group. I refer here to a subset of seven cases out of 149 documented raids. While the number is small, these cases illustrate how forces exogenous to the group can lead to religious demise. There are certainly other exogenous forces we could identify as catalysts of religious demise (war, genocide, territorial expansion, wholesale conversion to intruding missionary religion, etc.), but here I want to focus specifically on the aggressive and coercive actions of the state.

A brief overview of the seven cases of religious demise found in the Wright and Palmer study is provided below. These cases include the Branch Davidians, the United Nuwaubian Nation, the Yearning for Zion Ranch (a satellite community of the Fundamentalist Latter Day Saints), Horus, the Center for Teaching Biodynamism, Mandarom, and Amour et Misericorde. In each of the cases, the groups were targeted by state raids which resulted in their dissolution. I have separated the cases by country; three cases in the United States are covered first and differ from those in France because of the latter's unique policy of a "War on Sects." The French raids are all a result of *state-sponsored* anticult agencies tasked with monitoring new or nontraditional religions. There is no such parallel in the United States, though independent, third-party anticult movement organizations have had an outsize influence on state agencies.

Branch Davidians

On February 28, 1993, the US Bureau of Alcohol, Tobacco and Firearms (ATF) carried out a massive raid on a small Seventh Day Adventist sect known as the Branch Davidians near Waco, Texas (Wright 1995). The federal raid on the Branch Davidian religious community was the "largest enforcement effort ever mounted by ATF and one of the largest in the history of law enforcement" (US Department of Treasury 1993: 134). The raid was undertaken with the intent to serve search and arrest warrants for its leader, David Koresh, alleging that he and others had violated federal firearm laws. However, the raid was poorly planned as eighty members of the ATF's Special Response Team (SRT), which had trained at a nearby military base, Fort Hood, were determined to execute a "takedown" of the group (Wright 2005). A shootout ensued, and four ATF agents and six Branch Davidians were mortally wounded. In the wake of the failed raid, the FBI's Hostage Rescue Team (HRT) was called to Waco to take control of the incident which had now become a standoff. The standoff continued for fifty-one days as negotiators attempted to persuade barricaded sect members to surrender. FBI negotiators had some success; thirty-five sect members left Mount Carmel during the standoff, including a number of children. But as the siege wore on, the HRT's tactical commander grew impatient with negotiations and pressured FBI leadership and the Attorney General to use force to end the standoff. A deep rift developed between negotiators and the tactical units. The negotiators pointed to success in persuading some sect members to leave and lobbied the FBI Command Center in Washington to stay with peaceful negotiations. In the end however, the tactical unit prevailed. On the fifty-first day, the FBI launched a dangerous CS gas assault on the Davidian settlement using 29-foot, 52-ton M60 Combat Engineering Vehicles to breach the buildings. The military tanks effectively collapsed the structures driving the barricaded sect members into the back of the building where most of the children were gathered. There were no windows or ventilation to allow escape of the CS in this area of the building. After six hours of CS gas insertion and relentless tank assault, a deadly fire broke out killing seventy-six men, women, and children.

A congressional investigation later condemned the federal siege as an egregious overreach of law enforcement and openly criticized the manner in which the operations were carried out. Regarding the ATF investigation that served as the rationale for the initial raid, the congressional committees concluded that the affidavits filed in support of the warrants were filled with false and misleading statements. Moreover, the committees concluded that the raid was entirely unnecessary and that David Koresh could have been arrested when he was away from the property, thus avoiding endangering the lives of the other residents at Mount Carmel.

> The ATF's investigation of the Branch Davidians was grossly incompetent. It lacked the minimum professionalism expected of a major Federal law enforcement agency. While the ATF had probable cause to obtain the arrest warrant for David Koresh and the search warrant for the Branch Davidian residence, the affidavit filed in support of the warrants contained an incredible number of false statements. The ATF agents responsible for preparing the affidavits knew or should have known that many of the statements were false.
>
> David Koresh could have been arrested outside the Davidian compound. The ATF chose not to arrest Koresh outside the Davidian residence and instead were determined to use a dynamic entry approach. In making this decision ATF agents exercised extremely poor judgment, made erroneous assumptions, and ignored the foreseeable perils of their course of action. (*Investigation into the Activities of Federal Law Enforcement Agencies toward the Branch Davidians* 1996: 3).

The congressional investigative committees were equally harsh in their condemnation of the FBI's actions at Waco. Specifically, they castigated the FBI/HRT for its use of CS gas in the final assault, noting the possible lethal effects, especially on young children, pregnant women (of which there were several), and the elderly.

> The CS riot control agent assault on April 19 should not have taken place. The possibility of a negotiated end to the standoff presented by Koresh should have been pursued even if it had taken several more weeks. ...

CS riot control agent is capable of causing immediate, acute and severe physical distress to exposed individuals, especially young children, pregnant women, the elderly, and those with respiratory conditions. In some cases, severe or extended exposure can lead to incapacitation. Evidence presented to the subcommittees show that the use of CS riot control agent in enclosed spaces, such as the bunker area, significantly increases the possibility that lethal levels will be reached and the possibility of harm significantly increases. …(t)he presented evidence does indicate that CS insertion into the enclosed bunker, at a time when women and children were assembled inside that enclosed space, could have been a proximate cause of or directly resulted in some or all of the deaths attributed to asphyxiation in the autopsy reports (*Investigation into the Activities of Federal Law Enforcement Agencies toward the Branch Davidians*, 1996: 4).

The Branch Davidian community at Mount Carmel was effectively extinguished by the 1993 federal siege. The government has steadfastly maintained that the Branch Davidians committed mass suicide. But there is ample evidence of government misfeasance (Wright 2009) and egregious violations of established hostage-barricade protocols by the FBI's Hostage Rescue Team (Wright 1999) that cast grave doubts on the mass suicide thesis. Only a handful of sect members survived. Though all nine Davidians who faced the more serious charges of murder were acquitted, five were convicted of lesser charges, including aiding and abetting the voluntary manslaughter of federal agents. Eight Branch Davidians were convicted on firearms charges; nine were sentenced to prison. As of July 2007, all of the sect members had been released from prison. Others not formally charged with crimes scattered or were deported. Some lifelong Davidian survivors died in the intervening years (Catherine Matteson, Bonnie Haldeman, Mary Belle Jones). Many of those who died in the fire had no immediate family living and were not afforded a burial plot by the city of Waco. In a final show of humiliation, the remains of these deceased sect members were buried in a pauper's grave (Wright and Palmer 2016: 249).

United Nuwaubian Nation

On May 8, 2002, the FBI executed a massive paramilitary raid on the United Nuwaubian Nation, a Black Nationalist community located in rural Georgia. The state raid was planned and carried out as a spectacular show of force.

Three armored vehicles accompanied by over 300 agents from the FBI, ATF, and the local Putnam County sheriff's office burst past guards and rammed through the flimsy painted obelisks that formed the front of the community known as Tama Re. The raid was predicated on charges of child molestation and racketeering. The invading army of police expected to face a heavily armed "cult." They found instead only a few guns legally registered: no stockpile of illegal weapons, no munitions. No weapons charges were filed against the group despite media reports trumpeting the dangers of the cult (Palmer 2010).

The group was founded by Dwight York (Dr. Malachi York to his followers) in Brooklyn, New York. York's spiritual organizations began in 1967 but went through multiple incarnations and name changes. The United Nuwaubian Nation first came into existence in 1993. It was in this year that the group sold its property in Brooklyn and moved to Georgia. They purchased a building for their headquarters in Athens and bought 473 acres of land in Putnam County near the town of Eatonton. York had created a highly eclectic religion borrowing from Nation of Islam, the Black Hebrews, the Five Percenters, the Yamassee Amerindians, and even some UFO beliefs. The property in Putnam County was named Tama Re and displayed Egyptian themes, with a 40-foot pyramid among other things. York claimed Tama Re as a sacred land—a safe haven for all black people in the impending apocalypse. It functioned as pilgrimage site for African Americans of modest means (Palmer 2010: 71–4).

The inevitable conflict between Black Nationalists from New York with odd religious beliefs and the largely white, rural Southern bible-belt residents of Putnam County, Georgia, developed almost immediately. Initially, conflicts centered on zoning and building permits for the construction on Tama Re. Another source of conflict was the Savior's Day festival which drew crowds of thousands of black supporters. Local media coverage was not favorable, to say the least. Tensions mounted with locals calling for the Nuwaubians to move back to Brooklyn and York calling white people "the Devil" and suggesting the Caucasians go home to Europe.

The most serious allegations against York pertained to child molestation and sex abuse. Accusations were lodged by former members who contacted Putnam County Sheriff's office anonymously. The sheriff launched an investigation and contacted the FBI. The raid and subsequent custodial detention of Nuwaubian children produced no forensic or medical evidence of sexual abuse. Nonetheless,

York was arrested and charged with an array of child molestation crimes. The trial produced enough evidence based on testimonies of ex-members to convict. York was convicted of child molestation and racketeering and sentenced to 135 years in federal prison. The racketeering (RICO) charges allowed the government to seize the Tama Re property. The Nuwaubian community is largely dissolved with a small number still communicating online.

Yearning for Zion Ranch

The Yearning for Zion Ranch (YFZ), a satellite community of the Fundamentalist Latter Day Saints (FLDS), was founded in 2004 near the small town of Eldorado, Texas. The site was in a remote part of West Texas where the group believed they would encounter little resistance or interference. It was envisioned as a vanguard community where only the most committed followers at the FLDS base community in Colorado City, Arizona would be invited to reside. FLDS leader Warren Jeffs, it was later learned, chose this site to expand his practice of polygamy to include underage girls. Though the FLDS under the leadership of Warren's father, Rulon Jeffs, had moved toward older ages for women marrying (Bradley 1993: 100), the younger Jeffs intended to reverse this trend. Largely through the dogged actions of organized opponents, allied with the local sheriff's office and state agents, a raid on the YFZ property was planned and executed on April 3, 2008 (Wright and Richardson 2011). A joint task force of five Texas state and county law enforcement agencies, accompanied by the Department of Family and Protective Services (DFPS), laid siege to the YFZ ranch that was now home to over 800 members of the FLDS. Jeffs (who was already in custody) and ten senior leaders of the community were charged with sexual abuse and other related charges (Wright and Richardson 2014: 86). Jeffs was convicted and sentenced to life plus twenty years. The other defendants received sentences ranging from six years to seventy-five years. All 439 children at the ranch were taken into state custody, the largest state custodial detention of children in US history.

While the courts remanded the children back to the parents, the District Court orders for state supervision were extraordinarily intrusive and unprecedented. The DFPS was given access to the residence of each child for unannounced home visits that could include medical, psychological, or psychiatric evaluations (Schreinert and Richardson 2011: 253). The state's custodial supervision of the FLDS children, however, was only a prelude to broader actions.

In April 2014, the state of Texas seized the YFZ property after a court granted a request for asset forfeiture. Under Texas law, authorities can seize property that was used to commit or facilitate certain criminal conduct. At the time that the State Attorney General filed a request for forfeiture in 2012, the YFZ property was valued on the tax roll at over $33 million. The property was later auctioned off by the state. Some of the YFZ members returned to the main community in Arizona, but parents with young children were required to remain in Texas for an indefinite period.

******

The following four cases all took place in France. As alluded to earlier, France is unique because it is the only Western democracy with an official policy of a "War on Sects" (*la lutte contre les sects*). Consequently, these religious communities were targeted and criminalized precisely because they were new or nontraditional religions.

Horus

Horus was a New Age farming community located near La Coucourde, France. The formal name of the community was the International Center for Parapsychology and Scientific Research of the New Age. The Center was founded in 1989 by Marie-Therese Castano, a 44-year-old Basque widow. Ms. Castano was a former real estate broker and radio show host who often featured arcane or esoteric subjects. Through organizing conferences on spiritual perspectives regarding ecology, medicine, and personal growth, she acquired a following of about 100, mostly women. Eventually, she and fifty friends bought 35 hectares of land in the south of France to start the community, each paying into an equal share. Most of the members held outside jobs and the community sponsored workshops in the summer (Palmer 2011a).

According to Palmer (2011a: 130), Ms. Castano gained a reputation as a healer and over time was believed by her followers to be the reincarnation of Queen Nefertiti. Under her leadership, the community embarked on the study of ancient esoteric methods of farming and animal husbandry. She launched breeding experiments where fruits and fowl were grafted onto "pure" or more ancient regional forms. Horus was dubbed the "Findhorn of France," after the utopian, spiritual community in Scotland. Horus gained a reputation for its remarkable production of enormous vegetables without the use of fertilizers. Palmer (2011a: 131) describes it as "a community of craftswomen—weavers, potters and agronomists—who made cheese, yogurt, and wine from their vineyard to sell in the local markets."

Horus became a target of state monitoring after Castano began claiming that fertilizers and pesticides were unnecessary for farming based on her esoteric practices. News reports began labeling Castano as a *gourelle* (a female guru). The first raid on the group occurred as early as 1991, predating the Guyard List. It is not clear what actions authorities took after the initial raid. It wasn't until 1995 that the Center appeared on the notorious *list noir*. Evidently, anonymous complaints were sent to government officials. Horus became the target of a state raid in February 1996 on the suspicion that the group was engaged in the "illegal practice of medicine," a criminal charge in France. Horus was raided a third time in June 1997 and Castano was arrested. Facing the prospect of perpetual state harassment, Castano announced the dissolution of the Center in 1997. She was put on trial in 1999 with two other leaders. The plaintiffs in the case were officials with UNADFI (National Union of Associations for the Defense of Family and Individual), a powerful state-sponsored anticult organization. Ms. Castano was convicted of "non-assistance to a person in danger," a result of treating ill members with alternative healing practices rather than referring them to conventional medical treatment. Castano's colleagues were convicted of "illegal practice of medicine." The defendants were sentenced to two years in prison with one year awarded for time served in pre-trial detention. The court ordered the Center closed and it was prohibited from reopening in the future. Horus was effectively dissolved by the actions of the state.

Mandarom

Between 1994 and 2001, Mandarom was the target of no less than four government raids, each motivated by a different deviance claim. Mandarom was one of the NRMs placed on the Guyard List and was referred to by the media as "the most dangerous secte in France" (Palmer 2011a: 34). The Holy City of Mandarom was an eclectic, Hindu-style ashram in the French Alps, founded by a Frenchman, Gilbert Bourdin, known as Hamsah Manarah to his followers. Members practice the path of Aumism, which they believe unites all world religions in a mission of peace.

Palmer observes that the "fierce intolerance of the French authorities toward Mandarom throughout the 1990s" might be explained "as a reaction to the group's flagrant display of alien religious symbols or an aesthetic revulsion to Mandarom's pious display of art" (2011a: 34). This included an onion-shaped dome of the Lotus Temple, statues of Buddha, and the Cosmic Christ, reaching high into the mountain skies. The statues were seen as an eyesore to communities in the surrounding environs of the beautiful French Alps. The effort to have them removed was led by a local environmental organization, the Verdun Protection Association (VPA). In the end, the VPA prevailed as authorities determined that Mandarom lacked proper permits to build the statues.

Multiple raids were executed by French gendarmerie for inspection of the temples, tax fraud, child abuse, and finally demolition of the statues. The most serious charge was child abuse. Bourdin was arrested and convicted on the charge of sexual abuse of a minor, though the trial testimony was highly problematic. Bourdin and his followers argued that the charge was manufactured by organized opponents, a claim that has some support (Introvigne 2004; Palmer 2011a: 33–55; Wright and Palmer 2016: 209–12). To the previous point, when defense attorneys asked the alleged victim in trial if Bourdin had any distinguishing marks on his body that she could recall, the woman said no. The court record shows that the defense attorney had Bourdin remove his shirt to reveal that he was covered with tattoos. It didn't matter in the end, however. Bourdin was depicted a *secte* leader and he was convicted and imprisoned. The raids and the incarceration of Bourdin severely diminished the community.

In January 2010, Mandarom won a temporary reprieve when the state recognized it as valid religion. But litigation of the land use continued until 2014 when the Verdun Protection Association won a settlement of 30,000 euros in a judgment against Mandarom that ordered an environmental assessment conducted on the property. In 2018, another decision by the French court ordered Mandarom leaders to pay 70,000 euros in damages and legal fees; they were given six months to restore the property to its natural condition. The group lacks such funds and is facing a crisis. The case is now in appeal to the *Cour de Cassation* and the future of the religious community is in serious jeopardy. In this regard, Mandarom has not ended in the same sense as the other cases, but it is certainly debilitated and at risk of dissolution.

Center for the Teaching of Biodynamism

On February 22, 2011, seventy armed police from CAIMADES (French paramilitary police) laid siege to the Center for the Teaching of Biodynamism in Nyons, France. The Director, Sophie Berlamont, and four of her assistants were arrested and taken into custody. The rationale for the raid was that Berlamont and her staff were suspected of "potential sectarian activity" and of "overcharging for training sessions" (Wright and Palmer 2016: 214). Berlamont was later charged with *abus de faiblesse* (abuse of weakness), a criminal charge in France.

Sophie Berlamont was a distinguished physiotherapist who worked in a hospital in Montpelier before moving to Nyons. She specialized in women's health problems, primarily involving pregnancy, menopause, and sexual dysfunctions. After a divorce, Berlamont purchased a house and vineyard overlooking the Nyons valley. She created the Centre for the Teaching of Biodynamism in 2007 which offered courses that culled elements from Chinese medicine, reflexology, and Quanrique medicine. Over a period of fifteen years she built up a clientele of around 200 students, most of whom were middle-aged women (Wright and Palmer 2016: 214–15).

The catalyst for the raid on the Centre was based on information supplied by a former member. The former member separated from her husband who then became romantically involved with Ms. Berlamont. The disgruntled woman may have blamed Berlamont for this development; she allegedly persuaded other young trainees to complain about the Center to the anticult organization, ADFI (Association for the Defense of Family and Individual). In turn, it appears that ADFI exploited the conflict to assail Berlamont and the Center as a dangerous sect. The raid was organized by officials with MIVILUDES (Interministerial Monitoring Mission to Fight against Sectarian

Deviancy), a state agency monitoring sects or cults. After the raid, an official with MIVILUDES told the press that Berlamont seemed to "exert mental control on the trainees and to abuse their weakness." The French court found Berlamont guilty of the misdemeanor of *abus de faiblesse*. She was ordered to stop practicing Biodynamics, to close down her business and have no communication with her students.

This lower court judgment was overturned by an appeals court in February 2012, but for a whole year Sophie Berlamont had no means of support and depended on her father to pay her mortgage. After winning her appeal, she was re-indicted by prosecutors. The case went to the *Cour de Cassation* (the highest court in France). In February 2019, she learned she had won her case. But eight years after the initial raid and arrest, Berlamont's community had collapsed, her reputation was impugned, and the members had moved on. The aggressive actions of the state had decimated the Center for Teaching Biodynamism.

Amour et Misericorde

On April 11, 2012, a small prayer group residing in the suburbs of Dijon, France, which called itself Amour et Misericorde, was raided by police investigators. Four persons were taken into custody for questioning and transported to Paris for a lengthy interrogation. The leader of the group, Eliane Deschamps and her secretary/spokesperson were charged with *abus de faiblesse aggrave* (aggravated abuse of weakness).

Beginning in 1996, Eliane Deschamps, a housewife and mother of five, began having regular apparitions of the Virgin Mary for a 24-hour period on the 15th of each month. She gathered a prayer group of 150 faithful Catholics, who referred to her as "La Petite Servante." Amour et Misericorde was a registered association according to the French law of 1901. An inner circle of around twenty members lived communally in Deschamp's home.

In 2002, members of the local chapter of ADFI began collecting complaints against the group. One individual in particular complained that his wife and daughters left to join the group. Also a network of ex-members, concerned relatives, officials from ADFI and MIVILUDES, and the town's mayor organized to oppose the group. Facing heightened media scrutiny and criticism,

Deschamps officially dissolved Amour et Misericorde as an association. But this didn't stop opponents and the media from carrying out a campaign to have the group declared a dangerous sect.

The group responded to the raid and the unwelcome publicity by going underground. Thereafter, the messages from the Virgin were distributed only by mail. Members changed their cell phone number frequently and kept their participation in the prayer group secret. The group has no public presence today and has remained underground.

Conclusion

In summary, we have seven cases of religious demise resulting from state actions in the form of raids. The Branch Davidian raid was the most extreme case; the community was thoroughly destroyed by a federal siege. Its religious structures were demolished by military tanks and destroyed by fire. Its leaders and nearly the entire membership—seventy-six men, women, and children—died in the fire. A few survivors were imprisoned or deported; the remaining remnant were scattered. The United Nuwaubian Nation was raided by a joint task force of federal, state, and county law enforcement. Its leader was imprisoned, its property seized, and the membership scattered. The Yearning for Zion Ranch was raided by five state agencies, 439 children were taken into custody, the leaders arrested and imprisoned, and the property seized by the state.

In France, where four of the cases took place, we find an extraordinary government policy of religious intolerance in the "War on Sects" (*la luttre contre les sects*). The New Age community of Horus was harassed by a state-sponsored anticult agency (UNADFI) and charged with "illegal practice of medicine." Marie-Therese Castano, the founder, was forced to dissolve the group in 1997 in the face of multiple state raids and criminal charges. Le Mandarom was the target of four raids by French gendarmerie between 1994 and 2001. Its leader was convicted of sexual abuse and imprisoned. The group's temples and statues were destroyed by the army. Its property has been tied up in litigation for several years and it faces steep fines that seriously jeopardize the future of the group. The Center for Teaching Biodynamism was raided in 2011 by the state agency tasked with monitoring sects (MIVILUDES).

Its founder, Sophie Berlamont, was charged with *abus de faiblesse* (abuse of weakness). She was ordered to stop practicing Biodynamics, to close down her business, and have no communication with her students. The *Cour de Cassation* later overturned the conviction but it was too late; the community had collapsed, her reputation was impugned, and the members had moved on. Finally, Amour et Misericorde, a small prayer group in the suburbs of Dijon, was raided in 2012 by local gendarmerie. It leader, Eliane Deschamps, and her secretary were charged with *abus de faiblesse aggrave* (aggravated abuse of weakness). In the face of organized opposition and state harassment, Deschamps officially dissolved Amour et Misericorde.

As historians and others have shown, some religions die through processes of cultural change, transmutation, organizational crisis, or conversion to a missionary religion (de Jong 2018; Robbins 2014). But in other cases, such has been outlined here, religions are weakened, diminished, or destroyed by the direct actions of the state. In examining the different ways in which religions die or dissolve, scholars need to be acutely aware of how states play a significant role in determining which religions succeed and which ones fail. It should be a concern to scholars and guardians of religious liberty alike that modern states have the power to pick winners and losers in the religious marketplace. We might expect to see this kind of social control in authoritarian regimes where the dominant religion or secular state ideology is a prop to support ruling elites. But the cases discussed in this chapter occurred in Western democratic countries with religious liberty guarantees and traditions. Indeed, all seven cases took place in either France or the United States. So in exploring religious demise, it is imperative to understand how democratic states may become harsh instruments of repression and even unwitting allies of partisan political interest groups seeking to restrict or discredit nontraditional religions.

References

Anthony, D. and T. Robbins (1992), "Law, Social Science, and the 'Brainwashing' Exception to the First Amendment," *Behavioral Sciences and the Law*, 10: 5–30.

Anthony, D. and T. Robbins (2004), "Pseudoscience versus Minority Religion: An Evaluation of the Brainwashing Theories of Jean-Marie Abgrall," in

J. T. Richardson (ed.), *Regulating Religion: Case Studies from around the Globe*, 127–49. New York: Kluwer.

Beckford, J. A. (2004), "Laicite, Dystopia, and the New Religious Movements in France," in J. T. Richardson (ed.), *Regulating Religion: Case Studies from around the Globe*, 27–40. New York: Kluwer.

Best, J. (1990), *Threatened Children: Rhetoric and Concern about Child-Victims*. Chicago, IL: University of Chicago Press.

Bradley, M. S. (1993), *Kidnapped from That Land: The Government Raids on the Short Creek Polygamists*. Salt Lake City: University of Utah Press.

Cookson, C. (2003), "Religious Freedom Issues Faced by Wiccans," in D. H. Davis and B. Hankins (eds.), *New Religious Movements and Religious Liberty in America*, 135–53. Waco, TX: Baylor University Press.

De Jong, A. (2018), "The Disintegration and Death of Religions," in M. Stausberg and S. Engler (eds.), *Oxford Handbooks Online*, 1–23. London: Oxford University Press.

Doherty, B. (2014), "Sensational Scientology! The Church of Scientology and Australian Tabloid Television," *Nova Religio*, 17 (3): 38–63.

Doherty, B. (2015), "Colonial Justice or Kangaroo Court?" *Alternative Spirituality and Religion Review*, 6 (1): 9–49.

Fautre, W. (2004), "Belgium's Anti-Sect Policy," in J. T. Richardson (ed.), *Regulating Religion: Case Studies from Around the Globe*, 113–25. New York: Kluwer.

Finke, R., D. R. Mataic, and J. Fox (2017), "Assessing the Impact of Religious Registration," *Journal for the Scientific Study of Religion*, 56 (4): 720–36.

Gordon, J. (1987), *The Golden Guru: The Strange Journey of Bhagwan Shree Rajneesh*, Lexington, MA: Stephen Greene Press.

Gregory, D. (1993), "Government Regulation of Religion through Labor and Employment Discrimination Laws," in J. Wood and D. Davis (eds.), *The Role of Government in Monitoring and Regulating Religion in Public* Life, 121–60. Waco, TX: J.M. Dawson Institute of Church-State Studies, Baylor University.

Grim, B. and R. Finke (2011), *The Price of Freedom Denied: Religious Persecution and Conflict in the Twenty-First Century*. New York: Cambridge University Press.

Introvigne, M. (2004), "Holy Mountains and Anti-Cult Ecology: The Campaign against the Aumist Religion in France," in J. T. Richardson (ed.), *Regulating Religion: Case Studies from Around the Globe*, 73–83. New York: Klewer.

Investigation into the Activities of Federal Law Enforcement toward the Branch Davidians. (1996), Thirteenth Report by the Committee on Government Reform and Oversight Prepared in Conjunction with the Committee on the Judiciary Together with Additional and Dissenting Views, August 2. Washington, DC: U. S. Government Printing Office.

Jenkins, P. (1998), *Moral Panic: Changing Concepts of the Child Molester in Modern America*. New York: Aldine de Gruyter.

Kirkham, D. M. (2013), *State Responses to Minority Religions*. Surrey: Ashgate.

Luca, N. (2004), "Is There a Unique French Policy of Cults? A European Perspective," in J. T. Richardson (ed.), *Regulating Religion: Case Studies from around the Globe*, 53–72. New York: Kluwer.

Ollion, E. (2013), "The French 'War on Cults' Revisited: Three Remarks on an Ongoing Controversy," in D. M. Kirkham (ed.), *State Responses to Minority Religions*, 121–36. London: Ashgate.

Palmer, S. J. (2010), *The Nuwaubian Nation: Black Spirituality and State Control*. Surrey: Ashgate.

Palmer, S. J. (2011a), *The New Heretics of France: Minority Religions, la Republique, and the Government-Sponsored "War on Sects."* New York: Oxford University Press.

Palmer, S. J. (2011b), "Rescuing Children? Government Raids and Child Abuse Allegations in Historical and Cross-Cultural Perspective," in S. A. Wright and J. T. Richardson (eds.), *Saints under Siege: The Texas State Raid on the Fundamentalist Latter Day Saints*, 51–79. New York: New York University Press.

Palmer, S. J. and C. E. Hardman (eds.) (1999), *Children in New Religions*. New Brunswick, NJ: Rutgers University Press.

Passas, N. (1994), "The Market for Gods and Services: Religion, Commerce, and Deviance," in A. L. Greil and T. Robbins (eds.), *Between Sacred and Secular: Research and Theory in Quasi-Religion*, 217–40. Greenwich, CT: JAI Press.

Richardson, J. T. (1985), "The Deformation of New Religions: Impacts of Societal and Organizational Factors," in T. Robbins, W. Shepherd, and J. McBride (eds.), *Cults, Culture, and the Law*, 163–75. Chico, CA: Scholars Press.

Richardson, J. T. (1988), *Money and Power in New Religions*, Lewiston, NY: Edwin Mellen.

Richardson, J. T. (1992), "Public Opinion and the Tax Evasion Trial of Reverend Moon," *Behavioral Sciences and the Law*, 10: 53–63.

Richardson, J. T. (1999), "Social Control of New Religions: From Brainwashing Claims to Child Sex Abuse Accusations," in S. J. Palmer and C. Hardman (eds.), *Children in New Religions*, 172–86. New Brunswick, NJ: Rutgers.

Richardson, J. T. and M. Introvigne (2007), "New Religious Movements, Countermovements, Moral Panics, and the Media," in D. G. Bromley (ed.), *Teaching New Religious Movements*, 91–114. New York: Oxford.

Robbins, J. (2014), "How Do Religions End? Theorizing Religious Traditions from the Point of View of How They Disappear," *Cambridge Anthropology*, 32 (2): 2–15.

Sarkissian, A. (2015), *The Varieties of Religious Repression: Why Governments Restrict Religion*. New York: Oxford University Press.

Schreinert, T. and J. T. Richardson (2011), "Pyrrhic Victory? An Analysis of the Appeal Court Opinions Concerning FLDS Children," in S. A. Wright and J. T. Richardson (eds.), *Saints under Siege: The Texas State Raid on the Fundamentalist Latter Day Saints*, 242–64. New York: New York University Press.

U. S. Department of Treasury (1993), Report of the Department of Treasury on the Bureau of Alcohol, Tobacco, and Firearms Investigation of Vernon Wayne Howell, Also Known as David Koresh. Washington, DC: U.S. Government Printing Office.

Wright, S. A. (ed.) (1995), *Armageddon in Waco: Critical Perspectives on the Branch Davidian Conflict*. Chicago, IL: University of Chicago Press.

Wright, S. A. (1999), "Anatomy of a Government Massacre: Abuses of Hostage-Barricade Protocols during the Waco Standoff," *Terrorism and Political Violence*, 11 (2): 39–68.

Wright, S. A. (2005), "Explaining Militarization at Waco: Construction and Convergence of a Warfare Narrative," in J. R. Lewis (ed.), *Controversial New Religions*, 75–97. New York: Oxford University Press.

Wright, S. A. (2009), "Revisiting the Branch Davidian Mass Suicide Debate." *Nova Religio*, 13 (2): 4–24.

Wright, S. A. and S. J. Palmer (2016), *Storming Zion: Government Raids on Religious Communities*. New York: Oxford University Press.

Wright, S. A. and S. J. Palmer (2018), "Countermovement Mobilization and State Raids on Minority Religious Communities," *Journal for the Scientific Study of Religion*, 57 (3): 616–33.

Wright, S. A. and J. T. Richardson (eds.) (2011), *Saints under Siege: The Texas State Raid on the Fundamentalist Latter Day Saints*. New York: New York University Press.

Wright, S. A. and J. T. Richardson (2014), "The Fundamentalist Latter Day Saints after the Texas State Raid: Assessing a Post-Raid Movement Trajectory," *Nova Religio*, 17 (4): 83–97.

10

Mass Suicides and Mass Homicides: Collective Violence and the Demise of New Religious Movements

Carole M. Cusack and James R. Lewis

With regard to processes of change which are indicative of decline, loss of membership or social and political influence, weakening or fragmentation, and final demise or extinction, in the study of new religious movements (NRMs) no agreed vocabulary has emerged to map the particular trajectories of specific groups or to craft a model that has application across either the "class" of NRMs as a whole, or of certain sub-classes (UFO religions, ephemeral "spiritual" clusters, or neo-Hindu guru focused groups, for example). The language used to describe such negative developments among all religions may be strong and definite (e.g., death, end, eradication) or more modest, as in the use of "demise" as a broad catch-all that can encompass everything from decisive, datable ends to attenuated trends and indicators that bode ill, but where no endgame has been reached (de Jong 2018). The difficulty in identifying unambiguous ends was noted by Bryan R. Wilson more than three decades ago; he linked the failure of new religions to endogenous issues (while acknowledging exogenous pressures might also contribute), and proposed ideology, leadership, organization, constituency, and institutionalization to be the crucial factors (Wilson 1987). The recognition that new religions do not come into existence *ex nihilo*, but rather were embedded in the culture(s) of the charismatic founder and the early convert community, and that NRMs drew upon existing religious and spiritual concepts and trends (Ashcraft 2018), renders beginnings and endings fluid and mixed, with ambiguity about all but the simplest types of origins and endings being the norm not the exception. The clearest case for "endings" in new religions appeared to be in acts of violence, including mass suicide and mass murder (Richardson 2001), upheavals sufficient to make it impossible for the group to continue. This chapter will examine four NRMs—Peoples Temple (1978); the Order of the Solar Temple (1994); Heaven's Gate (1997); and the Movement for the Restoration of the Ten Commandments of God (2000)—which met unambiguous ends in mass murder, mass suicide, or a combination of both.

Jonestown, Guyana: A Charismatic Leader, an Isolated Community, and the Birth of the "Violent Cult" Stereotype

Scholars of NRMs have traditionally opposed the popular journalistic image of the "violent cult." The popular view of a "cult" generally includes these clichéd elements: a charismatic male leader of questionable sanity who has total control over his followers, a control that includes predatory sexual behavior, monetary dominance, and provocation to deviance and crime; a group of unstable and socially marginal disciples who are disaffected and irrational; the isolation of members from family, friends, and mainstream society; and a doctrinal vision of the end times or the need for the current order to be destroyed, which pushes the group toward extreme violence (Laycock 2013). A survey of media coverage of "violent cults" demonstrates that the archetype for almost all popular accounts of NRMs and violence is the murder-suicides in 1978 at Jonestown in Guyana. This incident, in which 918 people died, effectively ended Peoples Temple, a Christian church founded by Reverend James Warren (Jim) Jones (1931–1978) and his wife Marceline Baldwin Jones (1927–1978) in Indianapolis in 1953 (Moore 2018).

In its early years Peoples Temple was focused on civil rights, racial integration, and Jones's charismatic preaching and faith healing. In 1965 Jim Jones moved the church to California, where counter-cultural values were more socially acceptable. It is important to understand that Jones and Peoples Temple were not seriously regarded as problematic or dangerous right up to the time of the murder-suicides. The young Jones had "left a Methodist pastorate when his congregation resisted the inclusion of blacks in their midst" (Hargrove 1989: 30). In the mid-1970s membership was between 5,000 and

7,000 people, and "in 1975, Jones received positive endorsements from San Francisco's mayor for humanitarian work. In 1977, he received the Martin Luther King Jr. Humanitarian Award" (McCloud 2007: 221). It is true that there were detractors: Hugh B. Urban notes that:

> the *San Francisco Examiner* published a series of articles attacking Jones's messianic pretensions and the authoritarian structure of the movement; and in 1977, *New West* magazine published an exposé suggesting that Peoples Temple should be investigated for financial misdealings, coercive practices, and questionable involvement in San Francisco politics.
>
> (Urban 2015: 253)

The events of 1978 reversed this positive image forever. A group of family members of some of Jones's followers, Concerned Relatives, had requested an enquiry into the church, and a United States Congressman, Leo Ryan, flew to Guyana to visit Jonestown, the commune that Peoples Temple had built. He and four companions were shot dead as they prepared to fly back to America; Ryan's visit caused some members to try to escape with him, which prompted the murders at the air-strip, and that functioned as the proximate cause for the mass deaths at Jonestown (Hall 1989), although Jones's failing health and increasing paranoia were long-term factors of importance (Lewis 2005: 310).

Eileen Barker has argued that the Peoples Temple mass death at Jonestown, Guyana on November 18, 1978, in which 909 died, all but two from poisoning (the aforementioned five murders and four further suicides complete the total of 918 deaths), triggered a "cult panic":

> In November 1978 nearly the whole of the Western world had the 'cult' problem brought starkly and vividly to its attention. US Congressman Leo Ryan was shot dead at a jungle airport following an investigative visit to Jonestown, a community in Guyana built by members of the People's Temple. A religious group founded in 1953, the People's Temple was led by an ordained minister of the Disciples of Christ, the Reverend Jim Jones. A few hours after the murder of Ryan and 4 of his companions, Jones and over 900 of his followers were dead. First, the babies had cyanide squirted down their throats by syringe, and then the older children, followed by the adults lined up to drink from cups of Kool-Aid laced with cyanide—it was a suicide

ritual that the community had rehearsed on several previous occasions. It was not certain, however, that all Jones' followers had been entirely willing to make this final gesture … Nearly 300 of the victims had not reached their seventeenth birthday; a further 200 were over 65.

(Barker 1986: 329–30)

Perhaps the most important thing about Jonestown is that the mass death event was both an instance of both religiously motivated suicide and mass murder. Over the years Jones had developed a rhetoric of martyrdom termed "revolutionary suicide," which he asserted was "preferable to being taken prisoner, becoming a slave, or returning to the United States" (Moore 2014: 84). In 1978, discussions of revolutionary suicide intensified, and Peoples Temple members went through frequent "White Night" drills and "rehearse(d) a ritual in which they drank what they were told was poison and waited to die" (Moore 2018: 6). That the final drill on November 18 was not an entirely voluntary suicide on the part of all is indicated by Barker, who drew attention to the fact that almost one-third of the group were under seventeen years of age and were thus (particularly in the case of babies and young children) incapable of giving informed consent (Barker 1986). It is a fact that parents gave poison (Flavor Aid laced with cyanide) to their children before drinking it themselves. Two hundred members of Peoples Temple were over sixty-five years old; Rebecca Moore, whose sisters Carolyn Layton and Annie Moore were involved in the planning of the event and died at Jonestown, considers it "likely that many senior citizens were also murdered" (Moore 2018: 7).

The events of Jonestown were originally reported as suicides and were immensely shocking. Jones was a Christian minister, so his drug addiction, sexual promiscuity, and the violent fate of his followers were scandalous, and media interest was intense (Krause 1978). As Jason S. Dikes notes that "until the September 11 2001 attacks, Jonestown represented the largest single mass death event of civilians in U.S. history" (Dikes 2019: 95). It is possible that the Jonestown event may not have resulted in the demise of Peoples Temple, given the remaining 4,000–6,000 members who were in America not Guyana. However, the loss of the charismatic leader, Jones, and of much of the church's leadership (including Jones's wife Marceline and lover and second-in-command, Carolyn Layton), was a grievous institutional blow. Furthermore, the negative publicity, which fueled the anticult movement and created a climate of anxiety and increased monitoring of "fringe" groups, proved fatal to Jones's church. Peoples Temple died unambiguously with its founder (Feltmate 2018; Hall 1989).

The Order of the Solar Temple

The Order of the Solar Temple (OST) was an esoteric group founded by Joseph Di Mambro (1924–1994) which ended in a series of murder-suicides between 1994 and 1997. Di Mambro joined several initiatory bodies in the 1950s and 1960s, and founded "the Center for the Preparation of the New Age in 1973" (Bogdan 2014: 57). This group came to public attention as a "violent cult" in 1994 when the fifty-three bodies of members (and a family of three murdered ex-members) were found by police in Switzerland and Canada (Introvigne 2006). Fifteen, the "Awakened," had willingly taken poison. A further thirty, the "Immortals," had been shot or smothered (perhaps unwillingly), and eight "traitors" were murdered (Bogdan 2014: 56).

In 1995, a further sixteen bodies were found near Grenoble in France, and on the 1997 spring equinox five members committed suicide in Canada. Henrik Bogdan says that "the violence of the Solar Temple led to the death of 77 individuals in Canada, France and Switzerland between September 30, 1994 and March 20, 1977" (Bogdan 2014: 56).

Di Mambro was a member of the Ancient and Mystic Order of the Rosy Cross (AMORC) from 1956 to 1969. After years as a seeker he began to lead groups. The Centre for the Preparation of the New Age and a commune, La Pyramide, morphed into the Golden Way Foundation in 1978 in Geneva (Lewis 2005: 301). He met Luc Jouret (1947–1994), a doctor and homeopath born in Zaire (formerly Belgian Congo), and by the 1980s "the Golden Way became ... the parent organization of the Atlanta, Amenta and later Archedia clubs and groups" (Introvigne 2006: 29) that Jouret had established as a popular lecturer on the New Age circuit. The Order of the Solar Temple was founded in 1984. Massimo Introvigne proposed Di Mambro and Jouret linked three ideas in the OST: (1) a looming ecological catastrophe; (2) the renewal of the world by the Ascended Masters of the Grand Lodge of Agartha; and (3) a final war of the type propagated "by survivalist groups both on the extreme right and the extreme left" (Introvigne 2006: 30). The crisis that precipitated the mass deaths seems to be the failing health of Di Mambro, which combined with the group experiencing persecution, an intense apocalyptic vision, and internal dissent (Bogdan 2014; Introvigne and Mayer 2002).

By the 1990s the younger and more charismatic Jouret had assumed an increasingly public role with the Order's members. James R. Lewis has argued that failing health in leaders is key in tipping groups toward suicide. He compared three cases—Peoples Temple, the Order of the Solar Temple, and Heaven's Gate—and developed a list of factors that made suicide a probability:

1. Absolute intolerance of dissenting views.
2. Members must be totally committed.
3. Exaggerated paranoia about external threats.
4. Leader isolates him/herself or the entire group from the non-believing world.
5. Leader's health is failing—in a major way, not just a transitory sickness; or, alternately, the leader believes he or she is dying.
6. There is no successor and no steps are being taken to provide a successor; or, alternately, succession plans have been frustrated.
7. The group is either stagnant or declining, with no realistic hopes for future expansion (Lewis 2005: 311).

In the case of the Solar Temple there is no doubt that Di Mambro had deliberately isolated himself from members, using Jouret as the direct means of communication, a situation he later came to regret and resent. Moreover, he had grandiose ideas about himself, asserting that he was "the reincarnation of Osiris, Akhnaton, Moses, and Cagliostro" (Wessinger cited in Lewis 2005: 302). His daughter Emmanuelle was groomed as the messiah of the new era, while his son Elie became a vocal critic of the Order from 1990, when he discovered the "special effects" that accompanied OST rituals were created by a technician, Tony Dutoit. The same year Rose-Marie Klaus, whose husband was a member of the OST, began speaking to the Quebec police and the anticult group Info-Secte (Hall and Schuyler 2006: 71). These problems resulted in at least fifteen members leaving the group.

Dutoit and his wife Nicki defied Di Mambro (who had banned them from having a child) and had a baby, Christopher Emmanuel, in 1994. His name was viewed by Di Mambro as an affront to his daughter Emmanuelle. The Dutoits, ex-members, were the first victims of the OST demise; three-month-old Christopher Emmanuel had a stake driven through his heart, as Di Mambro seemingly believed he was the Antichrist (Bogdan 2011: 134). Di Mambro's authority was such that the murder of an infant was not questioned by his followers. Di Mambro was the channel for communication with the Ascended Masters and demanded absolute obedience from members (Lewis 2005: 308). By 1994, Di Mambro was under pressure on three fronts: the Order was losing members; ex-members and critics assailed him, including the Dutoits and his own son Elie; and he was in failing health. He had diabetes, kidney failure, and was incontinent, and also believed he had cancer (Bogdan 2011: 140). This was a vital factor in the rapid and violent demise of the Order.

It is reasonable to say that the OST dissolved rapidly, despite an interval of thirty months between the first murder-suicides and the final suicides. The initial violent events involved fifty-six deaths (fifty-three members and the Dutoits) at two Swiss villages, Cheiry and Salvan, and in Morin-Heights, Quebec. Of these, eleven were clearly murdered (counting the Dutoit family), and fifteen "Awakened" unambiguously committed suicide (Bogdan 2014: 56). The thirty "Immortals" were assisted by the "Awakened," revealing a similar blurring of boundaries between suicide and murder that characterized Jonestown (Lewis 2005: 296). The remaining twenty-one deaths in France and Canada in 1995 and 1997 were suicides. Jouret and Di Mambro died with their partners and family members, which effectively ended the OST (Hall and Schuyler 2006: 81–2). The later suicides were members who wished to have made the "transit" in 1994 but were left to go it alone.

Heaven's Gate: Voluntary Mass Suicide and the End of a UFO Religion

The suicide of thirty-nine members of Heaven's Gate, a UFO religion founded by Marshall Herff Applewhite (1931–1997) and Bonnie Lu Nettles (1927–1985), is usually understood to have ended this NRM (Balch and Taylor 1999). The bodies were discovered on Wednesday, March 26, 1997 in a large rented house in Rancho Santa Fe, San Diego County, California (Lewis 2003: 123). Two ex-members who left in 1987, Mark and Sarah King (Mrcody and Srfody),[1] told Benjamin E. Zeller that suicide was not part of the plan until after the death of Nettles (Zeller 2014: 123). Suicide was discussed by Applewhite in the context of Jesus's death (members believed Applewhite was the second coming of Christ), and ex-member Rio di Angelo (Neoody) was tasked with alerting the authorities. The suicide strategy was not coercive, and members left the group during the time when Applewhite began to teach it and the actual suicide date, which coincided with the visibility of the Hale-Bopp comet and the Christian festival of Holy Week (Urban 2011: 117). Zeller notes that the Heaven's Gate suicides are unusual in a number of ways:

> Unlike the members of the Peoples Temple living in Jonestown, Guyana, who committed mass suicide and murder in 1978, no network of hostile outsiders sought to take down the group. Nor did government forces raid the home of Heaven's Gate, nor did its leaders face any sort of criminal or civil charges, as happened in the cases of the Branch Davidians and Christian survivalists at Ruby Ridge, Idaho. In each of those examples, outside forces combined with inside ones to lead to violence and death among members of a new religious movement. This leads to a curious point: in most cases of millennial violence, something or someone instigated the final violent end of the group. This is precisely what appeared *not* to have happened in the case of Heaven's Gate, which makes it all the more surprising that thirty-nine people— plus more later—chose to end their lives.
>
> (Zeller 2014: 172)

Robert W. Balch and David Taylor (1999: 209–10) argue that the suicides were religious acts and members died willingly, but that they did not understand their actions to be suicides, but rather the opposite. The teachings of Heaven's Gate were "opposed to suicide *per se*, but redefined it as turning 'against the Next level when it is being offered', claiming that ... bodies were mere 'vessels' and 'vehicles', so that the destruction of these containers was an action of little importance" (Cusack 2014: 92).

Heaven's Gate began in 1972 when Nettles and Applewhite met in a psychiatric hospital in Houston; she was working as a nurse and he was receiving treatment for his homosexual desires. They recognized each other as spiritual partners and in 1973 Applewhite realized they were the two witnesses from *Revelation*, ushering in a new era of teaching involving public meetings in which "the Two" (known as "Bo and Peep," "Guinea and Pig," and "Ti and Do") taught a *mélange* of Christianity and UFOlogy (Chryssides 2005: 356–7). Their followers were urged to give up human life and focus on the "Level above the Human." To this end they were assigned a partner, forbidden to have sex, drink alcohol or take drugs, refused contact with family or friends (Balch and Taylor 2011 [1977]), banned from watching television, wearing jewelry and having beards, and were required to take a name in religion. This period ended in "February 1976 [and] resulted in mass apostasy, and the organization lost approximately half its members" (Chryssides 2005: 357). Nettles's death in 1985 from cancer was a sign for Applewhite, who interpreted her passing as a return to the Next Level, demonstrating that this could be achieved even if the human body died, and that she awaited him and the "class" (Balch and Taylor 1999: 217–19). In the 1990s the group exhibited renewed vigor: seven males including Applewhite underwent castration to overcome sexual desires; ex-members were invited to return; and Applewhite's message that the earth would be "spaded over" became more apocalyptic with every communication. It is important too that Applewhite by 1994 was seriously ill with cancer (Lewis 2003: 129). When news of the Hale-Bopp comet became available in November 1996, the group prepared to exit this world (Chryssides 2005: 358).

Preparations intensified in Holy Week 1997, when thirty-five of the thirty-nine members recorded farewell videos, in which they explained how meaningful their actions were and expressed regret that family members would not understand (Zeller 2014: 90–1). Glnody and Srrody prepared "Earth Exit Statements," and a press release was drafted on March 22, 1997. The videos and computer files were mailed to ex-members who were on good terms with Applewhite. This resulted in "Mrcody and Srfody—whom Applewhite had charged to operate the group's TELAH Foundation and website—Rkkody, Neoody, and other ex-members … [uploading the videos and files], creating a post-mortem Internet existence for Heaven's Gate that continues to exist" (Zeller 2014: 216). The suicides were reported in the press in sensational terms, emphasizing the identical new Nike shoes, black uniforms, purple shrouds, "Away Team" patches (referencing the science fiction series *Star Trek*), bags beside each bed, and small change and five-dollar bills in members' pockets (Zeller 2014: 1). Twenty-one women and eighteen men aged from twenty-six to seventy-two died in three groups of fifteen, fifteen, and nine over three days, between March 22 and March 26. Ex-members Rkkody (Chuck Humphrey), Jstody (Wayne Cooke), and Gbbody (Jimmy Simpson) committed suicide in the first year after the group suicides, but Neoody, Mrcody and Srfody, Crlody and Swyody continue to draw upon the group's beliefs and to debate and memorialize Heaven's Gate (Zeller 2014: 62).

Thus, Heaven's Gate ended in voluntary suicide, but the digital archives make it possible for interested parties to learn much about the religion and to keep its ideas alive. Heaven's Gate's website is maintained by ex-members and hosts an abundance of teaching materials. Online archives make the unfamiliar (and usually unpopular) beliefs and practices of a fringe group accessible to a far-larger audience than Heaven's Gate reached during its active years. The reduction of lived reality to texts is an issue in the academic study of religion that often focuses how the "ideal" text fails to comprehend the "religion of the everyday," but in the case of defunct groups, it may prove a surprisingly productive and valuable approach.

The Movement for the Restoration of the Ten Commandments of God: Mass Murder Disguised as Suicide?

The Movement for the Restoration of the Ten Commandments of God (MRTCG) was an apocalyptic group founded in Nigeria in the late 1980s by Credonia Mwerinde (b. 1952) and Joseph Kibweteere (b. 1932), among others. The Virgin Mary allegedly appeared to protest the lack of obedience to the Ten Commandments and over the next nine years "instructed her [Mwerinde] to take the Virgin's message to the world" (Walliss 2005: 52). In early 1989, Mwerinde's visions were reinforced by those of her sister Angela Migisha (b. 1947), and in June of that year by messages received by Migisha's daughter Ursula Komuhangi (b. 1968). From this point onwards, Mwerinde attracted hundreds of followers. However, by 1992, there were family tensions that led one of Kibwetere's sons to attempt to separate the Movement from his family properly.

The group, now approximately 200 members, moved to land near Kanungu, where they established the *Ishayuuriro rya Maria* ("Rescue Place for the Virgin Mary"). In this group home members refrained from sex, worked hard, and adhered to a severe routine of prayer and fasting. John Wallis sensibly insists that critics labeling the MRTCG a "cult" are incorrect; throughout its existence it was always a Catholic sectarian organization (Walliss 2005: 53). The group was ruthlessly hierarchical, with neophytes wearing black, "those who had seen the commandments" wearing green, and "those who were ready to die in the ark" wearing green and white (Walliss 2005: 54). Mwerinde and the leadership taught an eschatological doctrine that preached natural disasters, famine, civil disorder, unnatural births, demonic possession, and other signs characterizing the Period of Chastisement (Walliss 2014: 115). At the end of this time of tribulation, they proclaimed, there will be a new heaven and a new earth, and a quarter of the earth's populace will survive to see the new world. Uganda will be the "new Israel" and will "in turn convert all over nations" (Walliss 2014: 115).

The period of violence within the MRTCG which led to the fiery conflagration in which an unknown number of members perished is poorly documented. However, Mwerinde had a vision of the Virgin who informed her that "the world would end on March 17" (Walliss 2014: 117). Various complaints and requests from members regarding the return of their donations indicated a level of dissatisfaction with the group's leadership. John Walliss posits that at this point "the MRTCG leaders then began to plan for a collective suicide of the faithful" (Walliss 2014: 117). He argues that the failed prophecy that the world would end on December 31, 1999 (which he notes was announced as a means to get further monies from members) resulted in the leadership "murdering hundreds of dissidents, burying their bodies in the mass graves subsequently discovered by the police" (Walliss 2005: 56). On March 17, approximately 340 members were lured to the church in Kanungu, around 350 kilometers south of Kampala, where they died when the church was sealed and set on fire. On March 15, they had a feast of bull meat and soft drink "to celebrate the building of their new church" (Venter 2006: 155). They prayed through the night of 16 March and met in the new church on 17 March. Just before 10 AM the faithful went into the old church (which was boarded up) and the doors were locked. At 10.30 "an explosion was heard and a fire quickly consumed the building and all those inside" (Venter 2006: 156).

In addition to those in the church, the Ugandan police discovered many other bodies, and the total of the victims is usually given as 780 (Mayer 2001: 204). Jean-Francois Mayer has noted the pronounced Marian apocalypticism of the MRTCG and that Mwerinde's communications with members in

2000 stated that "we will soon be going to heaven, and you will be hearing about us on radio and reading about us in newspapers" (quoted in Mayer 2001: 208). The fact remains that the MRTCG was experiencing pressure from the Ugandan Catholic church. The membership was expecting an eschatological event (which caused them to sell their possessions cheaply, settle debts, and make preparations for departure), and the leadership engineered a massacre (with elements of suicide, perhaps, as followers expected to leave this world, though not to be burned to death) (Walliss 2005: 62).

It remains to state that other interpretations of the crisis that enveloped the MRTCG exist, and by late April 2000 the Ugandan police had issued warrants for the arrest of the group's six leaders (Associated Press 2000). It is assumed that Mwerinde, Kibwetere, the Catholic priest Dominic Kataribabo, Joseph Kasapurari, John Kamagara, and Ursula Komuhangi all escaped from Uganda over poorly defended borders, and that they absconded with the MRTCG funds. Yet there are disagreements over the correct interpretation of the MRTCG demise: P. M. Venter (2006: 160) believes the leaders died in the fire, and Richard Vokes argues that the mass graves contained those who died during a 1998 malaria plague and not murder victims, and further that the suicides were voluntary in the main (cited in Walliss 2014: 123). One fact remains; the act of violence on March 17, 2000, brought the Movement for the Restoration of the Ten Commandments of God to an end.

Conclusion

This chapter has considered four case studies in which a decisive act of violence (mass murder, mass suicide, or a combination of both) brought about the end of a new religious movement. Jonestown in 1978 undoubtedly provided the template for the popular image of controlling "cults" and predatory, irrational "charismatic leaders"; the mass death event that killed over 900 members of Peoples Temple remains the largest such incident more than forty years on (Dikes 2019). Both suicide and murder were in evidence at Jonestown, as in the case of the Order of the Solar Temple in 1994 (Bogdan 2011). The mass death event of the Movement for the Restoration of the Ten Commandments of God in 2000 is ambiguous; some scholars suggest that the group was prepared for suicide by eschatological messages that they would soon leave this world (Walliss 2014), whereas others view it as a mass murder planned by the leadership group, who survived the event and absconded with the funds. Heaven's Gate in 1997 emerges as the only likely case where suicide was clearly voluntary and undertaken by all members in a cooperative and consensual manner (Zeller 2014).

All four of these groups were largely motivated by endogenous factors (Wilson 1987), though all except Heaven's Gate had experienced some negative publicity and external social pressure. In explaining the motivations that tip groups toward suicide, Lewis's ideas about the authority wielded by the charismatic leader, and the disastrous effects of his/her physical decline or fatal illness (Lewis 2005) have proved useful as a refinement of Gordon Melton's contention that the death of a charismatic leader is the most traumatic event in the life cycle of a new religion (Melton 1991). It remains to note that two other groups are usually included in the religions that have potentially ended in extreme violence: the Branch Davidians at Waco in 1993 (Wessinger 2018) and Aum Shinrikyo's sarin gas attacks in Tokyo in 1995 (Repp 2005). Both were omitted from this chapter because the Branch Davidians' end was caused by external government actions, and the Aum attacks were not directed toward its membership, but toward random people on the subway. In terms of the demise of new religions, there is also a small remnant of Branch Davidans that still exist despite the destruction of the Mount Carmel property,[2] and there are questions as to whether Aum Shinrikyo ever ended (Baffelli 2020). The four groups discussed in this chapter definitely engaged with suicide as a potential eschatological act: the violence they enacted was directed toward the membership itself; the teachings of a powerful leader reified and elaborated on the benefits of leaving this world; and a group of dedicated followers were willing to follow. That some of these followers possibly changed their minds, or had to be "assisted" to die, blurs the trajectory toward suicide with murder in all cases apart from Heaven's Gate.

Notes

1   The suffix "ody" was understood by Heaven's Gate members to mean "child of the Next Level."

2   Charles Pace leads a group that lays claim to the Branch Davidian name, but none of the survivors from the Koresh-led group are affiliated with Pace, nor do they recognize his group as legitimate.

References

Ashcraft, W. M. (2018), *A Historical Introduction to the Study of New Religious Movements*. London and New York: Routledge.

Associated Press (2000) "Uganda Issues Warrants for 6 Cult Leaders," *Deseret News*, April 6. Available online: https://www.deseret.com/2000/4/6/19556601/uganda-issues-warrants-for-6-cult-leaders (accessed March 3, 2020).

Baffelli, E. (this volume), "Did Aum Shinrikyō Really End?," pp. 49–66.

Balch, R. W. and D. Taylor (1999), "Making Sense of the Heaven's Gate Suicides," in D. G. Bromley and J. G. Melton (eds.), *Cults, Religion and Violence*, 209–28. New York: Cambridge University Press.

Balch, R. W. and D. Taylor (2011 [1977]), "Seekers and Saucers: The Role of the Cultic Milieu in Joining a UFO Cult," in G. D. Chryssides (ed.), *Heaven's Gate: Postmodernity and Popular Culture in a Suicide Group*, 37–52. Farnham and Burlington, VT: Ashgate.

Barker, E. (1986), "Religious Movements: Cult and Anti-Cult since Jonestown," *Annual Review of Sociology*, 12 (1): 329–46.

Bogdan, H. (2011), "Explaining the Murder-Suicides of the Order of the Solar Temple: A Survey of Hypotheses," in J. R. Lewis (ed.), *Violence and New Religious Movements*, 133–45. Oxford and New York: Oxford University Press.

Bogdan, H. (2014), "Purification, Illumination, and Death: The Murder-Suicides of the Order of the Solar Temple," in J. R. Lewis and C. M. Cusack (eds.), *Sacred Suicide*, 55–71. Farnham and Burlington, VT: Ashgate.

Chryssides, G. D. (2005), "'Come On Up, and I Will Show Thee': Heaven's Gate as a Postmodern Group," in J. R. Lewis and J. A. Petersen (eds.), *Controversial New Religions*, 353–70. Oxford and New York: Oxford University Press.

Cusack, C. M. (2014), "Individual Suicide and the End of the World: Destruction and Transformation in UFO and Alien-Based Religions," in J. R. Lewis and C. M. Cusack (eds.), *Sacred Suicide*, 91–108. Farnham and Burlington, VT: Ashgate.

De Jong, A. (2018), "The Disintegration and Death of Religions," in M. Stausberg and S. Engler (eds.), *The Oxford Handbook of the Study of Religion*, 1–23. New York: Oxford University Press.

Dikes, J. S. (2019), "Media Review: Jonestown Documentaries on the Fortieth Anniversary," *Nova Religio: The Journal of Alternative and Emergent Religions*, 23 (2): 94–104.

Feltmate, D. (2018), "Peoples Temple: A Lost Legacy for the Current Moment," *Nova Religio: The Journal of Alternative and Emergent Religions*, 22 (2): 115–36.
Hall, J. R. (1989), *Gone from the Promised Land: Jonestown in American Cultural History*. London: Transaction.
Hall, J. R. and P. Schuyler (2006), "The Mystical Apocalypse of the Solar Temple," in J. R. Lewis (ed.), *The Order of the Solar Temple: The Temple of Death*, 55–89. Aldershot and Burlington, VT: Ashgate.
Hargrove, B. J. W. (1989), "Jonestown and the Scientific Study of Religion," in R. Moore and F. McGehee III (eds.), *New Religious Movements, Mass Suicide, and Peoples Temple*, 23–40. Lewiston, Lampeter, and Queenstown: The Edwin Mellen Press.
Introvigne, M. (2006), "Ordeal by Fire: The Tragedy of the Solar Temple," in J. R. Lewis (ed.), *The Order of the Solar Temple: The Temple of Death*, 19–38. Aldershot and Burlington, VT: Ashgate.
Introvigne, M. and J.-F. Mayer (2002), "Occult Masters and the Temple of Doom: The Fiery End of the Solar Temple," in D. G. Bromley and J. G. Melton (eds.), *Cults, Religions and Violence*, 170–88. New York: Cambridge University Press.
Krause, C. A. (1978) "Survivor: 'They Started with the Babies,'" *The Washington Post*, November 21. Available online: https://www.washingtonpost.com/archive/politics/1978/11/21/survivor-they-started-with-the-babies/ec559372-be60-4355-a5fc-f5e306370992/ (accessed March 3, 2020).
Laycock, J. (2013), "Where Do They Get These Ideas? Changing Ideas of Cults in the Mirror of Popular Culture," *Journal of the American Academy of Religion*, 81 (1): 80–106.
Lewis, J. R. (2003), *Legitimating New Religions*. New Brunswick, NJ and London: Rutgers University Press.
Lewis, J. R. (2005), "The Solar Temple 'Transits': Beyond the Millennialist Hypothesis," in J. R. Lewis and J. A. Petersen (eds.), *Controversial New Religions*, 295–318. Oxford and New York: Oxford University Press.
Mayer, J.-F. (2001), "Field Notes: The Movement for the Restoration of the Ten Commandments of God," *Nova Religio: The Journal of Alternative and Emergent Religions*, 5 (1): 203–10.
McCloud, S. (2007), "From Exotics to Brainwashers: Portraying New Religions in Mass Media," *Religion Compass*, 1 (1): 214–28.
Melton, J. G. (1991), "Introduction. When Prophets Die: The Succession Crisis in New Religions," in T. Miller (ed.), *When Prophets Die: The Postcharismatic Fate of New Religious Movements*, 1–12. Albany, NY: State University of New York Press.
Moore, R. (2014), "Rhetoric, Revolution, and Resistance in Jonestown, Guyana," in J. R. Lewis and C. M. Cusack (eds.), *Sacred Suicide*, 73–90. Farnham and Burlington, VT: Ashgate.

Moore, R. (2018), "Jonestown, Forty Years On," *Nova Religio: The Journal of Alternative and Emergent Religions*, 22 (2): 3–14.
Repp, M. (2005), "Aum Shinrikyo and the Aum Incident: A Critical Introduction," in J. R. Lewis and J. A. Petersen (eds.), *Controversial New Religious Movements*, 153–94. Oxford and New York: Oxford University Press.
Richardson, J. T. (2001), "Minority Religions and the Context of Violence," *Terrorism and Political Violence*, 13 (1): 103–33.
Urban, H. B. (2011), "The Devil at Heaven's Gate: Rethinking the Study of Religion in the Age of Cyberspace," in G. D. Chryssides (ed.), *Heaven's Gate: Postmodernity and Popular Culture in a Suicide Group*, 105–38. Farnham and Burlington, VT: Ashgate.
Urban, H. B. (2015), *New Age, Neopagan, and New Religious Movements: Alternative Spirituality in Contemporary America*. Oaklad, CA: University of California Press.
Venter, P. W. (2006), "Doomsday Movements in Africa: Restoration of the Ten Commandments of God," *Theological Studies*, 62 (1): 155–73.
Walliss, J. (2005), "Making Sense of the Movement for the Restoration of the Ten Commandments of God," *Nova Religio: The Journal of Alternative and Emergent Religions*, 9 (1): 49–66.
Walliss, J. (2014), "Apocalypse in Uganda: The Movement for the Restoration of the Ten Commandments of God," in J. R. Lewis and C. M. Cusack (eds.), *Sacred Suicide*, 109–27. Farnham and Burlington, VT: Ashgate.
Wessinger, C. (2018), "Collective Martyrdom and Religious Suicide: The Branch Davidians and Heaven's Gate," in M. Kitts (ed.), *Martyrdom, Self-Sacrifice and Self Immolation: Religious Perspectives on Suicide*, 54–84. Oxford ad New York: Oxford University Press.
Wilson, B. R. (1987), "Factors in the Failure of the New Religious Movements," in D. G. Bromley and P. E. Hammond (eds.), *The Future of New Religious Movements*, 30–45. Macon, GA: Mercer University Press.
Zeller, B. E. (2014), *Heaven's Gate: America's UFO Religion*. New York and London: New York University Press.

Index

abuse 9, 19, 72, 76–9, 105, 110–11, 121–32, 157, 161–2. *See also* violence
   of children 9, 104, 109–11, 115 n. 31, 158, 162, 166
   sexual 9–10, 23, 67, 71, 104, 109–11, 120, 127, 162–3, 166, 169
   spiritual 121, 128–32
   of weakness (*abus de faiblesse*) 157, 167–8, 170
African American 162. *See also* nationalism, black
Agonshū 52
Aleph 23, 50, 54–6, 59, 61 n. 8
America. *See* United States
Amerindian 162
Amour et Misericorde 158, 168–70
Amsterdam, Peter 105, 108
Ancient and Mystic Order of the Rosy Cross (AMORC) 179
Ancient Egypt 21, 162, 164
Anglicanism 8, 94. *See also* Church of England
Ansaaru Allah Community 17
Antichrist 181
anti-authoritarianism 137
anti-cultists 8, 23, 53, 76, 102–3, 157–9, 165, 167, 169, 178, 180
anti-religion 6, 147, 149
anti-sorcery 39–40, 45
apocalypticism 19, 20–1, 97 n. 13, 103–4, 107–8, 148, 162, 180, 182–5. *See also* endtimes
Applewhite, Marshall Herff 181–3
arrest 17, 22, 49, 51, 56, 61 n. 6, 150–1, 155–6, 159–60, 163, 165–9, 186. *See also* police; raid
Ascended Masters 179, 181
asceticism 49, 54, 57–9, 137, 139. *See also* renunciants
ashram 139–40, 142, 151, 166
ATF (United States Bureau of Alcohol, Tobacco and Firearms) 159–60, 162

atheism 138
Aum Shinrikyō 7–8, 17, 22–3, 25, 27, 49–60, 61 n. 6, 62 n. 10–11, 166, 187
Austin, J. L. 43–4
Australia 24, 32, 157
authoritarianism 121, 123, 155, 170, 177

Bainbridge, William Sims 13, 22, 57, 108
bigotry 143
birth control 107
Bahai 5
baptism 99, 101, 148
Baptist 32–3, 99–101
Barker, Eileen 9, 89–90, 96, 104, 107–8, 177–8
Barltrop, Mabel. *See* Octavia
Bedford 83, 89–90, 92
Bellah, Robert 91
Berg, David Moses 103–7, 113
Berger, Peter 13
Berlamont, Sophie 167–8, 170
Bible 4, 33, 103–4, 107–8, 123, 127–9
   of Rajneesh 147–8, 150–1
   School 69–70
bible-belt 162
Biodynamics 24, 158, 167–70
blog 113, 121–2, 124–7, 131
Böhme, Jacob 94
Bombay 137–8, 140, 149. *See also* India
Bourdin, Gilbert 166
brainwashing 23, 76, 157
Branch Davidians 60, 158–61, 169, 182, 187, 188 n. 2
Bride of Christ 70, 72, 77, 79–80
Buddha 5, 136, 140, 151, 153, 166. *See also* Buddhism
Buddhism 3, 7, 49, 52, 55, 135–6. *See also* Buddha; Zen
Bugbrooke Baptist Church 99–100
bullying 110, 119

California 9, 17, 20, 99, 103, 176, 181
Canada 179, 181
capitalism 137
Castano, Marie-Therese 164–5, 169
castration 183
Cathars 25
Catholicism 18, 23, 110–11, 168, 185–6
celebrity 9, 15, 22, 51, 102, 109, 121–2, 124, 132
celibacy 2, 102, 183–4. *See also* asceticism
Center for Teaching Biodynamism. *See* Biodynamics
charismatic leader 8, 20, 52, 68–9, 75, 77–80, 86, 92, 99, 105, 121, 123, 132, 175–6, 178, 180, 186–7
charismatic movement 33, 39, 100–1
charity 84, 93, 95–8, 101, 113, 140–1, 143
charlatan. *See* fraud
Charter, The 105, 109
Chiho Shōkō 51. *See also* Pana-Wave Laboratory
children 9, 17–18, 34, 39, 41, 68–9, 71, 83, 90, 100, 104, 106–7, 109–10, 113, 114 n. 20, 115 n. 31, 125, 129–30, 143, 158–64, 169, 177–8. *See also* abuse, children
Children of God (CoG) 9, 99, 103–8, 111–12
China 6, 155
Christ the Saviour Brotherhood 23
Christian Science 15, 94
Christianity 3–4, 6–7, 9, 21–2, 25, 32–5, 37–9, 41–2, 45, 69, 94, 99–100, 102, 104, 106–8, 112–3, 114 n. 17, 120, 122, 125, 130–2, 139, 143, 145, 176, 178, 182–3
Church of England 83, 94. *See also* Anglicanism
Church of Latter-day Saints (Mormonism) 5, 158, 163. *See also* Fundamentalist Latter Day Saints
Churches' Child Protection Advisory Service 110
Circle of Rainbow Light. *See* Hikari No Wa
clergy 3, 8–10, 25, 41–2, 67–80, 99, 119–32, 138, 144–5, 148–51, 176, 186. *See also* high priestess; nun
clothing 103–4, 142, 149, 183
cognitive disconfirmation 7, 19, 26

cognitive dissonance 20, 74
colonialism 6, 32, 35
communal living 9, 17, 55–6, 58–9, 84, 100, 102–3, 105–6, 108, 141, 156, 168
commune 10, 49, 96, 108, 140–3, 145–7, 149–52, 177, 179
confession 88–9, 121–2, 124, 132
conversion 5–6, 22, 32–4, 39, 92, 106, 108, 158, 170
converts 33, 90, 96 n. 12, 100–1, 103, 107–8, 124, 175, 185
counter-culture 176. *See also* hippies
court case 8, 24, 53, 57, 61, 67, 69, 74, 76, 104–5, 109–11, 120, 145–8, 150–1, 156, 163–6, 168
cult 22–4, 34, 104, 110, 135, 141, 143, 155–8, 162, 168, 176–7, 179, 185–6. *See also* anti-cultists

darshan 140
De Jong, Albert ix, 46, 50, 91–2, 95–6, 170, 175
death 1–4, 8, 10, 15, 17, 19, 38, 47, 51–4, 61 n. 1, 67, 70, 72, 84–96, 99, 102, 115 n. 31, 144–5, 147, 150, 152, 161, 175, 177–87. *See also* murder; suicide
democracy 6, 10, 155, 158, 164, 169
deprogramming 103–4
Deschamps, Eliane 168–70
Devil, The 70, 162
Di Mambro, Joseph 179–81
disaffection 53, 176
disaffiliation 7, 13–14, 53, 55
Divine Mother 88
dream 70
dress. *See* clothing
Driscoll, Mark 119–32
drug use 17, 100–1, 113, 123, 178, 183

Ellwood, Robert 94
endtimes, the. *See* eschatology
England 4, 8–9, 83, 94, 104
eschatology 11, 14, 103, 107–8, 176, 185–7. *See also* apocalypticism; heaven; hell; reincarnation
esotericism 8, 23, 94, 157, 164–5, 179
Ethiopia 119

Evangelical Alliance 100–1
evangelical Christianity 33, 69, 99–101, 103, 112, 119–32
evil 39, 41, 49, 69, 72–3, 79, 138, 162
ex-members 8–9, 50, 53–4, 57–63, 67–9, 75–7, 100, 102, 109–11, 113, 119, 121–2, 125–6, 131–2, 157, 163, 168, 179, 181–4
execution 49, 54, 56, 58, 60–1

Facebook 106, 119, 124, 130–1
FBI (Federal Bureau of Investigation) 159–62
femininity 127–9
Festinger, Leon 20, 78
Findhorn 165
Finnegan, Ruth 44
Flirty Fishing 104, 109
Fontaine, Maria 105
Fossmo, Helge 67, 69–70, 77–80
Foundation Faith of God 22
Foundation Faith of the Millennium 22
France 6, 10, 24–5, 156, 158, 164–70, 179, 181
fraud 19, 120, 143, 149. *See also* tax, fraud
medical 157, 165, 169
Freud, Sigmund 137
Fundamentalist Latter Day Saints (FLDS) 163–4

genocide 25, 92, 158
Georgia 161–2
Germany 3, 6, 123, 149
God 20, 33–4, 36–9, 41–2, 46, 67, 69, 70, 73, 74, 79, 84, 102–3, 111–12, 122, 124–5, 127, 129–30, 136–40, 142, 145–6, 148, 150–1. *See also* Buddha; Jesus Christ
goddess 96 n. 10. *See also* Virgin Mary
gods 22, 140
Golden Way Foundation 179
Goodwin, Emily 84–9, 92–3
government intervention 6, 23–5, 32, 35, 60, 117, 145–7, 151, 155–70, 182, 187. *See also* ATF; FBI; raids; police
guru 10, 136–7, 139, 142, 165, 175
Guyana. *See* Jonestown
Guyard List 156, 165–6

Hale-Bopp comet 182–3
Hanegraaff, Wouter 94
healing 20, 31, 41–2, 45, 84–6, 90–2, 96–7, 125, 132, 165, 176
heaven 20, 35, 84, 123, 185–6
Heaven's Gate 18, 20, 176, 180–4, 187
hell 59, 126
high priestess 10, 149–50. *See also* clergy
Hikari No Wa 23, 50, 54–9
Hinduism 135–40, 166
neo- 175
hippies 100, 103
HIV 106
Holy Order of MANS (HOOM) 22–3
Holy Order of Sophia 23
Holy Week 182–3
homelessness 101, 106
homicide. *See* murder
homosexuality 182
Horus 24, 158, 164–5, 169

immigration 10, 142, 150, 156
immortality 73, 84
Immortals 179, 181
imprisonment 25, 166, 169, 178
India 2, 119, 135–40, 146, 151. *See also* Bombay; Pune
indigenous culture 1–2, 6, 25, 32. *See also* Lakota; Native American; Sioux
Info-Secte 180
Institute of Applied Physics 20
institutional facts 22, 42–6
International Center for Parapsychology and Scientific Research of the New Age. *See* Horus
ISIS 6, 25
Islam 7, 25, 162
Israel 24
new 185

Jainism 136
Jamaica 90
Japan 3, 7, 15, 24, 50–1, 53–5, 60, 61 n. 1, 61 n. 3, 61 n. 6, 62 n. 10.
Jeffs, Warren 163
Jehovah's Witnesses 15, 21
Jesus Army. *See* Jesus Fellowship
Jesus Christ 4, 41–2, 70–80, 83–4, 88, 99, 101–4, 106–8, 124–6, 130, 140, 143, 145, 166, 182

return of 35, 70–1, 73–4, 75–6, 84, 88, 104, 107–8, 182
Jesus Fellowship (JF) 9, 99–103, 106–7, 109–13
Jesus Fellowship Survivors Association 111
Jews 6
Jiu 51, 60
Jones, James (Jim) Warren 18–19, 60, 176–9
Jonestown 19, 60, 104, 142, 148, 176–8, 181–2, 186
Jouret, Luc 179–81
Judaism. *See* Jews

Kehrer, Günter 91, 94
Kerista 16
Kibweteere, Joseph 19, 184, 186
Knutby Filadelfia 8, 17, 67, 69–71, 74–7, 79–80
Kōfuku no Kagaku 52
Koresh, David 60, 159–60, 188

La Fontaine, Jean 44
Lakota 25
language 5, 7–8, 14, 32, 57, 60, 92, 96, 122, 130, 139–40, 152, 175
  extinction 1–2, 4
law of love 104
lawsuit. *See* court case
Lead, Jane 94
Lear, Jonathan 43
legal trial. *See* court case
Lewis, James R. 11, 23, 104
linen 84, 96
"litnessing" 104
London 101, 115 n. 31, 139
Love Israel Family 17

magic 34, 36–7, 39, 42, 45. *See also* sorcery
  hunting 36–7, 39
Mandarom 158, 165–7
manipulation 76–7, 129, 157
marketing 119, 122, 124, 128
marriage 71, 74, 78–80, 102, 107, 109, 127–9, 131–2, 144, 163. *See also* polygamy
Martin, David 93
martyrdom 178
masculinity 36, 127–9

massacre 19, 25, 186
Matsumoto Chizuo. *See* Shōkō, Asahara
medical
  assistance 94, 101, 106, 143, 163–5, 167, *see also* psychiatric care
  evidence 162, *see also* fraud, medical
meditation 137, 139, 141, 144
megachurch 9, 119, 123, 125, 132
Melton, J. Gordon 17, 75, 85–6, 92, 187
messiah 83, 140, 177, 180
Methodism 176
millennialism. *See* apocalypticism
millenarianism. *See* apocalypticism
millennium 70, 182
missionary activity 6, 9, 17, 22, 24, 32–3, 104, 158, 170
Mitsu, Shimamura 51
modernization 6, 13, 93
Mount Carmel 159–61, 187
Movement for the Restoration of the Ten Commandments of God 18–20, 176, 184, 186
murder 6–8, 11, 18–19, 25, 41, 55, 57–8, 67, 70, 75, 79, 80 n. 3, 96, 110, 129, 149, 156, 160–1, 175–9, 181–2, 184–7. *See also* genocide; suicide
Mwerinde, Credonia 19, 184

Nation of Islam 162
nationalism 6, 122
  Black 161–2
  hyper- 123
Native American 25, 43. *See also* Lakota; Sioux
Neo-Phare 17
Nettles, Bonnie Lu 181–3
New Age 24, 94, 169, 179
New Creation Christian Community. *See* Jesus Fellowship
"new religions" (*shinshūkyō*) 17, 50, 147, 187
New York 20, 143, 162
New Zealand 33
nun 145. *See also* clergy
Nuwaubian Nation 17, 158, 161–3, 169

Octavia (Mabel Barltrop) 83–8, 96 n. 1
Ōkawa Ryūhō 52
online community 59, 112, 130–2, 163

Operation Lifeboat 110
Order of the Solar Temple 18, 156, 176, 179–80, 186
Oregon 10, 61 n. 2, 141–3, 145–9, 152, 153 n. 3
Orthodox Church 23
Osho. *See* Rajneesh, Bhagwan Shree
overwork 68, 71–2, 75

paganism
    Norse 21
    Polynesian 22
    in the Process Church 22
Palmer, Susan 6, 17–18, 20, 23–4, 53, 104, 138, 144–5, 149–50, 155–8, 161–2, 164–7
Pana-Wave Laboratory 51
Panacea Society, The 8, 83, 85–96
Panawēbu Kenkyūjo. *See* Pana-Wave Laboratory
Papua New Guinea 7, 21–2, 32–3
parody 9–10, 128, 130–2
patriarchy 129–32
Pentecostalism 8, 33, 39, 67, 69–70, 79, 95
Peoples Temple 18, 60, 176–80, 182, 186
police 19, 49, 51–2, 56, 60, 67, 73, 76, 106, 110–11, 115 n. 31, 120, 156, 158, 162, 167–8, 179–80, 185–6
polygamy 37, 163
pornography 127–8
possession 185
pressure
    endogenous 15, 16, 18, 26, 51
    exogenous 15, 16, 18, 23, 26, 51–2, 158, 175
prison 67, 106, 161, 163, 165. *See also* imprisonment
propaganda 122
prophecy 20, 70, 75, 83, 92, 94, 103–5, 108
    failure of 8, 19–21, 61 n. 2, 68, 74–5, 77, 79, 108, 185
proselytization 18, 74, 104. *See also* Flirty Fishing; missionary activity
Protestantism 5, 15, 114
provisioning 104, 109
Psychiana 17
psychiatric care 67, 182
PTSD (post-traumatic stress disorder) 124
Public Security Intelligence Agency (PSIA) 55, 61 n. 7

Pune 140, 143
punishment 25, 73, 78, 107

Quakers 4
Quebec 180–1

raids 6, 10, 24–5, 49, 51–2, 56, 60, 96 n. 5, 104, 111, 157–63, 165–70, 182
Rajneesh, Bhagwan Shree (Osho) 61 n. 2, 135–53
Rajneeshpuram 141, 143, 145–9, 151
Rappaport, Roy 44
Rasmussen, Peter 85
Rastafarianism 36
Reboot 105–6, 112–13
Reich, Wilhelm 137
reincarnation 60, 164, 180, 182
religiocide 5, 7, 24–6
religious corporation law 51, 56
Renmonkyō 51
renunciants 49, 59, 139. *See also* asceticism; *sannyasins*
residence permit 143, 146
resurrection 87–8, 144. *See also* reincarnation; Jesus Christ, return of
revolution 105, 157, 178
rights
    animal 22
    civil 68, 175
    human 53
    members' 105
    religious 51, 147, 155
ritual 3, 19, 25, 31, 34, 36, 38–9, 41, 44–5, 87, 178
Robbins, Joel 7–8, 13, 19, 21, 46–7, 50, 95, 170
Rosicrucianism 23

sacred texts 144
sacrifice 7, 22, 31, 34, 39, 41–2, 45, 123, 143
salvation 33, 69, 104, 144
Sami 25
sannyasins 139, 141, 144, 146–50
sarin gas attack 23, 49, 52–3, 56, 58, 187
schism 17, 22, 51, 135
science 141, 144, 148
Scientology 5, 57, 157
sealing (membership) 85, 87–9, 91–2, 96 n. 5
Searle, John 32, 42–5

Seattle 17, 119, 127–8, 131
sect 9, 114 n. 17, 135, 138, 141, 156–9, 161, 164, 166–9
secularization 13, 93–4
Seventh-day Adventism 15, 159
sex 9, 16, 38, 70–1, 74, 77–9, 80 n. 4, 104, 107, 109–11, 114 n. 11, 126–9, 131–2, 137, 139–40, 149, 167, 178, 183–4. *See also* abuse, sexual
sexual predators 110, 114, 176
Shakers 2–3, 8
Shaw, Jane 83, 85, 87–8
shinshūkyō. *See* "new religions"
Shōkō, Asahara 22, 49, 51, 54–6, 60, 61 n. 1
Sioux 2, 25
social media 9, 106, 119, 121, 131–2. *See also* Facebook; Twitter
Soka Gakkai 5
Sophia Wisdom (Mystical Christ) 23
sorcery 38–31, 45. *See also* magic
Southcott, Joanna 83–4, 94
Spiritualism 15, 94
"standing wrong" 73
Stanton, Noel 99, 102, 110, 113
Star Trek 183
suicide 19, 113, 129, 148
    collective 11, 18–20, 23, 156, 175, 173–87
Sweden 67, 69, 76, 80 n. 4
Switzerland 179, 181
Synanon 17
syncretism 91

Taiwan 20
Tambiah, Stanley 44
tantra 137
Tao, Chen 20
tax
    exemption 17, 51, 140, 143
    fraud 17, 155, 157, 166
    roll 164
Teens for Christ. *See* Children of God
TELAH Foundation 183
testimony 9, 57, 121–2, 124–5, 127, 132, 163, 166
Texas 20, 60, 159, 163–4

The Family International. *See* Children of God
theology 23, 70, 77–9, 87, 91, 123, 126, 131, 148, 151
Theosophy 15, 23, 94
therapy 8, 17, 68, 76–7, 79, 129, 140
Trappists 3
trauma 7, 50, 68, 129, 187. *See also* abuse; PTSD
Twitter 119, 121, 128, 130–2

UFO 20, 162, 175, 181, 183
Uganda 19, 184–6
United States 3, 6, 10, 15, 25, 43–4, 90, 103, 120, 140, 143, 146, 152, 158–9, 170, 177–8
Urapmin, the 21–2, 32–9, 41–2, 45–6
Urban, Hugh 5, 137–8, 140–1, 143, 145, 177, 182

Victor Programmes 107
violence 6–7, 11, 18–19, 25–6, 49–50, 52, 55–60, 67, 72–3, 75–6, 92, 101, 147, 162, 175–6, 178–9, 181–2, 185–7. *See also* abuse; murder; suicide
Virgin Mary 168–9, 184–5
vision 70, 72, 103, 179, 184–5. *See also* prophecy

Waco. *See* Branch Davidians
Waldau, Åsa 69–79, 80 n. 5
Weber, Max 85
Wild Wild Country 149–50
Wilson, Bryan R. 15, 71, 74, 114, 175, 187
Word of Life 69
World War II 24, 32, 84
Wright, Stuart A. 6, 10, 18, 20, 23–4, 51, 53, 61 n. 2, 61 n. 4, 71, 104–5, 166–7

Yearning for Zion Ranch 158, 163–4, 169
Yezidis 6, 25
yoga 23, 49, 54–5, 135
York, Dwight 162–3

Zeller, Benjamin E. 182–4, 187
Zen 3, 136, 151–2

www.ingramcontent.com/pod-product-compliance
Lightning Source LLC
Chambersburg PA
CBHW070637300426
44111CB00013B/2144